The Prudence of Love

The Prudence of Love

How Possessing the Virtue of Love Benefits the Lover

Eric J. Silverman

LEXINGTON BOOKS

A division of

ROWMAN & LITTLEFIELD PUBLISHERS, INC.
Lanham • Boulder • New York • Toronto • Plymouth, UK

Published by Lexington Books
A division of Rowman & Littlefield Publishers, Inc.
A wholly owned subsidiary of The Rowman & Littlefield Publishing Group, Inc.
4501 Forbes Boulevard, Suite 200, Lanham, Maryland 20706
http://www.lexingtonbooks.com

Estover Road,
Plymouth PL6 7PY,
United Kingdom

British Library Cataloguing in Publication Information Available

Library of Congress Cataloging-in-Publication Data

Silverman, Eric J., 1971–
   The prudence of love : how possessing the virtue of love benefits the lover / Eric J.
Silverman.
      p. cm.
   Includes bibliographical references (p.   ) and index.
   ISBN 978-0-7391-3930-1 (cloth : alk. paper) — ISBN 978-0-7391-3932-5 (electronic)
   1. Love—Philosophy—History. I. Title.
BD436.S48 2010
177'.7—dc22   2009032224

Printed in the United States of America

∞ ™ The paper used in this publication meets the minimum requirements of American
National Standard for Information Sciences—Permanence of Paper for Printed Library
Materials, ANSI/NISO Z39.48-1992.

Dedicated to Kristina, Allison, and Julia

Table of Contents

Preface

This book addresses two topics that are of great importance: the nature of love and love's connection to the lover's happiness. While my arguments are intended primarily for philosophers, I have also drawn upon resources in religion and psychology that would make many of my arguments interesting to those who specialize in those disciplines as well.

I begin by arguing that Thomas Aquinas provides a model of love that is more plausible than other contemporary accounts in analytic philosophy. My own account of love is largely shaped by his influence. The latter part of the book makes three distinct claims about the connection between love and the lover's happiness, which is sometimes referred to as subjective well-being. First, I claim there are at least five distinct ways that possessing the virtue of love contributes to the well-being of the lover. Second, the conjunction of these five benefits typically results in a net increase in a person's overall well-being. Third, developing a loving disposition is a more prudent strategy for increasing one's overall well-being than cultivation of the vicious alternative dispositions. Significantly, I argue that these three claims are true according to each of the four dominant views of well-being in contemporary philosophy. Furthermore, while my view of love is shaped by Aquinas's account, my arguments will not rely upon any other Thomistic philosophical commitments. I hope that placing these two constraints upon my argument will make my conclusions convincing to a broad cross section of the academic community.

Chapter One examines the current state of the philosophical debate on foundational components of my thesis, including traditional views concerning the connection between love and well-being, theories of well-being, and the definition of virtue. Chapter Two critiques and rejects four important contemporary conceptions of love. Chapter Three examines Thomas Aquinas's account of love. Chapter Four develops and defends my own account of the virtue of love derived from Aquinas's views. Chapter Five investigates the various ways possessing this Neo-Thomistic virtue of love benefits the lover. The benefits examined include love's role in providing the lover with enjoyable and meaningful final ends, engendering the lover's psychic integration, motivating his self-improvement, increasing his self-knowledge, and attaining and improving the lover's other relationships. Chapter Six investigates how various types of agents who lack the virtue of love fail to flourish. I hope that the pages that follow are thought provoking and encouraging to those who study love, *eudaimonism,* and medieval philosophy.

This book is a revised version of the dissertation that I wrote during my PhD studies at St. Louis University. Eleonore Stump, Daniel Haybron, and John Kavanaugh provided an enormous amount of insight and feedback to aid my work. I cannot thank St. Louis University's philosophy department and its chair, Theodore Vitali, enough for their commitment to me throughout my studies. I am also deeply appreciative of my current department at Christopher Newport University, of our dean, and our school's provost for the encouragement and support they have provided to help me develop this project during the past year. Jason Poling provided extensive help in proofreading the final manuscript. Finally, I must thank my wife, Kristina, and my daughters, Allison and Julia, for their unfailing support and patience while I've written this book over the past three and a half years.

I presented a paper based on the argument in Chapter 5.2 concerning the beneficial nature of love's final ends at the Eastern Division Meeting of the American Philosophical Association in 2008. Paul Prescott offered helpful comments during this session. I also presented papers related to the argument in Chapter 2.2 critiquing David Velleman's account of love at Baylor University's conference on friendship in 2007 and at the Tenth International Conference on Ethics Across the Curriculum in 2008. I am thankful to all who attended these presentations and for the suggestions that they offered. The presentation at Baylor University led to a particularly helpful conversation with Alexander Pruss concerning the nature of love.

Chapter 1

Foundational Issues

This book makes a simple claim: love contributes to the well-being of the loving person. More precisely, possessing the virtue of love directly and indirectly contributes to the well-being of the virtuous agent. Whether virtues, such as love, contribute to their possessor's well-being has been an issue for both historic and contemporary debate. While I am sympathetic to the broader *eudaimonist* position, I limit this project's scope to an investigation of whether love is an *eudaimonistic* virtue. I defend the position of the *eudaimonists*, such as Aristotelians and Thomists, against the claims of sentimentalists, Kantians, and others who see no necessary connection between virtues like love and the lover's well-being. I argue that the virtue of love benefits its possessor in at least five distinct ways, that possessing the virtue of love typically increases the lover's overall well-being, and that developing a loving disposition is a more prudent strategy for increasing well-being than cultivating any of the vicious alternative dispositions. This chapter proceeds by examining the current state of the philosophical debate on foundational components of my thesis with particular attention to traditional views concerning the connection between love and well-being, theories of well-being, and the definition of virtue.

1.1 HISTORICAL PRECEDENTS TO CONTEMPORARY VIEWS OF THE RELATIONSHIP BETWEEN LOVE AND WELL-BEING

Love is highly valued in ethics, in religion, and in most personal lives. However, the question of why love is valuable remains unresolved. Accounts of why love is valuable vary from one conception of love to another. While it is relatively uncontroversial that love benefits the beloved in numerous ways,[1] whether, how, and how likely love is to benefit the lover remain unresolved issues. Some of the historical precedents to contemporary views are found in Immanuel Kant, Plato, and Thomas Aquinas.

Kant's account of love and well-being is the most hostile to my own views, since he explicitly rejects any necessary connection between virtue and well-being. He construes love as practical sacrifice and describes it as service based upon moral duty. Love is embodied in action, apart from and even against the lover's personal inclinations:

> For love out of inclination cannot be commanded; but kindness done from duty—although no inclination impels us, and even although natural and unconquerable disinclination stands in our way—is practical, and not pathological, love, residing in the will and not in the propensions of feeling, in principles of action and not of melting compassion; and it is this practical love alone which can be an object of command.[2]

Thus, the Kantian account focuses on love expressed through sacrificial action, unaided by personal inclination, and sometimes even against the desires of the loving individual's heart. Love is not part of the lover's personal fulfillment. It does not necessarily contribute to the lover's happiness or well-being. Indeed, it may cause the lover to risk his own happiness and well-being for the sake of the beloved. This account reflects Kant's broader view that virtue often conflicts with an agent's pursuit of personal happiness. He explains why there can be no necessary connection between virtue and happiness:

> Consequently, either the desire for happiness must be the motive to maxims of virtue or the maxim of virtue must be the efficient cause of happiness. The first is *absolutely* impossible because (as was proved in the Analytic) maxims that put the determining ground of the will in the desire for one's happiness are not moral at all and can be the ground of no virtue. But the second is *also impossible* because any practical connection of causes and effects in the world, as a result of the determination of the will, does not depend upon the moral dispositions of the will but upon knowledge of the laws of nature and the physical ability to use them for one's purposes; consequently, no necessary connection of happiness with virtue in the world, adequate to the highest good, can be expected from the most meticulous observance of moral laws.[3]

The only ways Kant believes virtue and happiness could have a necessary connection would be if the proper motive for virtue were the desire for happiness or if virtue necessarily causes happiness. Since he believes duty is the only morally appropriate motive, he views the desire for personal happiness as a vicious motivation. He also asserts that attaining happiness is based upon one's practical abilities for achieving desires rather than one's degree of virtue.[4] Since possessing virtue does not entail the practical ability to fulfill desires, there can be no necessary connection between virtue and well-being. In Chapter Five, I will return to Kant's objection, but for now it is enough to note his rejection of *eudaimonism.*

In contrast, one common model of love claims that while it may require sacrifice, a life without love is inferior to one with love. One such theory is presented by Aristophanes in Plato's *Symposium.* He offers an overwhelmingly positive account of the nature of love, personifying it as a god. He extols love and its intimate connection to happiness:

> Mankind, he said, judging by their neglect of him, have never, as I think, at all understood the power of Love. For if they had understood him they would surely have built noble temples and altars, and offered solemn sacrifices in his honor; but this is not done, and certainly ought to be done: for of all the gods he is the best friend of men, the helper and healer of the ills which are the great obstruction to the happiness of the race.[5]

Aristophanes portrays love as the most central component of happiness. He goes on to explain love's importance in light of the myth of the divided person. It claims humans have been divided into two halves by the gods. Love is the only way to regain wholeness. It provides the ultimate mutual fulfillment of two selves. Without love, emptiness remains as one goes through life as an incomplete person. Fulfillment is only possible for those who love, regardless of the sacrifices it requires. He describes that the great joy lovers find in one another ultimately masks the deeper, opaque needs love fulfills:

> And when one of them finds his other half, whether he be a lover of youth or a lover of another sort, the pair are lost in an amazement of love and friendship and intimacy, and one will not be out of the other's sight, as I may say, even for a moment: these are they who pass their lives with one another; yet they could not explain what they desire of one another. For the intense yearning which each of them has towards the other does not appear to be the desire of intercourse, but of something else which the soul desires and can not tell, and of which she has only a dark and doubtful presentiment.[6]

While Aristophanes's account of love portrays love and well-being as deeply connected, it is ultimately vague concerning how it benefits the lover. While the myth claims that humans have been literally divided from their other halves, this metaphor obscures the actual benefits of love. We are left to infer what foundational problem love solves. Is the problem that each person is ultimately incomplete in himself and unable to reach happiness alone? Does love benefit by making valuable relationships possible, which in turn fulfill the lover? Is love then only valuable as a means for attaining desirable relationships? Aristophanes's account acknowledges that love benefits the lover, yet the nature of those benefits remains vague and limited to their role in improving relationships.

In contrast to these accounts of love, Thomas Aquinas's construes love in terms of personal fulfillment and gives a clear reason for why love benefits the lover. He views love as part of humanity's eternal destiny. The virtue of charity, which results in loving action, brings joy and peace to the charitable person. Furthermore, love is construed as a perfection of personal will that is needed for happiness. He offers an account that shows how love expressed in the lover's will is inevitably connected with his own happiness. He explains,

> Rectitude of the will is required for happiness both antecedently and concomitantly. Indeed, antecedently because rectitude of the will is needed to order one to the ultimate end.... And therefore no one is able to reach happiness without having rectitude of the will. Also it is required concomitantly, because ultimate happiness consists in the vision of the divine essence, which is itself the essence of goodness, as argued elsewhere. And therefore, the one who wills to see God's essence necessarily loves whatever he loves, in subordination to God.[7]

For Aquinas, happiness requires the proper ordering of a person's will toward her final end. The proper ordering of the will includes loving people as God loves. Therefore, happiness and the ultimate fulfillment of human purpose are only possible for those who love. However, the concept of a final end for humanity has fallen out of favor in contemporary philosophy. Many philosophers also reject the existence of God. Using these concepts to prove a necessary connection between love and well-being will not be acceptable to many thinkers. Instead, I hope to demonstrate that the virtue of love benefits the lover without relying upon these controversial claims.

I develop Aquinas's account more deeply in Chapters Three and Four. My account of love, which is heavily influenced by Aquinas's, claims that part of love's value is due to its contribution to the lover's well-being. Therefore, I reject any account of love that finds no necessary connection with the lover's well-being. At least part of love's desirability is due to its contribution to the lover's well-being. I also avoid relying upon vague metaphors like those used by Aristophanes. Finally, I avoid basing my thesis on claims about the existence of God or humanity's final end.

1.2 AN INITIAL OBJECTION: LOVE IS NOT SOUGHT FOR THE LOVER'S OWN SAKE

Someone might object that my project is paradoxical, because there is nothing more contrary to love than seeking relationships for self-benefit. This caricature of love is often described as "using people" since it treats other persons as means to less important ends. This attitude is incompatible with love. Agents who care about others primarily to gain some benefit from them do not truly love. This objection coincides with Kant's intuition that virtue for the sake of one's own happiness is not virtue at all.

The distinction between the first- and third-person perspectives helps show why examining love's benefit to the lover is not paradoxical. The first-person perspective is that of the loving person, while the third-person perspective is that of a detached objective observer. My project examines the benefits of love from the detached third-person perspective. From the third-person perspective, examining the benefits a loving person gains provides insight into the nature of love and the source of love's value. However, this examination is distinct from the loving person's motivations for seeking love. I do not claim that a loving person seeks to use others to gain these benefits.

From the lover's first-person perspective, he may be unaware of love's benefits. If he is aware of them, he does not seek love to attain these benefits. The benefits of love do not motivate love. From the first person perspective, the loving person may not understand some of the concepts used in explicating love's benefits such as "psychic integration" or "final ends." The loving person's desires toward the beloved are necessarily disinterested in that love is never sought for selfish reasons, despite any benefits an agent actually gains through love. Obviously, I do not deny that the lover's concern for the beloved is "interested" in the sense that the lover actually does benefit from loving. Yet, love benefits the lover in the same way that a marathon runner's training benefits his cardiovascular health, whether he seeks or is aware of this benefit. My examination of love's benefits does not imply that the lover enters relationships motivated by these benefits or that the lover ought to be motivated by these benefits. Love is necessarily an unselfish pursuit. The lover cares for others regardless of love's consequences.

There are three preliminary concepts to clarify before proceeding: the concept of well-being, the concept of virtue, and the concept of love.

1.3 AN INITIAL ACCOUNT OF THIS THESIS'S COMPATIBILITY WITH VARIOUS CONCEPTIONS OF WELL-BEING

There are competing accounts of well-being, and it might appear that this project will rely upon a particular view. However, my thesis does not rely upon a particular conception of well-being because several of love's benefit are compatible with most mainstream accounts of well-being. Some of love's other benefits are only compatible with particular theories of well-being.

Examining the leading theories of well-being will demonstrate that love plausibly benefits the lover on each account, thereby showing my thesis is compatible with each major theory. The three most popular theories of well-being are hedonist, desire fulfillment, and objective list accounts of well-being.[8] There are also perfectionist accounts of well-being, but they are less popular.

Hedonistic accounts claim that attaining pleasure and avoiding pain are the only aspects of a person's well-being. Love will contribute to well-being if and only if possessing it brings pleasure or reduces pain. The virtue of love may do so directly or indirectly; for example, love may constitute a benefit directly if being a loving person tends to be pleasant rather than painful. The lover may have a more enjoyable and pleasant life since love changes how he experiences it. Love may make life's everyday experiences more meaningful and pleasurable since caring for others adds larger meaning and purpose. For example, some parts of one's daily routine may be tedious. Yet if tedious activities are viewed as a way to love others, they may become more enjoyable.

Some events that would be painful or neutral to a nonloving person are pleasant instead. The lover views benefits received by the beloved as benefits for herself as well, resulting in pleasure for the lover. When a loving parent observes a child's success, it results in pleasure for both parent and child. Similarly, experiences that would be painful to a nonloving person might be neutral or even pleasurable for the lover. For example, when a beloved friend receives an honor that the lover desires for himself, this event can be pleasurable for the lover rather than painful. The lover's experience of hardship may be less painful because her focus on other people distracts from her own troubles.

A loving person may also have a tendency to be involved in different, more pleasant activities. For example, the lover might be involved in more social activities with her beloved, which might be highly pleasurable. A loving person may be involved more frequently in altruistic activities to ease the troubles of others. Love benefits the lover by making her less likely to hold grudges and meditate on wrongs suffered, thereby avoiding unnecessary painful experiences.

Love could also be indirectly beneficial in that some of the lover's actions instrumentally lead to other, more pleasurable experiences long-term. A trip to the dentist is a classic example of an instrumentally valuable action. Dental work typically causes short-term pain but reduces overall long-term pain. Love similarly contributes to well-being if it leads one to sacrifice short-term preferences, thereby encouraging long-term relational harmony. Increased harmony in relationships makes relationships more pleasurable long term. Restraining one's desires out of love for others may not be pleasant, but self-restraint allows for pleasurable lifelong harmony. Love may also result in greater self-knowledge, which later aids the lover in attaining pleasure or avoiding pain.

In contrast to the hedonistic account of well-being, the desire fulfillment account claims that fulfilling an agent's desires contributes to his well-being, whether or not it brings him pleasure.[9] Brad Hooker explains that this conception of well-being "takes into account the *number* of desires that get fulfilled, the *relative importance to you* of your various desires, and *how long* they last."[10] The desires relevant to this conception are goals valued as ends, rather than goals desired as means to some further end. If someone wants World Series tickets in order to meet famous baseball players, attaining the tickets themselves does not contribute to her well-being. Only achieving her ultimate goal of meeting famous players contributes to her well-being. Since agents typically prefer pleasure over pain, many events that contribute to well-being on the hedonistic account also contribute to well-being according to the desire fulfillment account. However, not all fulfilled desires lead to pleasure, such as desires fulfilled without the agent's knowledge, desires with unforeseen unpleasant consequences, or self-destructive desires.

According to the desire fulfillment account of well-being, love contributes to well-being if it leads to a larger number of more important desires being fulfilled for a longer period of time. There are numerous ways love might accomplish this requirement. Loving agents will have different preferences from nonloving agents. These desires might be more easily satisfied, be more fulfilling when satisfied, be more important to the lover, or stay satisfied longer. For example, both loving and nonloving people may desire marriage, but a lover's marriage may be longer lasting and more important to him than a nonlover's marriage. Loving agents typically have additional resources for satisfying desires, such as relationships that enable them to fulfill important preferences more often and more permanently than nonlovers. The lover may also have fewer extraneous goals than a nonloving person so a greater proportion of her remaining goals can be fulfilled.

Objective list theories of well-being simply list various goods that contribute to well-being. There are numerous list theories, but Hooker says their usual components include "autonomy, friendship, knowledge of important matters, achievement, and perhaps the appreciation of beauty. List theorists can add that our pleasure also constitutes a benefit to us."[11] Therefore, if love enables one to attain goods on the list, such as friendship or pleasure, then it contributes to well-being.

If pleasure is on the list of goods that contribute to well-being, then anytime love provides a benefit on the hedonistic account it also provides a benefit according to the objective list theory. Similarly, if desire achievement is on the list, then when love benefits the lover according to the desire fulfillment account, it also provides a benefit according to the list theory. Friendship is also a common component of objective list theories, so if love contributes to the formation of friendships, then it benefits the lover.

A fourth, but less popular, account of well-being is perfectionism, which claims that virtue constitutes a benefit to the agent. According to this account, becoming an ideal specimen of its species contributes to an agent's well-being. Typically, perfectionist accounts stipulate that there are numerous potentials in humanity that are only actualized as the agent develops virtue. If love actualizes an ideal human potential, then possessing it benefits the loving person. It is unsurprising that the virtue of love constitutes a benefit according to a perfectionist account of well-being since it counts virtue itself as a basic constituent of well-being.

To illustrate why my thesis does not rely on a particular theory of well-being, consider one of love's benefits: love is a necessary condition for certain desirable relationships, which Alasdair MacIntyre calls relationships of mutual giving and receiving.[12] Only a loving person may develop these relationships. Loving agents desire these relationships as ends in themselves. They are mutually beneficial, mutually enjoyable, long-term relationships in which each person is committed to and cares for the other.

On a hedonistic account of well-being, love benefits the lover because relationships of mutual giving and receiving are pleasurable. Long-term interaction with others who are committed to one's own well-being is pleasurable. On a desire fulfillment account, love is beneficial because it fulfills a necessary condition for the widely held desire for these relationships. Furthermore, these relationships also aid an agent in achieving other preferences. Even unloving agents typically desire the intimacy and mutual support of these relationships, though they may also have strong conflicting desires. If virtue itself constitutes well-being, as in perfectionist theories and some objective list theories, love benefits its possessor simply because it is a virtue. Objective list accounts typically include pleasure, desire fulfillment, friendship, or virtue in their list of objective goods. These relationships can be beneficial because of their role in bringing about any of these goods. Thus, my thesis is compatible with each of these accounts of well-being, and there is no reason to commit to a particular view of well-being.

This examination of theories of well-being is not an attempt to prove definitively that love contributes to the lover's well-being. Instead, it is meant to provide strong *prima facie* evidence that the upcoming discussion of love's benefits need not depend on a particular account of well-being. It demonstrates that, in principle, the claim that love benefits the lover is plausible on all accounts of well-being. Furthermore, it elucidates the various accounts of well-being, which set the success conditions for proving my thesis.

While my argument does not rely upon virtue itself directly constituting well-being, it is worth critiquing a recent argument against this position. Brad Hooker proposes the "sympathy test" to determine whether we view virtue as constitutive of well-being. He claims that when agents lack a good, we view their lives more sympathetically. Therefore, if we do not view people lacking virtue with greater sympathy than those with virtue, this fact demonstrates it does not constitute well-being. He argues:

> How sorry we feel for someone is influenced by how badly from the point of view of his own good we think that person's life has gone, that is, by whether we think his life has lacked important prudential goods ... We could try applying this line of thought to the question of whether we think moral virtue is a fundamental category of prudential value. Consider two persons who lead sad and wretched lives. Suppose that one of those two people is morally virtuous, and the other is not.... We would not feel sorrier for Unscrupulous [the person without virtue]. This suggests that we do not really believe that moral virtue has the same status on the list as pleasure, knowledge, achievement, and friendship.[13]

Hooker claims that if two lives are equal in every way except that one life is distinguished by virtue and the other by vice, we are not more sympathetic to the one lacking virtue. Therefore, virtue is not part of well-being.

Hooker acknowledges at least two limitations to his argument. First, it will only appeal to thinkers who are not more sympathetic toward vicious individuals than virtuous individuals. Second, it will not convince those who are already committed to viewing virtue as constitutive of well-being.[14]

There are several problems with Hooker's argument. First, the sympathy test is flawed and misleading. While one reason we view a person sympathetically is that we believe he lacks a good that contributes to well-being, many other factors influence sympathetic emotions. Even if we are not more sympathetic toward the Unscrupulous individual, there are explanations for this fact that do not require rejecting virtue as constitutive of well-being. For example, Hooker assumes that emotions are directed by a high degree of rationality, since sympathy is assumed to reveal what we actually value. Yet, not all people possess the psychic integration between values and emotions assumed by this test. Even if we grant that sympathetic emotions are largely guided by our values, we need not grant Hooker's conclusion. Furthermore, there are at least two additional possibilities that undermine his argument.

First, sympathy may be hindered when someone is viewed as undeserving of happiness. If someone lacks well-being but that lack is attributed to

personal vicious choices, we may be less sympathetic. Some thinkers, like
Kant, believe virtue reflects a person's worthiness to be happy and do not
view happiness as unconditionally good. He claims,

> Now, inasmuch as virtue and happiness together constitute the possession of
> the highest good in a person, and happiness distributed in exact proportion to
> morality (as the worth of a person and his worthiness to be happy) constitutes
> the *highest good* of a possible world, the latter means the whole, the complete
> good, in which, however, virtue as the condition is always the supreme good,
> since it has no further condition above it, whereas happiness is something that,
> though always pleasant to the possessor of it, is not of itself absolutely and in all
> respects good but always presupposes morally lawful conduct as its condition.[15]

Someone with these moral intuitions may judge a vicious individual
to be worse off than a virtuous individual but lack sympathy because he
believes vicious individuals are not worthy of happiness. For example,
many people judge that Saddam Hussein lacked important goods during
his final years in prison but are not sympathetic toward him because of his
many vices. History records many societies that lack sympathy for vicious
individuals who turn to criminal actions, and express this unsympathetic
attitude through harsh judicial penalties intended to destroy the criminal's
well-being.

A second explanation for our lack of sympathy for vicious individuals
is that we may be less sympathetic toward individuals who lack goods as
a result of their own choices. For example, if two individuals lack friends,
and one consistently rejects good opportunities to develop friendships
while the other lacks friends due to circumstances outside his control, many
people are more sympathetic to the person without control over his undesirable fate.

Therefore, it seems that Hooker's argument that virtue is not a constituent
of well-being fails. It is based upon an overly simplistic account of sympathetic emotions, which incorrectly portrays sympathy as only based upon an
evaluation of another person's well-being. While he acknowledges that there
are other influences upon sympathy, he neither tells us what they are nor
offers a systematic account of sympathy. This fact alone would be a sufficient
reason to view his argument skeptically. Since he does not provide a more
systematic account of sympathy, the proper way to interpret a lack of sympathy for vicious individuals is unclear. This lack of sympathy could indicate a
belief that virtue does not constitute well-being, a belief that vicious individuals are undeserving of happiness, a belief that those who voluntarily reject
goods are inappropriate objects for sympathy, that sympathy is not actually
correlated with our views of well-being, or some other factor.

Hooker anticipates numerous alternate explanations for a lack of sympathy toward vicious individuals. For example, he rejects claims that we lack sympathy for Unscrupulous because he is at fault for not developing virtue:

> Fault does not *always* shut off sympathy. Sometimes we recognize that people are to blame for, say, ruining their lives, and yet we simultaneously feel sorry for them because of what they have brought on themselves. For example, we might blame Jack for being so imprudent as to marry (or divorce) Jill, but nevertheless feel sorry for him.... Now, given that in some cases fault and blame do not preclude sympathy, we should demand some explanation of why sympathy is absent in the case of our reactions to Unscrupulous.[16]

Hooker claims that since a vicious individual's blameworthiness does not universally result in an absence of sympathetic emotions, his interlocutor bears the burden of explaining this phenomenon. Of course, there are numerous plausible ways to account for this phenomenon. Perhaps, we might lack a general sympathy toward vicious individuals but still have sympathy toward those who bring a staggering amount of harm upon themselves, those who bring more harm upon themselves than we believe they deserve, or those with whom we have emotional bonds. His example of one's sympathy toward Jack despite his culpability in undermining his relationship with Jill could be explained in any of these three ways without concluding that virtue does not constitute well-being.

In any case, Hooker's response is question begging. He tries to establish that virtue is not constitutive of well-being based on the sympathy test, does not give a systematic account of sympathy himself, yet demands such an account from his objectors. It is even possible that sympathy is not consistently rational. If this is true, no systematic account of sympathy would be available to support either his view or his objector's, but Hooker's question begging biases the argument in his own favor.

1.4 CONTEMPORARY ACCOUNTS OF VIRTUE

Any conception of the virtue of love relies upon a more general account of virtue. My argument uses a traditional Neo-Aristotelian definition of moral virtue, construing a moral virtue as a human excellence. The moral virtues are excellent, desirable, ethically valuable human character dispositions. Virtues are acquired dispositions that actualize innate human potential for excellence.

This definition is agnostic concerning why virtue is generally desirable. Some thinkers view virtues as desirable because of benefits they bring their possessor, while others hold that virtues are desirable because they are generally beneficial to society. Utilitarians like Julia Driver claim that virtues necessarily benefit people in general but need not benefit the virtuous person himself. She explains, "On my theory, the value of all of these traits resides in their tendency to produce good consequences."[17] In contrast, egoists such as Ayn Rand view dispositions that are beneficial to the self as virtuous, whether or not they benefit others. From a third viewpoint, deontologists like William Frankena claim that virtues enable their possessor to fulfill deontic moral obligations whether or not these dispositions contribute to anyone's well-being. He explains,

> For every [deontic] principle there will be a morally good trait, often going by the same name, consisting of a disposition or tendency to act according to it; and for every morally good trait there will be a principle defining the kind of action in which it is to express itself.[18]

Since this paper only focuses on the virtue of love, the general basis for virtue's desirability is not important to this project. Since love is widely recognized as an excellent, desirable, ethically valuable human character disposition that actualizes an important human potential, we may conclude that it is a virtue on most accounts of virtue.

This conception of virtue is compatible with most contemporary mainstream accounts. For example, this definition is compatible with Christine Swanton's account, which claims, "A virtue is a good quality of character, more specifically a disposition to respond to, or acknowledge, items within its field or fields in an excellent or good enough way."[19] It is also compatible with Rosalind Hursthouse's definition of virtue: "The concept of a virtue is the concept of something that makes its possessor good; a virtuous person is a morally good, excellent, or admirable person who acts and reacts well, rightly, as she should—she gets things right."[20] It is compatible with Alasdair MacIntyre's account: "A virtue is an acquired human quality the possession and exercise of which tends to enable us to achieve those goods which are internal to practices[21] and the lack of which effectively prevents us from attaining such goods."[22] It is compatible with William Frankena's view: "Virtues are dispositions or traits that are not wholly innate; they must all be acquired, at least in part, by teaching and practice, or, perhaps, by grace."[23] While these thinkers describe virtue in slightly different ways, each of them directly states or implicitly suggests that virtues are excellent, desirable, ethically valuable human character dispositions. Furthermore, while most contemporary ethicists no longer describe virtue as an actualization of innate human potential, these concepts are still implicit in their claims since they typically agree that virtues are not innate, must be developed, and can be widely developed by human beings.

    I argue that love contributes to its possessor's well-being without arguing
for a broader *eudaimonistic* theory that all virtues necessarily contribute to
the virtuous agent's well-being. Historically, there have been a number of
thinkers who reject *eudaimonistic* theory, especially in connection to virtues
like love. There are a number of reasons *eudaimonism* might be rejected.
Some deontologists believe that the moral obligations of rationality and self-
interest frequently conflict. Utilitarians believe that sometimes promoting
the greater good of all requires individuals to sacrifice their own well-being.
Virtuous dispositions in these theories do not necessarily benefit the virtuous
agent.

    One account of virtue I reject is Robert Solomon's view that some passions
are virtues. He argues, "This is the claim I want to pursue here, that passions
as such can be virtues.... I do not deny that virtues are typically states of
character (or for that matter, that passions can be states of character), but it
seems to me that passions (such as love) can also be virtues."[24] In particular,
I reject Solomon's claim that the passion of erotic love is a virtue. He ignores
traditional Aristotelian arguments against viewing passions as virtues.

    First, Aristotle argues that the development of virtue is voluntary while
passions are traditionally viewed as involuntary. Solomon's claim that passions are virtues is based upon an atypical construal of passions as voluntary
judgments. While he is correct that passions are not foreign entities thrust
upon the psyche from outside the self, neither are they strictly voluntary
judgments. Passions are derived, at least in part, from more foundational
aspects of the self such as dispositions. These foundational dispositions can
be developed through habituation, self-discipline, and the guidance of others.
Traditionally, these facts have been seen as reasons to view an agent's moral
dispositions as virtues rather than passions that are partially derivative from
those dispositions.

    Furthermore, Aristotle argues that passions in their simple sense are neither
virtuous nor vicious, but only reflect virtuous dispositions when they arise in
the right amount, for the right reasons, and in the right circumstances from
stable character dispositions. For example, in the traditional Aristotelian conception of courage, the person who never experiences fear or always experiences fear is not virtuous. The agent who never experiences fear despite great
danger is foolhardy and likely to die unnecessarily. The agent who experiences
fear in inappropriate circumstances is a coward. Only the agent who experiences the passion of fear in appropriate circumstances is virtuous. Therefore,
a person's dispositions ought to be viewed as virtues, rather than any passions
which arise from those dispositions.

    Accordingly, even if an agent has passionate love toward the right person,
in the right way, for the right reasons, it is the disposition that leads to the

passion should be viewed as virtuous, not the passion itself. The traditional Aristotelian argument claims that developing a disposition to love the right people in the right way for the right reasons is voluntary, while the passions that arise from that disposition are less voluntary, or even involuntary. Also, passionate love is virtuous not in itself, but only when experienced in the proper context. While there are disagreements concerning the proper relational context for passionate erotic love, virtually all thinkers and cultures agree that some relationships constitute a proper context for *eros* while others do not. For example, incestuous relationships are widely identified as vicious, improper, and destructive. Passionate love within these relationships is not virtuous. While Solomon is correct that passions reveal important aspects of an agent's character, passions are morally significant because they reveal voluntarily developed, foundational character dispositions.[25]

ENDNOTES

1. Surprisingly enough, even this modest claim might be disputed. J. David Velleman's assertion that love does not include a desire to benefit the beloved seems to conflict with the claim that love benefits the beloved. However, it is possible that such love still benefits the beloved, even if it is not the lover's intention. *Cf.* J. David Velleman, "Love as Moral Emotion," *Ethics* 109 (1999): 353.

2. Immanuel Kant, *Groundwork of the Metaphysics of Morals*, trans. H.J. Paton (New York: Harper and Row Publishers, Inc., 1964), 4:399.

3. Immanuel Kant, *Critique of Practical Reason*, trans. and ed. Mary Gregor (New York: Cambridge University Press, 1997), 5:114.

4. Elsewhere Kant defines happiness in terms of satisfying one's inclinations, committing him to a desire fulfillment account of well-being. *Cf.* Kant 1997, 5:73.

5. Plato, *The Symposium*, trans. Benjamin Jowett (Mineola, NY: Dover Publications, 1993), 189c–d.

6. Plato 1993, 192b–c.

7. Thomas Aquinas, *Summa theologiae*, I-II.4.4. I consulted the translation by the Fathers of the English Dominican Province and found it helpful.

8. *Cf.* Brad Hooker, "Is Moral Virtue a Benefit to the Agent?" in *How Should One Live?* ed. Roger Crisp (New York: Oxford University Press, 1996), 141–156.

9. There are also more nuanced versions of the desire preference account of well-being that stipulate the desires must be well-informed or developed in a similarly appropriate way.

10. Brad Hooker 1996, 143.

11. Brad Hooker 1996, 145.

12. *Cf.* Alasdair MacIntyre, *Dependent Rational Animals: Why Human Beings Need the Virtues* (Chicago: Open Court Publishing Company, 2002), 119–128.

13. Brad Hooker 1996, 149–150.

14. Brad Hooker 1996, 150.

15. Immanuel Kant 1997, 5:110–111.

16. Brad Hooker 1996, 153.

17. Julia Driver, *Uneasy Virtue* (New York: Cambridge University Press, 2001), 63.

18. William Frankena, *Ethics*, 2d ed. (Englewood, NJ: Prentice Hall, 1973), 65.

19. Christine Swanton, *Virtue Ethics: A Pluralistic View* (New York: Oxford University Press, 2003), 19.

20. Rosalind Hursthouse, *On Virtue Ethics* (New York: Oxford University Press, 1999), 13.

21. Of course, we would have to stipulate what is meant by "practices" in this context. To fit with MacIntyre's definition, I would suggest that the ideal way of interacting with other persons within various types of relationships would constitute the practices relevant to the virtue of love.

22. Alasdair MacIntyre, *After Virtue*, 2d ed. (Notre Dame, IN: University of Notre Dame Press, 1984), 191.

23. William Frankena 1973, 63.

24. Robert Solomon, *The Joy of Philosophy* (New York: Oxford University Press, 1999), 20.

25. I have made a similar argument against Solomon in an unpublished paper entitled "Why Emotions Cannot Be Virtues: An Aristotelian Response to Robert Solomon."

Chapter 2

Contemporary Philosophical Accounts of Love

Few concepts are more equivocal than love, and it can be difficult to adjudicate among the various accounts. Before examining the various views of love, we should decide upon the proper criteria for evaluating them. First, an adequate conception of love must be flexible enough to explain the first-person experience of love within a wide range of partial caring relationships. An adequate conception of love should at least explain the best type of mature romantic love, love between adult friends, as well as love in familial relationships between parents, children, and siblings.

In addition to love expressed within partial caring relationships, some ethical traditions value an agent's impartial care or love for all humanity. In the contemporary discussion, love for humanity is sometimes referred to as compassion or benevolence. Some accounts of love are only useful for examining partial caring relationships or a subset of partial relationships. It would be preferable to have an account that identifies the essential features of love in a broad range of relationships and toward humanity in general. This criterion tests the flexibility of an account of love.

Second, an account of love should explain common psychological experiences associated with love. Any plausible theory must be compatible with normative experiences such as the unique nonreplaceability of the beloved, the tenacity of loving relationships, emotional vulnerability in loving relationships, and the joy found in community with the beloved. To say that the beloved is nonreplaceable is to say that he is not fungible. Another person cannot replace the beloved without the significant loss of value. The tenacity of loving relationships refers to love's long-term consistency over time, even lasting through many changes in the beloved. While there is some disagreement on how tenacious love is, it is widely accepted that love does not easily wane. The joy found in day-to-day experiences with the beloved refers to the positive emotions that accompany everyday interaction with the beloved. Theories which fail to explain these paradigmatic experiences of love or are incompatible with them lose credibility. This criterion tests love's compatibility with experience.

Third, an ideal account of love should reconcile ethical concerns between partial love and impartial morality. Many ethical theories include moral duties that require impartiality toward everyone. For example, many versions of utilitarianism require that an action's consequences upon everyone are weighed equally. In contrast, love typically motivates individuals to give disproportionate concern to the well-being of the beloved. Also, Kantianism and other deontological views typically include moral duties that we have toward all others equally, not just those with whom we have loving relationships.

If moral duty requires impartiality in decision making, then how can the special attachments and obligations of love be reconciled with one's impartial moral obligations to all? Which partial actions of love are acceptable and which are not? A morally attractive account of love will show how partial love toward specific others and impartial concern for all are compatible. This criterion tests an account of love's compatibility with broader ethical concerns.

Fourth and finally, an ideal account of love must be compatible with construing love in terms of virtue, an excellent character disposition. An account of love should explain what is excellent and admirable within love and distinguish between the ideal love and inferior expressions of "love." Who one loves and how love is expressed are two components that are capable of excellence. Excellence can also be found in the rationality of love, in why one cares for those he loves. Practical wisdom may play a role in ideal love. An account of love should explain which, if any, motivations or reasons for love provide a normative rationale for why love exists between particular persons. Furthermore, an ideal account of love might explain why some people are better at loving than others. This criterion tests an account of love's compatibility with excellence.

To this last criterion someone might object there is no "right person" for love, "right way" for love, or "right reasons" for love. Furthermore, I admit that in friendship and romantic love, subjective preferences influence who we select for these relationships. Yet, even in these relationships, some agents love well and others love poorly. There are at least some objective criteria for excellence in friendship. "Friendship" based upon ulterior motives is not friendship at all. Friendships that are harmful to one or both parties are not excellent, such as "friends" who are criminal partners. Furthermore, friendships may be carried out excellently or poorly. Some friends are inconsistent, negligent, or inconsiderate of those they view as friends.

While there may be a range of "right people" who qualify for friendship, it is possible to choose friends well or poorly. A friend might be poorly chosen because the basis of friendship is misperception; the beloved friend simply does not have the traits the lover attributes to him. Choosing friends based upon ulterior motivations or upon criteria that have little to do with the friend's identity would be an improper basis for choosing friends. Furthermore, a particular friend might be a poor choice because that friendship conflicts with other important values held by the loving agent, such as when someone who values truthfulness befriends a compulsive liar.

Furthermore, there are relationships where there is an appropriate person for love, such as typical familial relationships: a child who fails to love a good parent through honor and care, a parent who neglects his young child, and an abusive spouse all fail to love well. There are also proper and improper motives for love. "Love" motivated by calculated self-interest is not love at all. Love expressed through unjust partiality and favoritism is an incorrect application of love.

An adequate account of love need not explain every common use of the word "love." An account of love needs to explain the morally significant use of the word, such as our care toward other persons and, perhaps, certain ideals. However, an adequate account of love need not address love in the sense that a person loves hometown football or his favorite candy bar.

Chapter Three argues that the account of love that best fulfills these criteria is one that views love as *a disposition towards relationally appropriate acts of the will consisting of disinterested desires for the good of the beloved and desires for unity with the beloved, held as final ends*. This account is similar to some contemporary thinkers' construal of benevolence or compassion in that the lover is disposed toward willing the good for every person. It will also reconcile partiality and impartiality since love is impartial in that the desires of love are present toward all others, yet these desires are expressed differently based upon the nature of each distinct relationship.[1] The particular ways the lover desires the good of the beloved and unity with the beloved and seeks to bring about these desires varies greatly based upon the relationship.

However, before giving an in-depth account of my view of love, we will examine the prominent alternative accounts of love. Four contemporary views of love that are used to explain partial relationships can be categorized based on the reason each offers for the agent's love of the beloved. The concept of "love" can refer to various rival concepts including the views of love developed by Harry Frankfurt, J. David Velleman, Hugh LaFollette, and Niko Kolodny.

2.1 HARRY FRANKFURT'S "NO REASONS" ACCOUNT OF LOVE

Harry Frankfurt offers an account of love that claims that neither the general human attributes of the beloved, such as personhood and rationality, nor the particular valuable attributes of the beloved, like a sense of humor, insight, or beauty, are the basis for love. Instead, the necessary connection between love and value is that love becomes the basis for the lover's valuation of a particular person. Someone who claims to love another person but does not value him misunderstands the nature of love. What is unusual about this account is that the beloved's value has no basis in any of his attributes, but rather love bestows value upon the beloved. Frankfurt claims,

> It is true that the beloved invariably is, indeed, valuable to the lover. However, perceiving that value is not at all an indispensable *formative* or *grounding* condition of the love. It need not be a perception of value in what he loves that moves the lover to love it. The truly essential relationship between love and the value of the beloved goes in the opposite direction. It is not necessarily as a *result* of recognizing their value and of being captivated by it that we love things. Rather, what we love necessarily *acquires* value for us *because* we love it.[2]

For Frankfurt, love is not a response to anything valuable within the beloved. Instead, love becomes the basis for the lover's valuation of the beloved. We do not love people because they are valuable, but they become valuable to us because we love them. Love bestows value upon the beloved.

Frankfurt emphasizes that whom we love is not simply voluntary. "What we love and what we do not love is not simply a matter of choice; it is not immediately up to us."[3] He explains that the overall structure of an individual's will, shaped by values, circumstances, and experiences, is the only possible measurement of love's rationality. The compatibility of one's loves with one another is the only test of whether a love is reasonable. There is no objective measurement of love's reasonableness:

> Love is not the outcome of any process of reasoning. It is not dictated by the necessities of logic or of rationality. It is shaped by the circumstances of individual experience and character. The desirability of loving one thing or another cannot be decisively evaluated by a priori methods. It can be measured only against requirements that are imposed upon us by other things that we love.[4]

He admits that we may find ourselves valuing something without good reasons for doing so. We may love something irrationally in the sense that loving it conflicts with our other important loves, but no other test of love's rationality is possible.

Frankfurt gives two common examples of love to illustrate his views: the love that a person has for her own life and the love of a parent for her children. He emphasizes that these loves seem innate and are not based on any reasoning but are caused by volitional necessity within the structure of the self's will:

> The fact that people ordinarily do not hesitate in their commitments to the continuation of their lives, and to the well-being of their children, does not derive from any actual consideration by them of reasons; nor does it depend even upon an assumption that good reasons could be found. Those commitments are innate in us. They are not based upon deliberation. They are not responses to any commands of rationality.[5]

While Frankfurt is correct that most people need no argument to convince them to love their own lives or their children, it does not follow that there is no objective rationality for evaluating such loves. Yet he quickly moves to this conclusion:

> We do not consider parents to be acting unreasonably or unjustifiably if they continue to love and to protect their children with unshaken confidence and devotion even after discovering that their children are regarded by others with distaste or contempt. Nor are parents generally condemned for doing this even when they are utterly incapable of arguing plausibly, much less of proving, that the hostility to their children is unwarranted. We do not think that a person is being irrationally stubborn, or that his behavior is reprehensibly arbitrary, if he insists upon defending his own life even when he cannot refuse the complaints against him of those who wish he were dead.[6]

Frankfurt implies that the only alternative to his "no reasons" view of love is to base love in some proof of worth of the beloved based upon the beloved's nonrelational attributes. If one's child or self is rightfully despised by others, which would undermine any claim that the beloved possesses objectively valuable attributes, the only alternative Frankfurt considers is that there must be no reasons for love.

Frankfurt's reasoning, however, is based in a false dilemma. An option he does not consider is that the value of an agent's children or his own life can be and is based in the nature of their relationship to the lover.[7] The agent's life has indisputable value to him because it is his self.[8] The agent's relationship to his self is an indisputable reason for him to value his life. We judge those who do not value themselves to be irrational, even if we believe their lives are without value to others. Those who do not value themselves are irrational because the relationship of one's self to one's self is indisputably valuable on all major accounts of well-being. The destruction of one's self destroys a necessary condition for any future goods such as pleasure, desires to be fulfilled, virtue, friendship, and so forth. This explanation differs considerably both from Frankfurt's claim that there is no reason for valuing one's self beyond the fact that valuing one's self is fixed by volitional necessity, and from theories locating the value of persons in their nonrelational qualities.

Similarly, those who do not love their own children except under extreme circumstances aren't merely odd in their desires. Their volitional structure is not trivially unusual or quirky, like someone who is obsessed with collecting bottle caps. A person who doesn't love his own children is typically viewed as vicious, sick, misguided, or even despicable. A person's children are valuable to her simply because they are her children. No *further* reason is needed, but the fact that they are one's children is a rational basis for their value.

Niko Kolodny offers a similar objection to Frankfurt:

> What if someone peering into the schoolyard, found himself caring about a stranger's child rather than his own child, Alice? Would we not think that he ought to care about something other than he does? Perhaps this parent's affections would be "unthinkable" for us, in the way that a normal parent's would not be. But this itself seems to tell against Frankfurt's view.... What we would be finding unthinkable is failing to love one's child: failing to love a person viewed as falling under a certain description. This seems to conflict not only with Frankfurt's analysis of love, which insists that it attaches to particulars as such, but also with his case that there are no reasons for love. For it offers us a possible reason for loving a person: that one shares a history of a certain kind with her, such as being her parent.[9]

Kolodny's objection emphasizes that someone who loves a stranger's child rather than his own isn't merely odd, but embraces something unthinkable for most people. His explanation is that Frankfurt has not considered a relational explanation for love. A relational explanation of love claims that relationships constitute the reasons for love. Thus, we should love our own children, rather than a stranger's, simply because they are our children.

Frankfurt provides an analysis of Bernard Williams's famous examination of the potential conflict between impartial morality and partial relationships, which unintentionally demonstrates this connection between relationships and love. Williams examines the dilemma of a man who sees two drowning people, one of which is his wife. Williams claims that if the husband searches for a reason to justify saving his wife first, he has "one thought too many."[10] He claims the relationship itself is obviously a sufficient reason for rescuing her first and there is something wrong if the man even thinks he needs further reasons for treating her preferentially. Williams uses this illustration to argue that deep personal attachments and impartial morality inevitably conflict. Frankfurt comments on this example, claiming that it is not the legal status of the rescuer and the drowner's relationship that provides a reason to rescue her first. After all, some marriages do become homicidally violent. Rather, the fact that the man loves her rather than the stranger provides a reason for treating her preferentially.[11]

The interchange between Frankfurt and Williams illustrates that we assume a person loves his spouse even if we know nothing about the couple other than their legal relationship. This association between love and marriage is hardly shocking since marriage vows include a commitment to love. When one does not love his spouse, we recognize the incongruity of the concept "unloved spouse." It is essentially saying that he does not love the one he has committed to love. In the marital relationship, it is easy to seize upon the vows as the reason we expect love to be present. We could hastily conclude that the concept of an "unloved spouse" is incongruous only because it implies a failure to fulfill a promise. Yet, there are other relationships that we expect to be marked by love. We recognize at least as much incongruity in the concept of an "unloved child" or "distant friend." Within marriage, the marital vow is one reason we expect the presence of love, but that's not because marriage vows constitute some arbitrary promise between two people. The marriage vow helps inaugurate and define the nature of the relationship between spouses. Most notably, it defines the relationship as one of committed and intimate love. However, there are also other relationships that are defined with an expectation of love.

As Frankfurt emphasizes, we expect a parent to love her offspring regardless of the child's character. However, like the spousal relationship, the nature of the relationship between parent and child itself is a reason for love. Similarly, it is expected that a person will love his own life, his self, at least in the barest form of protecting his own life. It is rarely necessary to offer reasons for love in these cases because the reasons are so deeply ingrained and so obvious that we are often blind to them. They are rarely salient in our everyday actions. However, that does not mean there is no reason for such love.

Kolodny offers a second criticism of Frankfurt, claiming,

> Besides having other problems, however, this view fails to characterize love as a distinctive state. Without in fact loving Jane, one can desire to do the same things for her that her lover desires to do. For example, one can desire to help Jane out of, say, duty, or self-interest, or simply because one is seized by a brute urge.[12]

If love is distinct and the actions associated with love can be engaged in for nonloving reasons, at least part of love's distinctiveness must be located in its reasons. Since Frankfurt's account gives no reasons for love, it cannot give distinct reasons for the actions of love. Therefore, the actions of love become indistinguishable from other unloving actions.

This objection, however, is overly simplistic. Frankfurt does not define love strictly in terms of "desires to do things" with or for the beloved, but as the source of the unique value of the beloved. Actions associated with love are motivated by the beloved's unique value. Implicitly, if an action is motivated by the unique value attributed to the beloved, it is not motivated by self-interest or duty. So the actions of love are at least distinguishable from actions motivated by self-interest or duty. Yet the difference between actions motivated by "love for no reasons" and "brute urges" is unclear on Frankfurt's account. Kolodny is correct that his view eliminates any distinction between these motives. Valuing something because of a brute urge becomes indistinguishable from love, which is a troubling implication.

Frankfurt's account of love is also inadequate in other ways. It provides no rational basis for a lover's choice of love for one person over another person. He denies the existence of an objective rational basis for love. Yet some loves are typically viewed as more rational or wiser than others. Loving one's own children in a distinct way from other children is a nearly universal phenomenon, while loving a stranger's children as one's own would likely be attributed to mental disease. The obvious exception to this pattern would be adoption, but adoption demonstrates the connection of love to relational reasons since adoption is a way to establish a new parent-child relationship. Developing friendships or romance with those who treat you well is more rational than developing these relationships with those who are verbally and physically abusive. We advise those who are mistreated by those they love to seek relational distance or even reconsider the value of the relationship itself. An account of love that fails to explain or justify this phenomenon is implausible.

Frankfurt's claim that the desirability of loving one thing over another is determined in light of our other loves illumines how agents subjectively evaluate the desirability of a particular love. However, we typically evaluate the desirability of other agents' loves under the modest presumption that every person loves himself and is concerned with his own well-being. For example, the expectation that each person loves himself is implied by Aquinas's account of natural law, which portrays self-preservation as one of its most basic dictates.[13] If a certain pattern of love for others is implicit in love for one's self, then an objective prudential evaluation of love is possible. Additionally, if the claims of *eudaimonism* are correct, then moral excellence in caring for others will coincide with its prudential desirability for the individual.

There is also a greater role for choice in love than Frankfurt's account allows. While he is correct that valuing inevitably follows love, there are times when love is marked by choice. Agents frequently make choices about love: choices that strengthen it, weaken it, or even quench it in its earliest stages. What does she value more: the vocational success allowed by a potential move or the romantic relationship that cannot be maintained if such a move is made? Does she value the relationships with a sister or parent enough to forgive a wrong in order to maintain a relationship? Does she value her relationship with this spouse enough to be faithful when other attractive opportunities are available? For Frankfurt there can be no correct answers for these questions, nothing admirable, rational, or excellent in how one loves.

Frankfurt's account also undercuts many aspects of discussing love as a virtue, a human excellence. For Frankfurt, it is possible to love what one happens to love excellently or for one's loves to be well-ordered in light of one another. However, there is nothing to measure the objective excellence in what one loves, and there are no excellences distinct to the various kinds of love. Alan Soble similarly objects that we would never allow hatred based upon no reasons, so why would we admit love based upon no reasons? He cleverly suggests,

> As an exercise, try all this out on hate. "I disvalue you because I hate you. Why do I hate *you?* I have no idea. It has nothing to do with you. It is not that you are antecedently hate-worthy, as if you did something nasty and cruel to me. I might even hate you were you especially *nice* to me." "Agapic" hate looks pathological, and we would help someone experiencing it to get over it. Not so for "agapic" love, according to its proponents.[14]

Soble illustrates that irrational hatred is something pathological to be overcome, not simply a volitional necessity to be accepted. Love is similar in that love without reason should not be accepted so easily. Some loves are widely viewed as excellent and others viewed as foolish or immature. Undying unrequited love for someone who hates us without reason is foolish. It is a pathology to be defeated, not a source of value to be embraced. There are also excellences in love that are closely connected to the distinct relationship one has with the beloved. For example, it is generally accepted that it is excellent to love one's spouse in ways that it would be foolish, unwise, defective, or vicious to love one's dentist. Even one's loves are not completely interchangeable. There are important differences between a particular person's love for a parent, a spouse, a child, and a sibling.

2.2 DAVID VELLEMAN'S "GENERIC ATTRIBUTES"
ACCOUNT OF LOVE

One alternative to Frankfurt's "no reasons" view of love identifies a reason for love found universally in all persons. On this account, love is based upon the recognition of the beloved's objective value. One such theory is advanced by David Velleman. In an attempt to reconcile the partiality of love with the impartiality of morality, he explains love in terms of the lover's emotional responsiveness to the beloved's humanity, personhood, and rational capacities. Since the basis of love is generic personhood, all humans are appropriate objects for love. His account focuses on mature adult loves, such as friendship, rather than irrational romantic love. He explains, "I do not want to claim that blind, romantic love has any special kinship with morality. When I say that love is a moral emotion, what I have in mind is the love between close adult friends and relations."[15] He argues that this love of friends is a morally valuable emotion since it is a response to the value of their personhood. Such a response does not conflict with the demands of impartial morality.

Velleman compares love to Kant's account of respect or reverence, which is also a response to the objective value of personhood. He models his account of love after the Kantian emotion of reverence. Both love and reverence are based upon the agent's awareness of the personhood of others. He explains, "Reverence for the law, which has struck so many as making Kantian ethics impersonal, is in fact an attitude towards the person, since the law that commands respect is the ideal of a rational will, which lies at the very heart of personhood."[16] Since the rational will is the essence of personhood, Velleman sees reverence for the moral law and love for others as paradigmatic examples of Kantian moral emotions. Both emotions have an impartial but personal basis.

Velleman explicates both love and respect as second order negative emotions. Based on the second formulation of the categorical imperative, which prohibits treating persons as a means, he describes respect as a negative second order motive. Respect prevents us from having first order motivations that treat persons only as means rather than ends in themselves. Respect is a second order motive because it is a motive concerning an agent's first order motivations. It leads the rational person to bring first order motivations in line with the second order guidance provided by respect. However, respect is a negative second order motivation because it prevents or discourages the agent from having morally unacceptable first order motivations. Respect for the moral law prevents an agent from immoral motivations such as greed, envy, hatred, and lust, each of which involves treating humanity as a means.

Velleman claims that love, like respect, is also a negative second order motive, but one that has particular other persons rather than all humanity as its object. He asks,

> Could this model of a negative second order motive apply to love? Let me return to Kant's description of reverence as the awareness of a value that arrests our self-love. I am inclined to say that love is likewise the awareness of a value inhering in its object; and I am also inclined to describe love as an arresting awareness of that value.[17]

Respect deters immoral motives that treat a person as a mere means to some further goal. If love is a second order motivation, what first order motives will it restrain? According to Velleman, love arrests a person's "tendencies toward emotional self protection from another person, tendencies to draw ourselves in and close ourselves off from being affected by him. Love disarms our emotional defenses; it makes us vulnerable to the other."[18] Thus, love is a second order motivation because it influences the loving agent's first order motives toward particular beloved persons. Love is a negative second order motivation because it restricts particular self-protective first order motivations. It restrains a person from acting upon self-protective motivations within relationships, such as fear, insecurity, and anxiety, allowing the lover to be open and vulnerable with the beloved. Simultaneously, he denies that love is focused on benefiting the beloved or aiding the beloved, rejecting such claims as "sentimental fantasy."[19]

There are numerous attractive features in Velleman's account of love. First, his account is correct that emotional vulnerability is a central normative experience of love in the broad range of loving relationships. A high degree of emotional vulnerability is present in most recognizable instances of love between friends, siblings, spouses, and so forth. Second, his strategy eliminates much of the tension between partial love and impartial morality, especially the Kantian account of morality. Since love has nothing to do with benefiting the beloved, it is not connected with actions in conflict with impartial morality. Finally, he provides an explanation for love that offers a compelling explanation for love's tenacity, unlike most accounts of love that explain love as a response to the beloved's attributes. Since love is based in an attribute that the beloved possesses in light of her personhood—her rational capacities—it is not easily lost. Beauty, personality, accomplishments, virtue, or even intelligence are more contingent personal attributes. In contrast, people possess rational *capacities* simply in light of being human.

While Velleman's account has these positive traits, it is inadequate in other ways. One obvious question raised by his account is why the lover cares for some people but not others since they are all appropriate objects for love in light of their personhood. Niko Kolodny offers this type of objection,

> In J. David Velleman's provocative and ingeniously argued proposal, the reason for love is the beloved's bare Kantian personhood, her capacity for rational choice and valuation. But no such non-relational feature works.... The claim that non-relational features are reasons for love implies, absurdly, that insofar as one's love for (say) Jane is responsive to its reasons, it will accept any relevantly similar person as a replacement.[20]

As Kolodny emphasizes, love is not transferable to others just because they have similar nonrelational traits. This problem is especially severe on Velleman's account since its reason for love is an attribute possessed by all persons. In an attempt to respond to such criticisms, Velleman explains that we love some people rather than others based upon our ability to grasp their personhood.

> One reason why we love some people rather than others is that we can see into only some of our observable fellow creatures.... Whether someone is loveable depends on how well his value as a person is expressed or symbolized for us by his empirical persona. Someone's persona may not speak very clearly of his value as a person, or may not speak in ways that are clear to us.[21]

Velleman suggests we love some people rather than others, because we can only see into the personhood of some people. If our interactions with another offer clear insight into his personhood, it is natural to respond to him with the love warranted by his status as a rational being. If we are less aware of another's personhood, it is easier to be self-protective. Yet this explanation seems strained and leads to unintuitive consequences. Daniel Calcutt, for example, objects that Velleman's response is flawed:

> This is *an* explanation of why we love only some people, but it is awfully far-fetched.... The fact that Velleman's account makes it so hard to explain the fact that we love only some suggests that something has gone wrong with the account. And the heart of the problem, it seems to me, is the marginalization of people's distinctive features in his conception of love.[22]

Calcutt goes on to suggest that greater attention to the specific attributes of the beloved would resolve Velleman's difficulty. We will examine Calcutt's type of view later when we examine Hugh LaFollette's account of love. Yet there are additional, unnoticed problems with Velleman's response. The most serious problem with Velleman's explanation for why we love some people rather than others is not its initial implausibility, but its difficulty explaining the nonsubstitutability of the beloved and the various types of loving relationships. Since he believes love acts identically in every loving relationship by restricting the agent's self-protective motivations, differing only in the degree of emotional openness based on our ability to see into the beloved's personhood, the beloved becomes too easily replaceable. The lover may recognize the personhood of his classmate, his spouse, and his child, but the normative experience of love clearly indicates that we should not accept them as substitutes for one another. Yet it is difficult to see what reason Velleman's account can give for not accepting such substitutions.

These potential consequences are seen in Velleman's claim, "The way to bring love in convergence with morality is not to stop thinking of morality as impartial but to rethink the partiality of love."[23] If love is impartial in this way, there is no reasonable basis for loving one person more than or in a distinct way from any other person. This implication is problematic since some aspects of love obviously differ from relationship to relationship. Love for a friend, a spouse, a child, and a parent differ significantly, and an account of love should offer some explanation for this common experience. A parent who is emotionally open to his child but has no further desire, emotion, or action toward him falls short of love. Love between spouses requires not only emotional openness, but also requires an ongoing commitment to maintaining the relationship and to sexual fidelity.

Velleman's account of love is also surprisingly minimalist. Love does not require a single positive action or motivation. He describes love as having an object in a particular other person, but no aim. Instead of an aim, love merely restrains the lover's self-protection motives. Love need not be instantiated in any action or desire-motivating action. Just as one may often carry out Kant's imperative to "never treat humanity as a means only" by interacting very little with a particular person, one can be emotionally open without many actions typically associated within love. It is also possible to be emotionally open to another but otherwise abusive. Such relationships do not embody the ideal of love. While emotional openness is a common trait within loving relationships, it is insufficient as a full and complete account of love.

Velleman's account of love as emotional openness seems to imply that some relationships should be recategorized as "loving." For example, an emotionally neurotic patient who pursues psychoanalysis faithfully may be "loving" toward his analyst on this account. So long as the patient views the analyst as a "safe" person and is vulnerable to her, the patient should be said to "love" the analyst. Similarly, the devoted parishioner who goes to a priest for confession participates in a loving relationship.[24] The new member of an Alcoholic's Anonymous Chapter who openly shares about his addiction with a room full of anonymous strangers "loves" them on this model.

While Velleman clearly works toward resolving the tension between impartial morality and partiality, it is not obvious that his account resolves the central issue of this debate. When ethicists worry about love's partiality, they aren't concerned with the partiality one shows through emotional vulnerability to friends, but with the practical benefits the lover offers the beloved. In Bernard Williams's illustration it is not the man's emotional vulnerability to his wife that is ethically troubling, but the husband's preferential treatment of her in saving her life rather than the stranger's life. Velleman's response to his example is revealing:

> Of course the man in William's story should save his wife in preference to strangers. But the reasons why he should save her have nothing essentially to do with love. The grounds for preference in this case include, to begin with, the mutual commitments and dependencies of a loving relationship.[25]

This response keeps love impartial by justifying the husband's partiality in terms of the mutual commitments and dependencies of a loving relationship, while denying these commitments and dependencies have any necessary connection with love. While it is trivially true that love as emotional vulnerability has no essential connection to marital commitments, this response doesn't really resolve the conflict between partial attachment and impartial morality, but merely separates the concept of love from partial attachment. While love no longer conflicts with impartial morality, partial attachment from the mutual commitments and dependencies of loving relationships still do.

2.3 HUGH LAFOLLETTE'S "SPECIFIC ATTRIBUTES" ACCOUNT OF LOVE

While Velleman's account claims the reason for love is the beloved's generic personhood, Hugh LaFollette[26] offers an articulate account of a more common view that claims the specific attributes of particular persons, such as their intellect, virtue, beauty, or humor, provide the rational basis for love. He explains,

> If Tom loves Barbara, he should have reasons for his love—even if he cannot completely articulate them. These reasons should make explicit reference to Barbara's characteristics. Tom should be able to say, for example, that he loves Barbara because she is funny, or interesting, or insightful, or kind. If he cannot, he would begin to doubt his love. So would Barbara.[27]

LaFollette claims the reasons for love are the beloved's specific attributes. While people may base love on a wide variety of attributes, obviously some attributes are a better basis for love than others. Some attributes are less central to the beloved's identity, are less permanent, are more easily repeatable, or have little relevance to the quality of the agent's relationships. He offers four conclusions about the reasons for love, claiming that the best reasons for love are the beloved's relationally helpful traits, particularly moral qualities. He concludes,

> (1) Love should be based on reasons; (2) reasons must make explicit reference to the beloved's traits; (3) the best reasons for love will make reference to those traits most conducive to close relationships; (4) the traits which will do that are generally moral traits. Therefore, the best reasons for love will be those which make explicit reference to the moral character of the beloved.[28]

LaFollette's view is neither new nor unusual. The idea that love is based upon the attributes of the beloved is an ancient idea that can be found at least as far back as Aristotle's account of friendship, in which one's friends are valued for their virtue, their pleasantness, or their utility.[29] Aristotle, like LaFollete, concludes that the best friendships are based upon the virtuous traits of the beloved.

LaFollette modifies this initial account of love since there are a number of obvious objections to basing love on specific attributes of individuals. For example, Kolodny's objection to Velleman's account also applies to LaFollette's: the normative experience of love suggests the beloved is unique and not substitutable with others, but the grounding attributes of love occur in many nonbeloved persons, often in superior quality. Similarly, love is more tenacious than this model seems to allow since it can last through changes in the beloved's attributes. Eleonore Stump raises similar objections to accounts like LaFollette's. She explains,

> But the responsive account implies that if the beloved loses the characteristics valued by the lover, then the lover's love must cease. On the responsive account, then, the well-known Shakespearean line is wrong: *pace* Shakespeare, love *must* alter when it alteration finds. This implication has the counter-intuitive result of making love very fragile, contrary to what we expect and find.[30]

These objections motivate LaFollette to offer numerous amendments to his initial account of love to explain love's tenacity and the perceived uniqueness of the beloved. While LaFollette claims the reasons for love are the beloved's personal attributes, he does not claim the reasons for love can be fully articulated.[31] He also adds that reason never dictates the formation of certain relationships or causes the initial formation of relationships, but that rational reflection merely approves or rejects, encourages or discourages, the maintenance and deepening of existent relationships.[32] Furthermore, once a relationship develops, the history of a successful shared relationship between lover and beloved becomes an important reason for maintaining love. He explains,

> A relationship is formed and shaped by relating: the sharing of activities, ideas, peeves, jokes, and, in deeper relationships, money and bodies. The interaction is the glue. The more we relate, the more intermingled our lives become. The more intertwined our lives become, the more each of us has a reason to continue the relationship.... If we have a successful relationship it is generally imprudent to abandon it to pursue a relationship with another.... The only way to know we can relate successfully is to successfully relate. [33]

Therefore, this history of a successful shared relationship makes it irrational to abandon this relationship, even if someone with similar or superior traits is available as a replacement.

While these modifications to LaFollette's account strengthen his account and address some of the previous objections, several problems remain. First, he admits this account of love is limited to adult friends, spouses, and lovers, but does not apply to other loving relationships such as those between family members.[34] He refers to his main account of love as "historical" love but describes family love as "rigid" love that does not fit this pattern. This limitation to his account is hardly devastating, but it at least demonstrates that his theory does poorly on the "flexibility" criterion for an ideal account of love.

While LaFollette's insight that shared relational history becomes a reason for maintaining an existent relationship helps explain love's "non-substitutability" and "tenaciousness," this factor also muddles his account. Since relationships aren't initially formed due to the beloved's specific attributes and because shared relational history becomes a central reason for maintaining relationships, the foundational role that personal attributes play in love vanishes. The role of the beloved's personal attributes becomes limited to briefly validating an existing relationship, which was not created because of attributes, until shared relational history becomes the reason for maintaining the relationship.

Lafollette's account also seems incorrect concerning the role of shared relational history. A history of successful interaction may be a reason for continuing a *relationship*, but this reason is hardly the basis for *love*. It is possible to have a wide variety of successful relational interactions and maintain a relationship without love. For example, spouses who fundamentally dislike one another may learn to interact well "for the sake of the children." Yet love is more than mere "successful relational interaction."[35] The true lover still cares for the beloved even when relational interaction becomes unsuccessful.

It is more appropriate to view the relationship itself as a central reason for love. While drawing on a similar intuition to LaFollette's view, this explanation has the advantage that it is not limited to friends, spouses, and lovers. A parent may love a child's beauty, playfulness, and good temperament, but first and foremost a parent's love for her children is based upon the simple fact that they are her children. If her children had other attributes, she would likely find some of those attributes attractive instead.

Even the voluntarily chosen relationships that LaFollette focuses upon are better explained if the relationship is taken as a reason for love. Perhaps a friend is initially chosen in part because of specific attractive attributes and the shared relational history becomes a reason for maintaining the relationship. However, the brute fact that this person has the relational status of "friend" quickly becomes an independent reason for caring about him, acting on his behalf, maintaining the relationship, and valuing the relationship through times of relational hardship. Friends act on each other's behalf, not only because of shared relational history, but also because of their current relational status. While friendship need not be lifelong, the fact that one is a friend or was once a close friend is a reason for caring about that person, regardless of the quality of current interactions.

2.4 NIKO KOLODNY'S RELATIONAL
ATTRIBUTES ACCOUNT OF LOVE

A final account of love, which captures some strengths of the previous views while avoiding many of their problems, is offered by Niko Kolodny. Unlike Frankfurt, he suggests there is a reason for love, but unlike Velleman and LaFollette, he claims that the only normative reason for love is the distinct relationship between lover and beloved. He claims, "One's reason for loving a person is one's relationship to her: the ongoing history that one shares with her."[36] Love is based upon neither a generic attribute that all persons possess, nor a specific attribute that a person possesses in herself, but a unique attribute that one person possesses due to her history with another.

Kolodny delineates the different aspects of love and its connection to beliefs about the nature of relationships. He explains,

> Love is not only rendered *normatively appropriate* by the presence of a relationship. Love, moreover, partly *consists* in the belief that some relationship renders it appropriate, and the emotions and motivations of love are causally *sustained* by this belief (except in pathological cases). Special concern for a person is not love at all when there is no belief that a relationship renders it appropriate.[37]

On this account, love is based in a unique attribute of the beloved, the beloved's distinct relational history with the lover along with the lover's belief that the relationship renders love appropriate. The desires and feelings associated with love are sustained by a belief that the nature of the lover's relationship with the beloved makes these desires and feelings appropriate. When love causes the lover to aid a beloved friend, the lover cares for and aids his friend because the beloved is a friend. He does not care if the friend is wise, funny, or possesses generic personhood. If one's beloved spouse dies, the lover does not weep primarily because his wife was beautiful, a great painter, or even because she was wise, kind, and virtuous. There are undoubtedly more beautiful, better painters, and more virtuous persons the loving husband did not mourn; he mourns the loss of his wife because the beautiful, virtuous painter that died was her, his wife.

Relationships are ongoing historical interactions between two particular people over time. Kolodny emphasizes that in a loving relationship the lover both is emotionally vulnerable toward the beloved and believes the relationship rationally justifies both her vulnerability to the beloved and certain types of actions toward the beloved:

> According to the relationship theory, love is a psychological state for which there are reasons, and these reasons are interpersonal relationships. More specifically, love is a kind of valuing. Valuing X, in general, involved (i) being vulnerable to certain emotions regarding X, and (ii) believing that one has reasons both for this vulnerability to X and for actions regarding X.[38]

This (still preliminary) account of Kolodny's view specifies that love is a species of valuing that one person has for another. Somewhat surprisingly, valuing necessarily includes a belief that one has reasons for this valuing located in the shared relationship between lover and beloved.

Kolodny also offers a fuller six-point account of love. He describes love saying:

> More precisely, A's loving B consists (at least) in A's:
> - believing that A has an instance, r, of a finally valuable type of relationship, R, to person B (in a first-personal way—that is, where A identifies himself as A);
> - being emotionally vulnerable to B (in ways that are appropriate to R), and believing that r is a noninstrumental reason for being so;
> - being emotionally vulnerable to r (in ways that are appropriate to R), and believing that r is a noninstrumental reason for being so;
> - believing that r is a noninstrumental reason for A to act in B's interest (in ways that are appropriate to R) and having, on that basis, a standing intention to do so;
> - believing that r is a noninstrumental reason for A to act in r's interest (in ways that are appropriate to R), and having, on that basis, a standing intention to do so; and

- believing that any instance, r*, of type R provides (a) anyone who has r* to some B* with similar reasons for emotion and action toward B* and r*, and (b) anyone who is not a participant in r* with different reasons for action (and emotion?) regarding r*.[39]

Kolodny's six criteria for love include four core beliefs the lover must hold, two of which lead to ongoing intentions toward the beloved and two types of emotional vulnerabilities associated with love. The first requirement states that the lover believes the beloved possesses an instance of an intrinsically valuable type of relationship with him. The second and third requirements stipulate that the lover is emotionally vulnerable both to the beloved and to their specific relationship in ways appropriate to that kind of relationship generally. Emotional vulnerability causes the lover to have a tendency toward experiencing a range of positive emotions concerning love's object. The fourth criterion requires is that the lover believes his relationship with the beloved is a sufficient reason to act on her behalf in relationally appropriate ways, and that the belief causes an ongoing intention to do so. The fifth requirement is that the lover believes his relationship with the beloved is a reason for acting in the relationship's interests and has ongoing intentions to do so. The sixth requirement is that the lover believes that anyone within the same type of relationship has similar reasons for emotion and action within that relationship, and believing that anyone outside of that type of relationship necessarily has different reasons for action and emotion.

There are many advantages to Kolodny's view. It gives reasons for loving that are truly unique to beloved individuals, instead of finding reasons in some trait that may be infinitely repeatable. Since the sole reason for love is the unique ongoing history of a shared relationship, no other person could be relevantly similar as a substitute for love. His view avoids the problems associated with giving nonrelational reasons for love. His account better explains love's tenacity than any account that focuses on nonrelational attributes of the beloved. Love often survives many changes within the beloved's attributes. Of course, certain kinds of changes within personal attributes, especially character changes, may undermine the relationship between lover and beloved. Yet Kolodny's view correctly identifies the relationship as the attribute most central to love. Finally, the "relational reasons" view is flexible and applies to a wide variety of relational contexts.

While Kolodny's view avoids the problems of the first three views, it has some difficulties of its own. One type of objection to his view attempts to find an instance of genuine love without a relationship. For example, Vellman rejects Kolodny's account, saying,

We probably cannot love people with whom we aren't acquainted, but I think that we can indeed love acquaintances with whom we have no significant relationship—love them at first sight or from afar. We can also love people whose relationship with us we do not value at all, as when divorcing couples still love one another despite looking back on their marriage as a disaster from day one.[40]

Velleman claims love for an acquaintance or divorced spouse does not fit Kolodny's account, but he underestimates the flexibility of the relational account of love. In the case of love for a former spouse, a lover may yet believe that a relationship with a divorced spouse from a disastrous marriage is a basis for some positive emotions or concern for him. Such a person may also be deeply double-minded and possess both strong positive and negative emotions toward the former spouse, but it is undeniable that he played an important role in her life. Anger with a former spouse may be rooted in an equally deep amount of care for her and an unfulfillable desire for intimacy with her. A rejection of the value of a specific kind of relationship with someone, in this case a marital relationship, does not necessarily entail rejecting the value of all types of relationships with him. The divorced spouse example is more complex than the objection permits.

Velleman is correct that love for a casual acquaintance presents difficulties for the relational account, since this case involves caring for a specific acquaintance in ways one does not care for all acquaintances. However, Kolodny will deny that unusually intense care for an acquaintance or emotions toward her constitute love. Perhaps, the "lover" in this case is merely attracted to the acquaintance, enjoys her company, or empathizes with her plight. These positive emotions need not be identified with love. His account has room for concern and positive emotions toward others that fall short of love. Yet the plausibility of this defense depends upon the specific details of the situation.

Eleonore Stump offers a specific relational example that causes problems for the relational account. She describes one famous medieval instance of love that doesn't fit Kolodny's pattern:

> For Dante and Beatrice, there was virtually no interaction at all, let alone a history of interactions, and so also no relationship, in the sense at issue for the relational account. Nor did Dante suppose that there was. The way Dante himself describes his connection to Beatrice is just that he loves her from a distance with unrequited love. On the relational account, we have to say not that there is something somehow defective or impaired about Dante's love for Beatrice, but just that he did not love her.[41]

Stump is correct that according to the relational account Dante does not love Beatrice, which is counterintuitive. Yet instances of unrequited love,

love from a distance, or love at first sight are certainly nonstandard cases of love. The relational account's inability to capture our full intuitions concerning these cases is not a devastating critique to his account.

Velleman offers a more threatening critique of the relational account and insists that it is egoistic. He explains,

> I find love as Kolodny conceives it to be self-centered, since it responds to a value the beloved has, not because of what he is in himself, but because of what he is to us. Love so conceived is a response to a fundamentally egocentric value, a value that others have in virtue of the part they play in our lives. I doubt whether love really is so egocentric.[42]

If this criticism is correct, it threatens the relational account more centrally than Stump's counterexample. He claims the relational account isn't merely less flexible than we might prefer, but outrightly immoral. Yet the objection's force seems based on an equivocation in the word "egocentric." The relational account of love is not egocentric in the ethically troubling sense of "selfish" or "only caring for one's self." Kolodny's lover cares for the beloved noninstrumentally and acts upon that care. This love is not self-seeking or selfish.

This objection, instead, claims the relational account of love is egocentric because love relies upon a role the beloved plays in the lover's life. Yet, due to the subjective nature of love, it is arguable that this "egocentrism" is found in all accounts of love, including Velleman's account. After all, for Velleman, we only love those people whose rational nature we are adequately able to perceive. It could be argued that we love them "egocentrically" since we would not love them if our interactions did not reveal their personhood. Furthermore, according to Kolodny's schema for love, the lover recognizes the value of certain types of relationships in general. This recognition is implied by his sixth criterion for love, which includes a belief that all relationships of certain types rationally justify love for anyone participating in them. The lover views such relationships as objectively valuable. The lover would love anyone who had the relevant type of relationship with him. Any person would be an appropriate object for love if the proper relational circumstances obtain. It is not egocentric, in any ethically troubling sense of the word, to place unique value on a specific instance of something objectively valuable that one experiences firsthand. For example, it is not irrational, unethical, or surprising if one attributes objective value to works of great art but uniquely values the Mona Lisa because he has personally experienced its beauty.

A more appropriate objection to Kolodny's account is that it simply has too many criteria for love. Must the lover have a detailed theory of love? His sixth requirement for love requires that the lover hold a "theory of love" applying to everyone, everywhere and not just to his own relationship. Many people are less theoretically inclined than this account requires. In a footnote, he acknowledges Wai-hung Wong's convincing counterexample of young children's love for parents as a genuine instance of love although it lacks an internalized schema concerning the nature of love and relationships.[43] It is also likely that there are many nonphilosophers in genuine loving relationships, who could not offer the type of theory of love required by criterion six. Not everyone who values a particular relationship immediately makes the universal inference that everyone in such a relationship should value it. There is also the counterintuitive implication that those who reject the relational theory of love do not truly love. For example, Frankfurt and Velleman do not believe that love is justified by specific relationships, thus failing criteria one and six of Kolodny's requirements for love. Perhaps these loves are imperfect, less fully rational, or less mature than loves that fulfill all six of Kolodny's criteria, but it is dubious to claim that these instances are not love at all.

Another objection to the relational account of love focuses upon counterexamples that fit the relational account of love but are obviously dysfunctional. In an attempt to ward off this possibility, Kolodny lists some experiences that are sometimes mistaken for love. His examples include concern for another based on a brute urge, pathological concern for another, and concern for another based upon relational misperception. He explains,

> Special concern for a person is not love at all when there is no belief that a relationship renders it appropriate. Such is the case with my urge to help Fred Simmons, who is a stranger to me. Love is inappropriate when there is such a belief, but the belief is false. Stalkers, for example, often believe that they have relationships to the objects of their obsessions. Sometimes this reflects a willful interpretation of the evidence, other times a full-blown psychosis. A different kind of inappropriate love results when a person is misled, say by someone who is just using her.[44]

Using these examples, Kolodny rules out the possibility of love based on mistaken beliefs about specific instances of relationship. However, this does not rule out love based on mistaken beliefs concerning what kinds of relationships in general render love appropriate. Someone may be vulnerable to intense emotions toward a celebrity and mistakenly believe that "owning all of a music star's albums" creates the basis for a loving relationship between fan and musician that gives the fan reason for undying devotion to the star, yet this kind of love is hardly an excellence. At best, such love is trivial and immature. At worst, it is a fetish. More disconcertingly, a slave owner might be vulnerable to certain emotions toward people he "owns" and believe that a master-slave relationship provides a relational basis for feeling and acting this way. However, such care and concern is hardly a relational and moral excellence. These instances are based upon mistaken beliefs concerning which kinds of relationships justify love generally, rather than mistaken beliefs concerning the details of a specific relationship.

Kolodny's account also fails to provide a basis for loving benevolence toward people generally. His account only justifies love if we have a relational history with the particular agent. He acknowledges that his account gives reasons for partiality in practical rationality. Yet he does not discuss whether such partiality is incompatible with impartial morality. His account has difficulty reconciling partial love for others with impartial morality. When discussing love, some ethicists believe we ought to have a degree of care and goodwill toward others generally. Recognizing that someone else is "a human being in need" does not create a shared historical relationship meriting "love," but an ideal account of love would show how partial love and impartial benevolence work together.

Michael Slote, for example, gives much attention to the moral importance of benevolence outside of particular relationships and views motivations of both partial caring and impartial benevolence as foundational moral motives. He explains, "I have also become convinced that an ethic of [partial] caring can take the well-being of humanity into all consideration just as easily as an agent-based virtue ethics grounded in universal (i.e., impartial) benevolence."[45] Similarly, Martha Nussbaum emphasizes the importance of general compassion toward others. She claims that the emotion of compassion toward others in general produces a vital link between the agent and broader community. She explains, "First, compassion, in the philosophical tradition, is a central bridge between the individual and the community; it is conceived of as our species' way of hooking the interests of others to our own personal good."[46] An account of love that captures the moral excellence of care both within partial relationships as well as relationships more generally would be superior to Kolodny's account.

ENDNOTES

1. This account of the virtue of love does not preclude the possibility that someone without the fully developed virtue of love could still be said to "love his child or spouse." However, this love is only one expression of a broader virtue, so an agent who loves well in only a few relationships would not have the full virtue of love.

2. Harry Frankfurt, *The Reasons of Love* (Princeton, NJ: Princeton University Press, 2004), 38–39.

3. Harry Frankfurt, *Some Mysteries of Love* (Lawrence, KS: University of Kansas Press, 2001), 6.

4. Harry Frankfurt 2001, 7.

5. Harry Frankfurt 2004, 29.

6. Harry Frankfurt 2004, 30–31.

7. J. David Velleman's view that love is based in the generic personhood of the beloved could also provide an account compatible with Frankfurt's observations. In fact, Frankfurt's objection only undermines a view like Hugh LaFollete's account of love, which identifies specific attributes of the beloved as reasons for love. *Cf.* Hugh LaFollette, *Personal Relationships* (Cambridge, MA: Blackwell Publishers, 1996), 61.

8. Some definitions of the word "relationship" may stipulate that a relationship can only be properly discussed between two different people. However, while speaking of one's relationship with one's self will not fit such strict definitions, this use of the word "'relationship" in this context is at least metaphorically useful.

9. Niko Kolodny, "Book Review: The Reasons of Love," *The Journal of Philosophy* 103 (2006): 49.

10. Bernard Williams, *Moral Luck: Philosophical Papers* (New York: Cambridge University Press, 1981), 18.

11. Frankfurt 2001, 2.

12. Niko Kolodny, "Love As Valuing a Relationship," *Philosophical Review* 112 (2003): 135.

13. ST I-II.94.2.

14. Alan Soble, "Love and Value, yet *Again*," *Essays in Philosophy* 6 (2005), http://fs.uno.edu/asoble/pages/soble2rev.html (11 June 2009).

15. J. David Velleman 1999, 351.

16. J. David Velleman 1999, 348.

17. J. David Velleman 1999, 360.

18. J. David Velleman 1999, 361.

19. J. David Velleman 1999, 353.

20. Niko Kolodny 2003, 135.

21. J. David Velleman 1999, 372.

22. Daniel Calcutt, "Tough Love," *Florida Philosophical Review* 5 (2005): 39.

23. J. David Velleman 1999, 342.

24. I do not deny that some relationships between priests and parishioners should be described as loving. I only deny that emotional openness is a sufficient condition for a loving relationship.

25. J. David Velleman 1999, 373.

26. LaFollette's views are arguably the least influential of the four alternative views examined here. This lack of influence is probably due to the fact that his views are more conventional than the others. However, LaFollette offers a sophisticated and articulate presentation of this fairly conventional position, so his views are worth examining as an attractive representation of a mainstream position.

27. Hugh LaFollette 1996, 61.

28. Hugh LaFollette 1996, 92.

29. Aristotle, *Nichomachean Ethics*, trans. J.A.K. Thompson (New York: Penguin Books, 1955), 1156.

30. Eleonore Stump, "Love, By All Accounts," *Proceedings and Addresses of the American Philosophical Association* 80 (2006): 25–26.

31. Hugh Lafollette 1996, 61.

32. Hugh Lafollette 1996, 61–62.

33. Hugh Lafollette 1996, 63.

34. Hugh Lafollette 1996, 5.

35. The importance of successful relational activities in LaFollette's views is probably due to a behaviorist trend in his view of the self.

36. Niko Kolodny 2003, 135–136.

37. Niko Kolodny 2003, 146.

38. Niko Kolodny 2003, 150.

39. Niko Kolodny 2003, 150–151.

40. J. David Velleman, "Beyond Price," *Ethics* 118 (2008): 198.

41. Eleonore Stump 2006, 26.

42. J. David Velleman 2008, 198.

43. Niko Kolodny 2003, 187, fn 22.

44. Niko Kolodny 2003, 146.

45. Michael Slote, *Morals From Motives* (New York: Oxford University Press, 2001), ix.

46. Martha Nussbaum, "Compassion: The Basic Social Emotion," Social Philosophy and Policy 13 (1996): 28.

Chapter 3

Aquinas's Account of the Virtue of Love

This chapter examines Aquinas's account of the virtue of love. He construes love as *a disposition towards relationally appropriate acts of the will, consisting of a disinterested desire for the good of the beloved and a disinterested desire for unity with the beloved, held as final ends.*[1] Of the contemporary views of love, it is most similar to Niko Kolodny's conception due to the role relational attributes play in love. My view of love is influenced by Aquinas's account of charity, which in turn is influenced by Aristotle's account of friendship. While Aquinas uses four different words for love: *amicitia, amor, caritas,* and *dilectio,* his account of *caritas,* or charity, is his most detailed and most important account.[2] In the *Summa theologiae,* Aquinas's discussion of charity spans twenty-four questions and contains over one hundred twenty-five articles.[3] While an exhaustive examination of charity is beyond the scope of this project, this outline of charity serves as a model for my own contemporary Neo-Thomistic account of love.

3.1 ARE THERE GENUINE VIRTUES WITHOUT CHARITY?

For Aquinas, charity is the greatest of the virtues[4] and the form of all virtues since charity directs them to their proper end.[5] Apart from the love of charity, other virtues might be misused and misdirected.[6] They might be used egoistically or in irrational service of appetites. For example, a thief is courageous in the sense that he controls his fear of danger; however, his "courage" is incompatible with charity because it undermines the objective good of others, and thus he is not deemed virtuous.

One important interpretive question is whether Aquinas claims there are genuinely good moral virtues that do not require charity. Eberhard Schockenhoff interprets Aquinas as claiming there are genuinely good virtues that are neutral regarding charity. He explains,

> Wherever the human being is oriented by the virtues of justice, prudence, courage, bravery, and generosity, or by human civility to the realization of such ends [genuinely good proximate goals not in conflict with charity], he or she brings about a provisional and imperfect happiness that can achieve a certain stability even when it is not directed by charity to the complete happiness of community with God. Not so much by the lack of charity, but only if the relevant partial goal proves to be only an apparent good, the pursuit of which destroys the orientation to the last end, do such prior inclinations lose their virtuous character.[7]

Schockenhoff suggests that a lack of charity does not necessarily undermine the goodness of the moral virtues, so long as goals pursued through these virtues are genuinely good. For example, it is good that a hunter faces danger courageously even if this virtue is not directed by charity. Such virtues that are neutral regarding charity direct the agent toward imperfect happiness, an earthly flourishing, but not toward perfect happiness found in the afterlife's beatific vision.[8]

While there are attractive aspects of Schockenhoff's interpretation, there are two compelling reasons to reject it. First, his criterion for this third class of virtues does not fit within Aquinas's larger account of love. Schockenhoff claims the lack of charity is an insufficient reason for rejecting a "moral virtue's" goodness. For a moral virtue to fail to be good, he believes the goal it aims toward must be merely an apparent good. Yet Aquinas recognizes that some genuinely good goals, such as pleasure,[9] can be pursued in vicious ways when not directed by charity.[10] The virtues used in such a pursuit meet Schockenhoff's criterion since they are directed toward a genuinely good goal, but Aquinas clearly rejects their goodness.

An additional problem for Schockenhoff's interpretation comes from Aquinas's belief in the unity of the virtues.[11] Just as prudence necessarily plays a role in all Aristotelian virtues,[12] infused virtues like charity necessarily play a role in all genuine Thomistic virtues. Aquinas insists that all true moral virtues are connected to infused virtues like charity. He explains,[13]

> Therefore, it is evident that neither infused prudence is able to exist without charity; nor are the other moral virtues able to exist without prudence.... Only virtues that have been infused are perfect, and deserve to be called virtues simply, because they order a man well to the ultimate goal. Certainly acquired virtues are virtues in an inferior sense, but not simply; they order a man well

regarding some final goal of another kind, but not regarding man's ultimate goal simply. Besides the words of Romans XIV, "All that is not out of faith, is sin," a gloss of Augustine says, "Where one fails in acknowledging truth, even virtue in good morals is deceptive."[14]

While Aquinas acknowledges we speak of "virtues" attained by Aristotelian habituation apart from the spiritual life necessary for receiving divinely infused virtue, these traits fall short of full excellence. He believes that the fullest virtues, including charity, are acquired through a process of supernatural infusion,[15] unlike the Aristotelian virtues that are acquired through habituation. The truest expression of prudence, infused prudence, provides practical wisdom guided by charity for directing a person's other virtues toward humanity's ultimate spiritual goal. For Aquinas, either one's dispositions are directed by charity and the other infused virtues to humanity's final end, or they are not. Therefore, Schockenhoff's interpretation claiming there are genuinely good moral virtues developed completely apart from charity should be rejected.

3.2 LOVE'S DISINTERESTED DESIRE FOR THE GOOD OF THE BELOVED

For Aquinas, the central feature of charity is a love for God.[16] This love leads the charitable person to love all that is capable of attaining happiness in God.[17] This includes all persons, since they possess a rational nature capable of attaining happiness in God.[18] This love permeates all of the lover's relationships. Apart from this love, humanity's true purpose and opportunity for happiness is subverted.[19]

Aquinas, citing Aristotle, defines charity as authentic friendship based upon disinterested motives of benevolence. He contrasts authentic love based upon benevolence with inauthentic "love" driven by selfish motives:

> The philosopher says, in the *Ethics VIII*, not every love has the method of friendship, but only love that is combined with benevolence, thus certainly when we love someone we will good to him. On the other hand, if we do not will the good to things we love for their own sake, but instead we will the good to them for our own sake (as we are said to love wine or a horse or anything of this sort) this love is not friendship, but a kind of concupiscence.[20]

A central desire of charity is a disinterested will for the beloved's good. For Aquinas, strong emotions and desires toward another person are not proof of charity. It is appropriate to desire some objects, such as food, for strictly self-beneficial reasons. But when the object of desire is a person, charity requires that we desire the good for her own sake. However, strong feelings can be motivated by selfishness instead of a disinterested concern for the good of the beloved. Such desires are incompatible with charity and express concupiscence, a form of covetousness. Similarly, Etienne Gilson explains that strong passions can be motivated by a disordered and irrational love of self or the love of pleasure, neither of which is compatible with charity.[21]

Under the subtopic of almsgiving, Aquinas offers a list of fourteen actions that express charity whereby the lover promotes the beloved's good[22] by meeting his physical, emotional, intellectual, and spiritual needs.[23] Since Aquinas has an objective view of the good,[24] an agent's desires toward others are evaluated on the basis of their actual rather than intended goodness. Therefore, someone may think he desires the good for another, but be mistaken if his desires for the beloved are not genuinely good. Similarly, someone may mistakenly believe his desires are not good for the beloved. Eleonore Stump offers the example of a battered spouse who wants distance from the abuser but mistakenly thinks this desire is unloving. Since temporary relational distance in such circumstances may be best for both abused and abuser, this desire may actually be an expression of love.[25]

Gilson similarly explains that loving desires consist in willing the same good for the beloved that is wanted for self, and in treating the beloved as another self out of a sense of unity with him.[26] He explains,

> The most immediate and general effect of love is the union between the lover and the beloved.... It is a union of feeling and purely affective if it is a question of the love of friendship, wherein one wishes for the other the same good as for oneself.... To will for another what we will for ourselves, to love another for himself as we love ourselves for ourselves, is to treat the beloved as another self.[27]

Gilson claims that Thomistic love results in a union with the beloved that causes the lover to desire the same goods for the beloved that he wants for himself. While this claim appears to rely upon a subjective account of the good, his suggestion is that the lover wants the same objective goods for the beloved that all people ultimately want for the self, especially happiness, charity, and the other virtues.[28]

Of course, there is a wooden sense in which Gilson's claim is incorrect. Clearly one does not desire all of the specific goods for the beloved that he wants for himself if relevant circumstances differ.[29] For example, a loving person who desires a graduate school education in art history, a fine meal featuring coconut shrimp, and a caring spouse may not wish these precise goods for a beloved friend in relevantly different circumstances, for example, a blind priest with a seafood allergy. While the lover does not always desire the same specific goods for the beloved, he typically desires that the beloved enjoy the same types of goods in a more general sense, in this case, goods associated with education, good food, and rewarding relationships.

3.3 LOVE AND UNION WITH THE BELOVED

Aquinas views the desire for the good of another person as insufficient for love. There must also be a desire for a type of union between lover and beloved. He expands on this theme:

> But love that is in the intellectual appetite actually differs from benevolence. Namely it brings about a certain union of affection of lover to beloved. The lover considers the beloved in a certain way one with himself, even extending to himself, and thus moved into himself. But benevolence is a simple act of will whereby we wish good to someone, yet not presupposing the previously mentioned union of affections to himself. So therefore in delight, that is an act of charity, benevolence is certainly included, but delight or love adds union of affections. And the philosopher because of this says in that very place [*Ethics IX*] that, "benevolence is the beginning of friendship."[30]

In addition to benevolent goodwill toward the beloved, a desire for union of affections with the beloved is also necessary for charity. This affective union is a bond that causes the lover to view the beloved's well-being as partially constitutive of the lover's own well-being. Therefore, a desire for permanent relational distance is incompatible with love.[31] This affective union is particularly relevant to the sharing of life's goods and troubles. While a degree of union between the lover's affections and the beloved's is necessary for love, this union need not be mutual since one person cannot control another's response. While some love will ultimately be unrequited, the lover desires a mutual relationship of goodwill with the beloved, even if such a relationship turns out to be impossible.

Aquinas specifies three types of union that are connected to love. He explains,

> I say that union has a threefold relationship to love. There is union which is the cause of love. Indeed this is substanial union, as regards the love with which one loves himself; while the love with which one loves others is the union of likeness, as argued elsewhere.
>
> There is also another type of union that is essentially love itself; and this second union is conjoined affections. Certainly, this union is compared to substantial union, inasmuch as the lover considers the beloved almost as himself ...

A third type of union is the effect of love. And this is real union, which the lover seeks with the beloved thing. And this union is in keeping with the convention of love. As the Philosopher says, in *Politics II:* "Aristophanes said that lovers may desire out of both to become one"; but because, "from this either one or both may be destroyed," instead they seek union that is appropriate and fitting for love; in order to dwell together, speak together, and share in similar things.[32]

Aquinas cites three relationships between love and union. Substantial union, the unity within a single object, causes an agent to love whatever is united to him since it is part of the self. For example, people love their own bodies due to their union with them. Aquinas explains the strength of one's love for blood relatives on a similar principle. Blood relatives are united by a similarity in substance that accounts for strong love between them.[33]

One sense of union relevant to charity is the aforementioned unity of affection, since the lover views the beloved as connected to himself. This union is based on a similarity between lover and beloved.[34] Recognizing this similarity causes an affective union leading the lover's passions to respond to the beloved's well-being as if it were his own. The lover has a sense of affective union with the beloved and desires the continuation of this union.

Aquinas describes the final sense of union as "real union," which brings lover and beloved together in ways such as physical time, shared attention, communication, and presence. In real union, the lover desires to share daily life with the beloved. In these latter two unions of love, the distinctness and autonomy of the beloved must be preserved to maintain the distinction between lover and beloved. While love's connection to union is a complicated matter for Aquinas, it includes an affective connection between lover and beloved and a desire for aspects of real union with the beloved.

3.4 LOVE'S CONNECTIONS TO THE INTELLECT, THE WILL, AND THE PASSIONS

Since charity is constituted by two desires, Aquinas views the will as the locus of love.[35] For Aquinas, the will is an appetite that is naturally inclined to desire the good.[36] When the will does not love well, it is in a state of disorder and misuse. Its proper function is to care for all persons.[37]

While love is an activity of the will, it has implications for the lover's emotions and intellect as well. While emotions and passions[38] do not constitute love, they are influenced by love.[39] Gilson claims that passions are guided by one's cares and desires.[40] Passions are directed and shaped by what one "loves" in an extended sense of the word. Strong passions and emotions typically result from whatever one wills, whether or not those desires express authentic love. Joy or happiness naturally results when desires are fulfilled.[41] Similarly, frustration or sadness typically results when desires are thwarted.[42]

For Aquinas there is a rationality to love. Since he portrays the will as an intellectual appetite, it is naturally drawn toward what the intellect presents to it as good.[43] Love is rational when the will's desires are directed by an accurate assessment of something's goodness and irrational when directed by an incorrect assessment of a thing's goodness.[44] However, despite the will's natural inclination toward whatever is perceived as good, it maintains freedom since nothing acts upon the will with efficient causality, thereby forcing its choices.[45]

Despite the intellect's influence in decision-making, the will can direct the intellect's attention to various aspects of something's goodness or lack of goodness.[46] An action may include numerous good and bad aspects, allowing the will to shape the decision-making process by choosing which aspects of the action the intellect will focus upon. For example, the intellect may present cheating on an exam as a "good" and useful way to pass a course, as a morally "bad" action, as a "bad" choice that undercuts the development of epistemic goods, or as a "bad" action that hinders one's spiritual life. The will plays a critical role in directing which aspects of the choice the intellect attends to, which in turn determines which factors are weighed most heavily in the will's final choice.

James Keenan makes an even stronger claim that the will is completely and foundationally free because it exercises the power of choice before reason attends to any particular object. He says,

> The will must first be willing to consider any object offered by reason for its acceptance. That the will must first be willing means that the will must first move itself and reason. Without that antecedent willingness, reason does not influence the will with its objects. By establishing this antecedent self-exercise of the will, Thomas distinguishes between God as final cause of the will, *quantum ad exercitium,* and reason as formal cause of the will's movement, *quantum ad specificationem.* This antecedent *exercitium* provides the foundation for Thomas's assertion that the will is free to move itself and reason.[47]

Keenan claims Aquinas believes the will has a foundational antecedent role in decisions that is entirely free from reason's influence. He believes the will's influence goes beyond controlling which aspects of an object are considered or choosing whether to consider an object already presented to it by the intellect. Keenan claims that for Aquinas, the will antecedently chooses whether the intellect considers an object at all. Therefore, it has foundational control in its loves because it can prevent reason from ever considering an object the person does not want to love.

Michael Sherwin offers a differing explanation of the dynamic relationship between the will's desires and the intellect's knowledge in the decision of love. First, loving desires must be based on some preexisting knowledge of the beloved as an appropriate object for love, since something must be known in order to be desired. Therefore, the will's role does not precede the intellect's role in love. Yet the will also influences the intellect since the will can influence the intellect's attention. Sherwin's account of the relationship between love and knowledge can be seen in these two passages:

> Notice that Aquinas does not define love's primary act apart from its object. Love is not merely *complacentia*, it is *complacentia boni:* it is an affective enjoyment and affirmation of some good thing made known to us by reason. In other words, love's object is the *bonum rationis*. Love's dependence on knowledge at this most basic level (the stage that I have called affirmation) has profound implications for Aquinas's theory of action. It means that for Aquinas love, and thus also human action, presupposes a voluntary receptivity to reality.[48]

This first passage indicates love's foundational dependence on the intellect. On Sherwin's account, the will's dependence on the intellect does not leave room for the antecedent type of freedom advocated by Keenan. Yet, Sherwin also acknowledges the importance of the will's free receptivity of knowledge provided by the intellect, thus avoiding determinism. He explains,

> What saves Aquinas' theory from determinism is his recognition that the will's receptivity toward any particular good is freely chosen. Love's primary act is rooted in a receptivity before the real, but this receptivity is not deterministic. We love the goods we perceive, but we can choose not to see them, or we can choose to consider them under the aspect of their limited goodness and thus as not good here and now.[49]

For Sherwin, the will's free choice to receive an object presented to it is not prior to the intellect's influence. Yet Sherwin still protects Aquinas from any charge of determinism in his theory.

Sherwin's account is the more correct of the two interpretations. Keenan's interpretation suffers from two problems. First, even if Keenan is correct that the will can antecedently prevent reason from attending to an object, it does not follow that the will makes this choice apart from the previous dictates of reason. If the will refuses to consider an object altogether, it does so in part because reason has previously presented such refusal as good.[50] For Aquinas, the will always has the perceived good as its object, and therefore it refuses what it perceives as bad.[51] Second, whenever the will refuses to attend to an object, this refusal implies an antecedent consciousness of the object's existence. This consciousness is dependent on, rather than antecedent to, the intellect's activities.

Regardless of whether we accept Sherwin's or Keenan's account, one important upshot of the dynamic relationship between intellect and will is that love is not restricted by the limits of the agent's knowledge. Love can reorder the lover's knowledge and guide her to view things more accurately and charitably. If knowledge influenced love, without love also influencing knowledge, the ability to love might be entirely constrained by the social conditioning that shapes one's beliefs.

A rational person's love is influenced by both the objective and subjective lovability of the object. Objectively speaking, personhood is a necessary and sufficient condition for being an appropriate object for love.[52] People are appropriate objects of love in that they are the most morally valuable objects in existence. Aquinas uses Boethius's definition of the term "person," "an individual substance of rational nature."[53] He goes on to describe personhood as the highest perfection in nature. He explains, "That 'person' signifies that which is most perfect in all nature, certainly that which subsists in a rational nature."[54] Since personhood represents the greatest perfection in existence, it has both the greatest moral value and is worthy of the will's strongest moral responsiveness. In the account of charity offered in *De caritate,* he specifies the rational nature as the proper object of charity.[55] Appropriate objects for charity are always persons, which possess a rational nature as an essential attribute, including God, neighbor, self, and even enemies.[56]

While all persons are appropriate objects for love, the intensity and expression of an agent's love ought to vary from person to person, since people differ both in themselves[57] and in their relationship to an agent.[58] It is possible to love the wrong thing, to express love in the wrong way, or to love with the wrong intensity.[59] One is irrational in her cares when love is based on misperception. One factor that influences love is that some persons are more appropriate objects for love than others based on how completely they fulfill their potential as human persons. Vicious persons are still appropriate objects for love as persons, but their character is not an appropriate object for admiration.[60] Furthermore, the subjective appropriateness of love depends on the relationship between two persons.[61] It is rational to love all but to possess stronger love toward those people most closely united to an agent. For example, it is irrational for a person to desire that Liza Minnelli win the Grammy for best song more strongly than he desires vocational success for his own parents.

3.5 LOVE'S UNIVERSAL SCOPE BUT
DIFFERING EXPRESSIONS

While many contemporary accounts of love view it as a phenomenon within a narrow scope of partially valued relationships, Aquinas broadens love's scope by claiming the charitable person cares for all humanity.[62] He implies the charitable person views no one as a stranger, a person with no relationship to the lover. Instead, the default relational status between two people is that of neighbors regardless of their spatial or relational proximity.[63] All humans are united with one another in the sense that they are potentially fellow partakers in happiness. Furthermore, Gilson explains that all love is based either on similarity or difference;[64] and the love of charity for other persons is a love of friendship based on their shared status as rational beings with happiness in the vision of God as their final end.[65]

While the lover cares for some people more intensely than others and expresses love in different practical ways based upon their shared relationship, the same ultimate good is willed for every person: happiness in the contemplation of God.[66] Factors that help shape the appropriate expression of love include the physical proximity of the beloved, the proximity of their blood relationship, whether they have benefited from the beloved's actions, and the beloved's degree of need.[67]

Aquinas claims that while we ought to will the good for all, we should will the good more strongly for those closest to us. An agent ought to love others in a way appropriate to their relationship. He explains,

> Therefore, it is right that we more greatly benefit those more greatly connected to us.
>
> The nearness of one man to another can be measured by what matters they share; just as kinsmen share in natural matters, fellow-citizens in political matters, the faithful in spiritual matters, and similarly concerning other matters. Various affinities are fitting to arrange different benefits, for it is fitting to produce a benefit to each one concerning the matters in which he is most closely connected with us, simply speaking. Yet this principal can be changed according to various places, times, and troubles; for instance, it is fitting for anyone to help a stranger in extreme need, rather than even one's own father if he is not in great need.[68]

Aquinas believes the nature of two persons' relationship determines both the proper strength and expression of the love's desires. Relationships unite people through their shared concerns. For example, co-workers are united in their shared vocational concerns, fellow citizens are united in shared political concerns, teachers are united with their students in their shared academic concerns, families are united in the shared concerns of everyday life, and so forth. It is possible for two people to have multiple aspects that unite them such as when a relative is a fellow citizen, working in the same vocation, and a member of the same religious faith.

Note that this use of the expression "shared concerns" refers to an objective aspect that is normative for a particular type of relationship. It is possible for someone to neglect a concern that normatively stems from a relationship. For example, it is possible for a teacher to neglect the educational needs of his students, but this does not make education any less of a "shared concern" between student and teacher in this sense of the expression.

Stump summarizes the role of love's relational contexts by claiming it shapes the nature of the union desired with the beloved.[69] However, Aquinas also thinks that the relationship helps determine how the lover seeks to benefit the beloved. For example, the lover gives priority to providing for his close relatives over giving to others. He explains,

> Just as Augustine says in *I de Doct. Christ.*, "It comes to us by a certain chance, that we ought to provide for those that are more nearly connected to us." Nevertheless, prudence about this matter should be employed, according to different amounts of connection, holiness, and usefulness. For instance, alms are more fittingly bestowed upon a holier person who is suffering great need, and is of greater use towards the common good; than a person more closely connected to us, especially if he is not very closely connected, whose concern is not imminent to us, and if he is not suffering great need.[70]

For Aquinas, those who are closely related to us often receive first priority in giving, which includes both corporeal benefits such as financial resources and spiritual benefits such as moral advice.[71] This priority represents additional responsibilities the lover embraces toward those who are most closely united to him.

While Aquinas claims that priority in generosity often goes to those closely related to the lover, circumstances sometimes warrant prioritizing the needs of strangers. Others without a close relationship may have priority when their need is much greater or when they are particularly virtuous.[72] Alasdair MacIntyre's interpretation of Aquinas emphasizes the importance of the virtue of *misercordia,* generosity toward people in great need, for the agent's own flourishing. He explains,

> Those in dire need both within and outside a community generally include individuals whose extreme disablement is such that they can never be more than passive members of the community, not recognizing, not speaking or not speaking intelligibly, suffering, but not acting.... The care that we ourselves

need from others and the care that they need from us require a commitment and a regard that is not conditional upon the contingencies of injury, disease and other afflictions.[73]

He believes that this unconditional commitment to others regardless of their ability and relationship aids in each person's flourishing since anyone may find himself in such circumstances. When one embodies universal benevolence, he can typically hope to receive such help when needed. However, MacIntyre does not acknowledge the contingency of this benefit of love. Certainly, there are unusual circumstances where dysfunctional communities undermine this benefit of love, such as in Nazi Germany. It is also possible to sacrifice so much for others that no earthly benefit is possible for the lover, as when Maximillian Kolbe sacrificed his life for a stranger in a concentration camp. In such cases, it is unwarranted to expect the community to provide aid to the lover when he is in need.

3.6 DIFFICULTIES WITH LOVE

One difficulty with extending the scope of love to all humanity is that humans are creatures of limited time and energy. It is impossible to have a loving relationship marked by shared time and personal attention with every person. Stump suggests that Aquinas overcomes this problem by positing the possibility of an ultimate union between all humanity in the afterlife through the shared beatific vision.[74] Similarly, Schockenhoff claims that the essence of love is found in desiring the same ultimate end and ultimate good for the beloved as one's self, union with God.[75]

A second difficulty with Aquinas's position is that it is counterintuitive to love some persons, such as enemies.[76] Typical moral intuitions claim an ideal agent has obligations of justice toward enemies but is not expected to love them. Aquinas specifies that the charitable person does not love others in their role as enemies, but as fellow persons created with a rational nature, with union with God as their final end.[77] Loving those who live as one's enemies does not require actions typically associated with friendship[78] such as shared time and attention, but still requires a desire for the same ultimate good for them that is willed for all, union with God.[79] If this desire becomes fulfilled, then negative elements of the current relationship would be eliminated.[80] By desiring the good of union with God for one's enemy, the lover wills the enemy's vicious character be changed to one of love, which would eliminate enmity in the relationship.

A final question of interest is how Aquinas balances the concerns of impartial morality with the priority of partial relationships. Since Aquinas views charity as the most important moral attribute, the central moral issue becomes whether or not an agent possesses loving desires toward other people in general. Therefore, Aquinas's morality is impartial first in that the ideal moral agent has the same desires of love toward all, including a desire for the same ultimate good for all, happiness found in attaining the final end of union with God through charity.

Moreover, Aquinas's account is impartial in that the criteria that justify treating people differently from one another are objective criteria based on areas of shared concerns that unite persons. For example, in civic matters, the source of unity between fellow citizens is the political bond derived from shared civil concerns. Therefore, the will for the good of all fellow citizens as fellow citizens ought to be similar whether the fellow citizen is a stranger, a friend, or a brother.

Finally, charity toward all others constrains how love is expressed to those closest to the lover. "Love" expressed through unjust preferential treatment of those close to the lover is not love at all. In fact, Aquinas identifies a misapplication of relationally motivated preferences that is incompatible with justice—and, by implication, with love—which he refers to as "respect of persons." Respect of persons takes place when the identity of an individual person is used as a reason to treat them preferentially, instead of a relevant trait. However, a relational bond is a morally relevant trait justifying preference in some matters:

> Respect of persons is opposed to distributive justice.... If anyone promotes someone to an official position because he has sufficient knowledge, this promotion attends to a proper cause, not the person; but if anyone confers anything focusing on the person himself, not because what he grants to him is proportionate and appropriate, but bestows this only because he is that specific man, such as Peter or Martin, this is respect of the person, because he is not granting because of any cause that makes him worthy, but simply granting because of the person.... Nevertheless, sometimes the circumstance of the person makes one worthy in respect to one thing, and not in respect to another, just as a blood relationship makes someone appropriate to be appointed as an heir of an estate, but does not make somone appropriate to be appointed to a church office. Therefore, consideration of the same circumstance of the person in one matter causes respect of the person, but does not cause it in another matter.[81]

Aquinas distinguishes between legitimate reasons for treating people in different ways and reasons that are incompatible with justice. For example, promoting someone to a professorship because of his great knowledge is a legitimate motivation, while granting a professorship on any other basis, such as his relational attributes, is unjust. A relationship is a just cause for granting certain benefits such as appointing one as an heir. Furthermore, the sacrifices entailed by certain relationships naturally require certain kinds of benefits in return. Those who fail to respond in thanks and service within these relationships are not only unloving, but also unjust. For example, Aquinas cites the Decalogue's command to honor one's parents as a command rooted in justice.[82]

As we have seen, Aquinas provides an intricate account of love that portrays it as an excellence of the will. He claims it consists of a disinterested desire for the good of the beloved and union with the beloved, in ways appropriate to the relationship connecting lover and beloved. He also provides a detailed account of love's relationship with the intellect and passions. In the next chapter, I develop a contemporary version of Aquinas's account of love and offer it as an alternative to the accounts examined in Chapter One.

ENDNOTES

1. This interpretation of Aquinas's account of charity has been influenced by conversations with Eleonore Stump. *Cf.* Eleonore Stump, "Love, By All Accounts," *Proceedings and Addresses of the American Philosophical Association* 80 (2006): 25–43.

2. Stump 2006, 27.

3. ST II-II.23–46.

4. ST II-II.23.6.

5. ST II-II.23.8.

6. ST II-II.23.7.

7. Eberhard Schockenhoff, "The Theological Virtue of Charity (IIa IIae, qq. 23–46)," in *The Ethics of Aquinas*, ed. Stephen Pope (Washington, D.C.: Georgetown University Press, 2002), 250.

8. Schockenhoff 2002, 250–251.

9. ST I.5.6.

10. ST I-II.2.6.

11. ST I-II.65.1.

12. *Cf.* ST I-II.65.2 and Aristotle, *Nicomachean Ethics*, 1144b.

13. Here and elsewhere I provide my own translations of Aquinas's *Summa theologiae*. However, I consulted the translation of the Fathers of the English Dominican Province, and I followed its example for certain ambiguous clauses. I also consulted Alfred Fredoso's translation (available online at http://www.nd.edu/~afreddos/summa-translation/TOC-part1.htm) concerning the ST I.29 passages.

14. ST I-II.65.2. Also, *Cf.* ST II-II.23.7.

15. ST I-II.55.4.

16. ST II-II.25.1.

17. ST II-II.25.12.

18. ST I.29.1.

19. ST I-II.4.4.

20. ST II-II.23.1.

21. Étienne Gilson, *Thomism: The Philosophy of Thomas Aquinas*, trans. Laurence K. Shook and Armand Maurer (Toronto, Canada: Pontifical Institute of Mediaeval Studies, 2002), 311.

22. However, these actions may also have complete strangers as their target.

23. ST II-II.32.2.

24. *Cf.* ST I.5.1, II-II.25.7. Stump also offers a discussion concerning how Aquinas's objective view of the good influences the desires of love. *Cf.* Stump 2006, 28–29.

25. Stump 2006, 40, fn 31.

26. Gilson 2002, 314.

27. Gilson 2002, 313–314.

28. *Cf.* ST II-II.25.2

29. I am uncertain which of these interpretations Gilson intended, but out of charity I assume the later interpretation is correct.

30. ST II-II.27.2.

31. This desire is in contrast with a desire for temporary relational distance, which can be motivated by an ultimate desire for union with the beloved.

32. ST I-II.28.1 ad 2.

33. ST II-II.26.8.

34. ST I-II.27.3.

35. *Cf.* ST II-II.23.2.

36. ST I-II.8.1.

37. ST II-II.24.1.

38. For purposes of this conversation, I lay the distinction between emotions and passions to one side. Yet, it is noteworthy that the medieval worldview does not view these two concepts as synonymous.

39. ST II-II.28.1.

40. Gilson 2002, 313.

41. ST II-II.28.1.

42. ST II-II.28.1.

43. ST I-II.10.1.

44. Note that Aquinas would view loving one's enemies as rational since they are still human beings. An example of irrational love would be if a person cared more for a rock than for a person.

45. ST I-II.10.2–4.

46. ST I-II.13.6.

47. James Keenan, *Goodness and Rightness in Thomas Aquinas's Summa Theologiae* (Washington, DC: Georgetown University Press, 1992), 50.

48. Michael S. Sherwin, *By Knowledge and By Love: Charity and Knowledge in the Moral Theology of St. Thomas Aquinas* (Washington, DC: The Catholic University of America Press, 2005), 95.

49. Sherwin 2005, 97.

50. ST I-II.8.1.

51. ST I-II.8.1.

52. The only persons Aquinas thinks we ought not love are demons, but even in this case, Aquinas's reasoning is not based on the claim that demons are abhorrent, but that the ultimate good of union with God is no longer possible for them. *Cf.* ST II-II.25.11.

53. ST I.29.1.

54. ST I.29.3.

55. Thomas Aquinas, *De caritate*, article VII.

56. ST II-II.25.

57. ST II-II.25.6.

58. ST II-II.26.7.

59. ST II-II.26.

60. ST II-II.25.6.

61. ST II-II.26.6–8.

62. ST II-II.25.1, 4, 6, 8, 12.

63. ST II-II.25.12.

64. Gilson's claim does seem dangerously vague. After all, all traits would seem to qualify as either a similarity or a difference.

65. Gilson 2002, 313.

66. ST II-II.44.7.

67. ST II-II.26.

68. ST II-II.31.3.

69. Stump 2006, 32.

70. ST II-II.32.9.

71. ST II-II.32.2.

72. ST II-II.32.9.

73. Alasdair MacIntyre, *Dependent Rational Animals: Why Human Beings Need the Virtues* (Chicago: Open Court Publishing Company, 2002), 127–128.

74. Stump 2006, 31.

75. Schockenhoff 2002, 255.

76. ST II-II.25.8.

77. ST II-II.25.8.

78. ST II-II.25.9.

79. ST II-II.25.1.

80. ST II-II.25.9.

81. ST II-II.63.1.

82. ST II-II.122.5.

Chapter 4

The Neo-Thomistic Account of the Virtue of Love

My account of love is based largely on Aquinas's depiction of *caritas*. Therefore, I view love *as a disposition toward relationally appropriate acts of the will consisting of disinterested desires for the good of the beloved and unity with the beloved held as final ends.* However, in order to make this account of love compatible with a wide variety of worldviews, it will not rely upon other controversial aspects of Aquinas's philosophy such as the existence of objective final ends for humans, the existence of God, or the four types of Aristotelian causation.

4.1 TWO INITIAL OBJECTIONS TO THE NEO-THOMISTIC ACCOUNT OF LOVE

One possible objection to the Neo-Thomistic account is that someone might think there is a contradiction within the definition. It might seem that a desire for the good of and union with another is necessarily interested. Since desiring the good for another and desiring union with another implicitly suggests the lover desires union with the good desired for the beloved, it might seem the lover is necessarily selfish. However, there is a difference between a person who wills the good for and union with another *in order to enjoy the good* willed for the other and the person who wills the good for and union with another *as ends unto themselves.*

For example, a husband may buy a new car "for his wife," either motivated by a desire to enjoy the car himself or motivated by the desire for her enjoyment of the car whether or not he also happens to benefit from the purchase.

In the first case, the husband's actions are unloving because they are motivated by an interested selfishness in gaining access to the car. However, in the second case, the husband's desire for his wife's good motivates his decision. The fact that his continuing desire for unity with his wife may cause him to benefit from the purchase need not play any role at all in his motivation. While there may be benefits that are directly constituted by or likely contingent results of fulfilling the desires of love, those benefits will not be salient in the formation of loving desires.[1]

Another objection to this account of love claims its emphasis on disinterested benevolence is defective and damaging to the lover. Ayn Rand offers this type of objection:

> By elevating the issue of helping others into the central and primary issue of ethics, altruism has destroyed the concept of any authentic benevolence or good will among men. It has indoctrinated men with the idea that to value another human being is an act of selflessness, thus implying that a man can have no personal interest in others—that *to value* another means *to sacrifice* oneself—that any love, respect or admiration a man may feel for others is not and cannot be a source of his own enjoyment, but is a threat to his existence, a sacrificial blank check signed over to his loved ones.[2]

This objection suggests that requiring the lover to have a disinterested desire for the good of the beloved necessarily undermines the lover's happiness and enjoyment in the beloved, consigning the lover to an unacceptable subservient existence. Yet this concern is unfounded. As Chapter Five will demonstrate, having a disinterested desire for the good of the beloved does not prevent the lover from enjoying and benefiting from this relationship. For example, on Aquinas's account of psychology, one enjoys the fulfillment of a disinterested desire in the same way one enjoys any other desire.[3] However, it is true that this enjoyment must not be one's primary reason for holding the desire or it would become an interested desire. When a loving parent desires that her children flourish, she enjoys watching them flourish, but she certainly does not want them only to flourish because she desires to experience this joy.

The Neo-Thomistic account of love also does not require that one's care for others be a "sacrificial blank check signed over to his loved ones."[4] According to this account of love, the desire for the beloved's good is modified by one's desire for the good of all humanity, including one's self, in appropriate ways. While love undoubtedly requires sacrifice at times, it does not require a subservient existence. Genuine love for others must be compatible with love for all people, including the self.

4.2 THE VIRTUE OF LOVE AS A DISPOSITION

Several components of my account of love warrant further explication. Like all virtues, love is a general character disposition, a consistent and ongoing personal habit. An agent does not possess love if she loves inconsistently or only loves well within some of her relationships. However, it is possible for someone to possess genuine "love toward his child" or "love toward her husband" without possessing the full virtue of love. A loving person habitually cares excellently within the many types of relationships, including distant impersonal relationships as well as close relationships.

My account of this disposition is similar to some contemporary accounts of benevolence, compassion, or caring in that the lover wills the good for every person. For example, it serves the same broad role in morality as Michael Slote's conception of partial benevolence, which includes caring for all but "caring *more* for some people than for others."[5] It is also similar to Christine Swanton's account of "universal love" in the breadth of its scope, in its desire for union, and in its impartial nature. She describes universal love explaining: "(i) It is a form of 'coming close.' (ii) It is particular. (iii) It is universal. (iv) It is impartial. (v) It is unconditional."[6] It is also similar to Martha Nussbaum's account of compassion in that it includes an impartial concern for the well-being of others who experience serious suffering.[7] As in these contemporary accounts of virtue, the lover is disposed to desire consistently the good for all others.[8]

This baseline amount of good will toward others is rooted in the recognition that all persons are appropriate objects for love, not just those who are relationally close. However, the strength of love's desires differs according to the closeness of each relationship. Impartial care for others demonstrates the breadth of an individual's love, while partial care within close relationships reveals the depth of a person's love. Important partial relationships associated with love include those with friends, spouses, children, and parents. Those who consistently love well within both partial and impartial relationships have the full virtue of love. Since an in-depth account of the term "virtue" construing it as a disposition is offered in Chapter One, there is no need to repeat those considerations.

4.3 LOVE AS AN ACTIVITY OF THE WILL

Harry Frankfurt's influential work describing the structure of a person's will in terms of various orders of desires is well-known;[9] however, describing the role a person's will plays in love can deepen our understanding of the virtue. The activities of a person's will are the choices, desires, and motivations that shape a person's volitional structure. A person's volitional structure includes which states of affairs a person desires, how strongly each state of affairs is desired, the relative strength of each desire, and what motivates a person's desire for these states of affairs. The lover holds disinterested desires for another's good and union with him as final ends. These desires are neither motivated by other interests nor are they pursued primarily as a means to any further end.

The content of a person's volitional structure reveals more about her character than the content of her emotional states alone. Aristotelians have long held that emotions alone reveal relatively little about a person's character.[10] A person's emotions are far more revealing when understood in the context of her internal desires, motivations, and external circumstances.[11] For example, experiencing the emotion of "happiness" could indicate virtue, vice, or neither. Mother Teresa's happiness based on her love for a flourishing orphan is qualitatively different from Adolf Hitler's happiness based on his fulfilled desire for increased power achieved in the conquest of France. A third agent might experience happiness due to a genetic predisposition toward positive emotions in general, not based in any other particular reason.

While a person's volitional structure is more central to love than emotional states are, desires do typically influence a person's emotions. As in Thomas's account, knowledge of fulfilled desires usually results in positive emotion. Knowledge of thwarted desires typically causes negative emotion. The lover does not merely act in the right way or desire the right thing, but experiences the proper emotions before, during, and after virtuous activities. Typically, joy, happiness, and satisfaction are experienced when love's desires are attained. When desires are thwarted, there tends to be sadness, disappointment, or a sense of loss. Love within close relationships, like those between spouses, children, and parents, tends to have a particularly strong emotional component. Under normal psychological conditions, the love of a person who does not experience these emotions in the appropriate circumstances is deficient. However, love does not require an agent to be unusually sentimental or emotional. An agent who experiences ecstatic feelings of happiness when desires are fulfilled and devastating feelings of disappointment when they are not fulfilled is not necessarily virtuous. He may simply have a hormone imbalance. While the virtue of love has strong requirements for the disposition of the will, the emotional component of the virtue is less essential and the emotional requirements of love are more flexible.

There are a number of reasons for defining love primarily in terms of volition rather than emotions. First, volitional structure is more foundational to moral character than emotions. As implied in our example comparing Mother Teresa's happiness to Adolph Hitler's happiness, a person's emotions tell us little about an agent's character outside of the context of his volitional structure. However, the reverse is not true. If we know much concerning a person's volitional structure but nothing about his emotions, we know quite a bit about his character. If we know that Mother Teresa wants a young orphan to flourish as a final end or that Hitler wants to conquer Europe as a final end, this information reveals something deeply significant about his character. The fact that Teresa or Hitler is happy, apart from the facts concerning the broader context of that happiness, reveals very little about that person's character.

Furthermore, love differs significantly from most emotions because it is more enduring. While a mature adult's emotions may fluctuate several times a day between happiness and sadness, love is considerably more tenacious. Passing fancy or infatuation may fluctuate erratically, but love does not.

4.4 THE DESIRES OF LOVE

The fact that the lover desires the good of the beloved implies that the lover wants her to possess the goods needed for a fully flourishing life.[12] These goods include whatever the lover is warranted in viewing as objectively beneficial to anyone in the beloved's circumstances. Goods a lover typically desire for any beloved include health, pleasure, happiness, knowledge, achievement, virtue, and friendship. These goods also include anything the beloved desires for her self, so long as they are compatible with other important aspects of her own flourishing. The goods the lover desires for the beloved include the sorts of goods people typically desire for themselves.

However, it is unclear whether some desires qualify as genuinely good for the beloved. What if the lover is incorrect in his view of the good? I claim that the lover's desires count as loving, so long as she is reasonably warranted in viewing these goods as beneficial to the beloved.[13] This view allows room for a lover to be sincerely incorrect in what he views as loving. However, this account still offers a sufficiently high threshold ensuring that desires that are clearly detrimental to the beloved are still identified as incompatible with love. Therefore, the virtue of love entails that the lover possess at least a minimal amount of prudence and intellectual virtue in recognizing what is beneficial to others as well as in how he attempts to bring about such benefits.

The lover also views the fulfillment of the beloved's desires as valuable contributors to her good. The lover recognizes that attaining subjectively desired goods is typically beneficial to the beloved. In close relationships of love, the lover deeply values the subjective desires of the beloved. Some specific goods a loving person wishes for a friend who wishes to be a successful lawyer, an emergency medical technician, or a professional basketball player vary greatly. The goods a lover desires for someone also depends upon the beloved's talents. Willing the good for a friend with an underdeveloped potential for art may take a different shape than if he had no artistic potential.

This account of the goods the lover desires for the beloved raises obvious questions. For example, what should the lover do when he disagrees with the beloved concerning something's desirability? What if the lover views virtue as an essential component of well-being, while the beloved does not? The loving person weighs many factors when she and her beloved have differing views of the good.

One important factor includes the nature of the relationship between lover and beloved. It is usually appropriate for loving parents, especially parents of young children, to trust their judgment over their children's since this relationship is not between equals. A loving parent desires health for her child and is highly motivated to advance her child's health. This desire often leads her to reject a child's requests for unhealthy foods. However, when a child's desires are compatible with other important goods, those desires are happily accommodated, such as when a child prefers to wear a particular color or play a particular sport.

In contrast, it is generally appropriate for friends to be fairly trusting of the beloved's judgment. While friends have a relationship of equality with considerable autonomy, it is sometimes appropriate to challenge a friend's choices. If a lover is convinced that a friend is undercutting his long-term happiness, she will try to intervene in an appropriate way that still acknowledges the beloved's autonomy.

The lover is also influenced by how essential she believes the disputed good is to the beloved's well-being. If the lover thinks the beloved is wasting a small amount of time or money in pursuing a false good or that the beloved is missing an opportunity for a small good, she will be relatively unconcerned by the beloved's action. In contrast, if the beloved appears to be undermining goods essential to his own long-term happiness, the lover is likely to take significant action to encourage the beloved to attain this essential good.

A third factor that influences the lover is her level of confidence in her view of the good. A loving parent may believe her son is better suited for teaching than accounting, but may not be confident enough to take significant action to steer her son toward teaching. In contrast, a parent or even a friend who discovers the beloved is using well-known, harmful, mind-altering drugs, such as LSD, will take substantial action to deter the beloved's involvement in the behavior.

Since the lover desires the good of the beloved, she promotes the good of the beloved in a way appropriate to their relationship. A loving mother not only wills the good for her child, but she wills to promote her child's good through her relationship of "mother" by providing nurture, guidance, and many practical goods. A loving spouse expresses practical cares for the beloved by helping with the day-to-day details and difficulties of life. Clergy promote the good of parishioners in religious matters. A teacher promotes the good of her students in academic matters. The lover's type of union with the beloved shapes the way she promotes his good.

Union is a type of bond between persons. The lover desires bonds with others appropriate for his relationships with them. There are many possible types of union between persons. The most intimate forms of union include shared life, residence, family identification, personal attention, affection, and sexual intimacy. Less intimate forms of union include shared human identification, dignity, and the recognition of value or status. The union relevant to impersonal relationships does not require considerable personal attention. Obviously, the limited nature of time and human attention makes it impossible for a person to be present and close to all others. Somewhere between the most and least intimate types of union would be bonds based on shared goals, vocation, and worldview with the beloved.

The lover desires union appropriate to his relationships with others. However, some people's bonds are inadequate for love. A friend who abandons friendships easily, a spouse who gives up on marriage due to normal difficulties, and siblings who make little effort to build and maintain a close relationship are inadequately bonded. Relationships of intimate and close connection warrant strong bonds that are not easily abandoned. Love requires maintaining these bonds when possible. Some circumstances may justify distancing one's self from a relationship, such as when another person becomes dangerously violent.

As in Aquinas's account of love, the desire for union must be accompanied by a desire for the good of the beloved; therefore, the lover seeks no type of union that would be bad for the beloved. Some people are unloving because they bond in ways that are not appropriate to their relationships. These bonds are incompatible with love because they have an improper scope to them. For example, some "friends" dominate the lives of other friends and leave inadequate room for other important relationships. These smothering friendships have an improperly large scope. Supervisors who interfere in their workers' personal lives or who attempt to expand work's scope so that it leaves no room for employees' personal lives are unloving.[14] Parents who do not expect their adult children to have a personal life outside of the family have inappropriately expanded the scope of the parent-child bond. The extreme case of incestuous relationships involves sexual bonds that are inappropriate for relatives. Agents who develop or desire these types of bonds are unloving since they are incompatible with the "beloved's" flourishing. Such bonds are typically motivated by selfishness rather than love.

In addition to having the proper strength and scope of bonds in existent relationships, the lover also develops new bonds wisely through the prudent development of these relationships. Voluntary relationships include friendships, marital relationships, and some vocational relationships. For example, it is possible to choose friends wisely or poorly. Some people are poor choices of friends for various reasons, such as their view of the good life is incompatible with the lover's, they are too geographically distant for the formation of friendship, they have numerous vicious characteristics, or their lives are simply too busy.

The lover's desire for union is influenced by his desire for the good of the beloved. However, there are circumstances where normally appropriate types of union with the beloved become harmful to him. For example, while it is bad for the lover to have a physically abusive spouse, it is also bad for the abuser to have union that enables the continuation of such abuse. While physical closeness, shared time, and shared residence are typically proper expressions of union in marriage, such union is harmful to both lover and beloved in these circumstances. Among other problems, such union obscures the beloved's need to change and mature.

Similarly, some specific aspects of union may become bad for the lover, rather than union more generally. For example, some sharing of financial resources between parents and children (even adult children) is a normal expression of the bond between parent and child. Yet, sharing financial resources becomes bad for the child if it is used to fund a drug addiction. Funding such an addiction is not an authentic expression of love. The two desires of love modify one another.

In cases where union with the lover becomes bad for the beloved, the lover desires to change circumstances so that union is no longer bad for the beloved. In the examples above, the lover might help the beloved see that some of his actions and attitudes are self-destructive.[15] The lover continues to seek unity with the beloved by encouraging character changes that are good for the beloved and necessary for union. Even in voluntary relationships such as those between spouses or friends, a serious character change in the beloved does not necessarily end the relationship.

Accounts of love that focus on personal attributes as reasons for love seem to imply that love should not continue when the beloved's character changes since he now has significantly different attributes from the person who was originally loved. On the Neo-Thomistic account, the desires of love should still exist but ought to be carried out differently since circumstances have changed. Even in extreme cases in which changes in the beloved cause long-term relational distance, the lover still wills the good of the beloved and desires unity with him but may sadly conclude that such desires cannot be fulfilled because the beloved's vicious character makes some types of union bad for him. In these cases, the lover seeks distance from the beloved motivated in part by a desire for the beloved's good.

Joseph Raz investigates one type of union between persons, which he describes as "attachment." An attachment is a partial and unique bond with another person.[16] It is based in the lover's view of the beloved as someone of value. While there may be general types of attachments, each is ultimately unique since it is formed by a unique individual and has a unique object. He discusses how some traditional accounts of morality ignore the ethical significance of attachments. He explains,

> The universality thesis [of morality] fails to explain our deepest attachments, the attachments of love and friendship, for example, or of the relations between parents and children, or people and their countries, attachments without which life does not have meaning.[17]

Just as an adequate conception of particular commitments must leave room for impartial morality, universal morality must have room for personal attachments.[18] While attachments add subjective personal value to their objects, persons are valuable whether or not one forms an attachment with them.[19] However, Raz acknowledges that not all attachments are valuable.[20] It is possible to be too attached to someone or attached in an inappropriate way. He deems such attachments to be pathological and harmful. There is also the moral problem that not all attachments are inherently disinterested. To the contrary, many attachments are formed for selfish reasons.

I view Raz's attachments as a type of union within close personal relationships. However, a desire for union is not always identical with a desire for an attachment with another person. The lover has no special Razian attachment within many ordinary impersonal relationships. Yet, he may desire unity with them through the recognition of their value as human beings by acknowledging that a personal attachment is not a necessary condition for their value. Furthermore, a desire for union with another is not exhausted by the desire for an attachment. While the lover often has unique emotional bonds with her close relationships based in positive attitudes toward them, there are morally relevant bonds between persons that differ from Raz's account of attachments, such as the bonds constituted by common concerns and shared resources.

The desires of love are necessarily disinterested. Desires are selfish when they are primarily motivated as means to the agent's good. The lover desires union with the beloved and the good of the beloved as final ends without an ulterior motive. An ulterior motive—an interest—exists when desires are held as a means to some further end. However, since human motivation is complex, it is possible for desires to have numerous motivations. For example, a wife may desire her husband's good health as a final end, but also because it is a means to her and her children's financial security. In this case, her desire for his good is overdetermined. Such desires are compatible with love when the beloved's flourishing is primarily held as a final end and that desire is sufficiently strong that it would be held in the absence of any other motivations. A spouse shows no vice by recognizing that her partner's death would have serious financial consequences so long as she would desire her husband's continued health even if it did not. In contrast, if an agent wants another to flourish primarily because she benefits from his flourishing this desire is unloving. For example, an employer may desire that her employees are happy because she believes that happy employees are more productive workers.

The desires of love are necessarily held as final ends, valued in themselves. It is possible for someone to desire the good for another and union with another as a means to some other final goal. For example, someone might desire the good of his unlikable stepmother because he views his stepmother's good as instrumental to his beloved father's flourishing. This desire is unloving because he does not desire his stepmother's good as a final end.

4.5 WHAT IS A RELATIONSHIP?

It is necessary to examine the general concept of a relationship before discussing its role in shaping the desires of love. How should the term "relationship" be defined? The definitions offered by contemporary social psychology are a worthwhile starting point. A summary of the three main conceptions of relationships in psychology is presented by psychologists Richard Lucas and Portia Dyrenforth.

> Although most people would agree that the bond that an individual shares with a romantic partner counts as a relationship, interactions that an individual has with other individuals are often not so clear. For instance, if someone has a brief discussion with a stranger on the street, is a new relationship formed? Do routinized, script-based interactions that occur on a regular basis (e.g. interactions with a checkout clerk at the grocery store) represent a meaningful, albeit nonintimate, relationship?
>
> … Some researchers have suggested that any simple interactions between two or more people counts as a relationship. Others argue that only repeated patterns of contact count. Still others maintain that the relationship partners must develop a mental schema of the relationship before a relationship can be said to exist.[21]

This summary offers three differing sets of criteria for relationships. The broadest account of relationships views them as constituted by any interactions between persons, the second uses stricter criteria requiring repeated patterns of interaction, and the strictest account requires the relationship partners' development of a mental schema concerning the relationship.

The first conception of relationships gives the broadest scope for the term, by construing any interaction at all between two persons as a relationship. Many relationships are deeply impersonal and cursory on this account. An anonymous bagger at a grocery store who hands a customer his purchases fulfills this bare definition of relationship. On the second account, this sole interaction would not establish a relationship, since relationships require repeated patterns of interaction. However, if the same customer came to the store every Tuesday morning and habitually came through the same line where the same bagger packs his groceries, then they would have a relationship. Note that this pattern of interaction does not guarantee increased interpersonal attention between them.[22] It is possible for people to remain anonymous despite a repeated pattern of interaction. According to the third conception, each member of the relationship must have a mental schema for his or her interpersonal interaction to qualify as a relationship. Perhaps, the customer comes to view the bagger as "his bagger" and seeks him out during each trip to the supermarket. In turn, the bagger might notice the unusual friendliness of one of "his regular customers." If both individuals develop a mental schema of their interactions, then their weekly exchanges constitute a relationship.

Since social psychology seeks to explain interpersonal phenomena, it is unsurprising that the first two definitions are distinguished by levels of interaction between people. However, these definitions are insufficient for our philosophical purposes of understanding how relationships shape the lover's desires toward all persons, since we have direct interactions with relatively few of the world's billions of persons. Furthermore, it is possible to have important relational connections with people we have not met. In some cultures, a marriage may be arranged with someone one has never met. A father may die before his child is born. A citizen has a relationship with his governor or president even if they have never met.

The third definition focusing on the relational members' possession of a mental schema of the relationship has greater philosophical potential. Since one may have mental schema toward people she has never met, such as rock stars, heads of state, and her unborn child, this definition is more flexible. Yet this account is still inadequate for our purposes since it requires both members of the relationship to have a mental schema concerning one another. Even if I have mental schema concerning my relationship with Pope Benedict, President Obama, and Phil Collins, it is quite unlikely that they have mental schema concerning me as an individual.

A more philosophical account of relationships may be useful. Niko Kolodny offers an account of relationships in his article on love. He suggests,

> When two people satisfy some two-place predicate, we can say that they stand in an interpersonal relationship. Not every interpersonal relationship, in this broad sense, is an interpersonal relationship, in the sense in which relations between friends, lovers, and family members are relationships. Some relations belong to a different ontological category.[23]

Kolodny adds that relations relevant to love necessarily fulfill at least three necessary criteria: they are ongoing, they are between particular people, and they are historical. Relationships are ongoing in that they persist over time. They are between particular people in that relationships are distinguished by the identities of their members. They are historical in that they depend in some part on facts about the past, unlike relations between persons that only depend upon some fact about the present such as "sitting to the left of." Kolodny explains that meeting these criteria is not sufficient to constitute an interpersonal relationship, but he offers no further criteria.[24]

Kolodny's criteria for relationships are not particularly helpful in identifying two-place predicates that represent relationships that ought to shape love. Obviously, two people must fulfill some two-place predicate in order to have a relationship with one another since any plausible relationship between them must be at least minimally describable. Yet, this requirement is not helpful since there are numerous two-place predicates that do not represent a relationship, such as "not in a relationship with," "being twice the height of," "having the same middle name as," or "living 200 miles east of."

Kolodny is also correct that relationships are historical in that they depend upon facts about the past. However, this criterion is far less discriminating than he realizes, since literally any two-place predicate about actual persons relies upon facts about the past such as "having been born" or "having come into existence." Even his example of a nonrelational, nonhistorical two-place predicate of "sitting to the left of" is flawed since this predicate depends upon past facts concerning one person entering the other's proximity and both people having come into existence at some previous time.

Kolodny's requirement that a two-place predicate connecting two persons must be ongoing to serve as a relationship is only minimally helpful. He is correct that relationships are not in an absolute state of fluctuation and have some temporal persistence. He compares an ongoing relationship with one that obtains only for an instant such as "being exactly twice the age of."[25] He also gives the example of friendship as something that is "not the momentary obtaining of some relation, but something that has persisted over time, and may continue to persist, over time."[26]

However, Kolodny offers no further clarification concerning this requirement, which leaves at least two significant ambiguities. First, must the connection between persons represented by the predicate have an indefinite duration in order to qualify as ongoing? His example of an ongoing friendship may suggest a predicate must be completely open-ended. Yet, even if a predicate must potentially persist indefinitely, quite a few nonrelational predicates persist for more than an instant and may continue indefinitely such as "being older than," "having the same name as," "being taller than," or "having the same birthday." In contrast, some predicates that are plausible candidates for relationships have definitive time frames such as "student of" in the context of a college course or "employee of" when fulfilling a nonrenewable contract.

Second, if a predicate does not need the potential for indefinite duration to qualify as ongoing, how long must it persist to count as a relationship? Is "governor of" a relationship if she is limited to a single four-year term? Does a "student of" predicate qualify as a relationship between student and teacher if it lasts a single semester? Is "employee of" a relationship when referring to a temporary substitute for a permanent worker during his vacation? Is "trainer of" a relationship when referring to a speaker at a one-day seminar? Kolodny's requirement that a two-place predicate must be ongoing is ultimately vague. The only predicates it clearly disqualifies are those that obtain for a single instant. Furthermore, it is unclear what duration or potential duration a predicate must have to satisfy this requirement.

Kolodny's requirement that a two-place predicate must be between particular persons is also only minimally helpful.[27] He claims, "Relationships are individuated by the identities of their participants; they cannot survive substitution of participants."[28] He offers the example that being "my dentist" may constitute a relationship if the predicate consistently refers to the same individual, but when it refers to a role where various people can substitute for one another, it is not a relationship in the relevant sense.[29] Even if this final criterion is correct, it does not significantly narrow the number of predicates that might represent a relationship. Since he has already stipulated that relationships are ongoing predicates between two persons, little is added by specifying that they must also be between particular persons since this particularity is already implied by the requirement that the predicate be ongoing.

While Kolodny's thoughts offer little help for defining relationships, a more useful conception is offered by Robert Kraut. He discusses relationships in terms of offices and officeholders. The role one person plays in another's life is an office. The officeholder is the person occupying this role in another's life. Kraut offers the example of Mrs. Smith and her only child Lisa:

> Lisa plays a certain role in her mother's life—she is her mother's only child. *Being Mrs. Smith only child* is, we might say, an office that Lisa holds, and Lisa is the unique holder of that office. Needless to say, no one else is going to "score higher on those characteristics"—mother's love is not likely to be transferred to someone else.... The distinction between offices and officeholders is as straightforward as the distinction between definite descriptions and the items that satisfy them.[30]

The idea of an office or role in someone's life is a flexible conception of what constitutes a relationship. Holding an office does not require direct interaction between the two people. Lisa has the role of her father's only child while she is in the womb even if he dies before she is born, if he spends five years overseas before meeting her, or if he never meets her because he abandons her mother before she is born. It also does not require that both members of the relationship have a schema for their relationship. The president of the United States has an office in his citizens' lives even if he is not aware of most of them as individuals.

According to Kraut's account, a relationship can be represented by a two-place predicate between people that specifies a role one plays in the other's life. This criterion eliminates quite a few nonrelational predicates such as "being taller than" or "having the same middle name as" since those predicates have no implications concerning roles. Yet, there is an ambiguity concerning the necessary and sufficient conditions for having a role in another's life. Does the farmer in Iowa who grows the wheat in my bread have a role in my life? Do fellow citizens who vote in the same elections have a role in each other's lives? Does someone play a role in another's life simply by being a fellow human being worthy of moral consideration? Kraut does not provide clear answers to these questions.

As we have seen, even in academic circles there is a broad range of uses for the term "relationship." Similarly, the popular use of the term relationship is equivocal and ambiguous. In one usage, a relationship is constituted by a history of shared personal interaction between two people. This account of historical relationships views relationships as constituted by a history of shared personal interaction, typically viewing positive and pleasant shared interaction as foundational to the relationship. On this model, relationships can be distinguished by shared interests motivating and sustaining the interactions: a work relationship is based upon shared vocational goals, a romantic relationship is based upon the pursuit of mutual romantic interest, a friendship is based upon shared recreational pursuits or shared pursuit of the good life.

A second use of "relationship" refers to culturally recognized roles people play in each other's lives. Some of these relationships are established by facts about the world. These facts often include connections based on shared heredity such as relationships between siblings, parents, and children. All humans also share a natural connection in light of their shared human capacities and ancestry. Unlike the first use of relationship, these connections can exist between persons without direct interaction. Other culturally recognized roles have nothing to do with heredity. For example, the connection between president and citizen or craftsman and apprentice are nonhereditary culturally recognized roles. In the Catholic culture, the connection between godparent and godchild would be such a relationship. Some, but not all, culturally recognized relationships will also be historical relationships marked by a history of interaction.

4.6 THE NEO-THOMISTIC ACCOUNT OF LOVE AND RELATIONSHIPS

Which conception of relationship should be used to shape the desires of love? An adequate conception must accommodate a broad range of relationships since love is an excellence of a person's will in each relationship. As Kolodny suggests, relationships can be expressed as two-place predicates obtained between persons that are at least ongoing, historical, and between particular people. As Kraut suggests, the predicates connecting two persons must constitute a role each plays in the other's life, though a role need not include direct personal interaction. From popular usage of the term relationship, I add that the two-place predicates expressing a relationship will either represent a historical connection of personal interaction or a culturally recognized role between persons. Therefore, *a relationship is an ongoing, historical connection between particular people constituting either a historical or a culturally recognized role one plays in the other's life that can be represented by a two-place predicate.*[31]

Implicitly, persons are the only appropriate object for love, since the relationships that shape love's desires are always between persons. The idea that persons are the proper object for love reflects a common ethical claim expressed in Kantianism, Thomism, and elsewhere that personhood is worthy of unique dignity. One reason persons are love's appropriate object is that only they have relational capacities enabling personal union. Nonpersons are incapable of personal relationships, thus willing personal union with them is inappropriate. Rational, conscious beings, capable of personal attention have unique relational capacities that make them appropriate objects for love.

Agents are capable of goodwill toward inanimate objects, plants, and nonhuman animals. However, this good will falls short of love.

It is possible that some nonhumans might count as persons. Since traditional theism offers a personal account of God, He would be an appropriate object for love. Nonhuman animals with advanced functioning might be appropriate objects for love to the degree that they are persons or are similar to persons in their possession of the distinctive capacities of persons such as rationality, will, self-awareness, emotions, ability to communicate, and so forth. While this account of love is open to the possibilities of nonhuman persons, I lay this issue to the side to focus exclusively on love between human persons.

It is useful to distinguish between voluntary and involuntary relationships. Voluntary relationships are roles in other people's lives that the agent chooses, while involuntary relationships are not chosen. Models of love that claim it is based upon the particular attributes of the beloved are partially motivated by the voluntary nature of some important relationships. The fact that these relationships are originally formed with some individuals rather than others may be partially due to their attractive features. Voluntary relationships with friends and spouses are typically chosen in contrast to involuntary relationships with parents, children, siblings, fellow citizens, and the self.

Once a voluntary relationship is established, it has considerable tenacity that is not based on attractive attributes that may have contributed to the initiation of the relationship. The relationship itself becomes a reason for the lover's continuing role in the beloved's life. Furthermore, voluntary relationships are often maintained because explicit or implicit commitments are made within the relationship. For example, adoption is voluntary but includes an explicit commitment to care for the child, establishing a tenacious parent-child relationship. The parent's commitment to the adopted child becomes a reason for maintaining the relationship regardless of the child's attributes and apart from the history of personal interaction between the persons.

Marriage has traditionally been viewed as this type of relationship. A voluntary commitment between spouses establishes an ongoing tenacious relationship between spouses. At minimum, this commitment provides a strong reason for a continued relationship between spouses even if there are considerations, reasons, or events that could override this reason. Friendship typically does not involve explicit commitments, yet it seems to involve implicit commitments, such as the commitment to open communication between friends, to the good of one's friends, and to loyalty between friends.

Since love is constituted in part by a desire for union with the beloved, the desire for union with the beloved can never be completely eliminated in a loving way. However, circumstances may warrant or cause distance within these relationships. For example, we have already discussed instances where union with the beloved becomes bad for him, warranting a degree of distance within these relationships. There are also circumstances outside the relationship that may cause relational distance. For example, moving to a new region due to a job change is often compatible with love, even if it causes distance within some relationships.

Many important relationships are involuntary. Humans generally do not choose their own parents, siblings, children, or fellow citizens. However, there are exceptions to this pattern, such as when children are adopted and chosen for adoption partially because of particular characteristics. Some individuals choose to emigrate and adopt a country as their own along with new countrymen. And while one's choice of residence determines the identity of one's neighbors, the personal identity of these neighbors is rarely a salient feature in choosing a residence.[32]

A person's relationship with himself constitutes an important involuntary relationship. This relationship is unusual in that one person fulfills both places in the two-place predicate describing the relationship. Like other relationships, the relationship with one's self is an ongoing, historical relationship fulfilled by a particular person representing a role he plays in his life. As in other relationships, the lover desires the good for himself and union with himself.

Someone might object that desiring the good for one's self is egoistic or morally problematic. Yet if all persons are appropriate objects for love, then it logically follows that the self should be loved, since the self is a person.[33] We do not blame someone who appropriately desires the good for the self. No one is vicious because she desires a healthy diet, exercise, or an appropriate wage for a day's work. Fears of egoism are raised when one loves only the self, loves the self with undue partiality, or loves the self in a way that is harmful to others. In order to possess the virtue of love, one must love one's self in a way compatible with loving all persons.

It might seem that everyone desires the good for himself. Yet although everything people desire must appear to have some attractive or good aspect to it, not everyone truly seeks the good for himself. It is not unusual for a person to desire goods for himself that he believes undermine his long-term well-being, such as addictive drugs or an unhealthy diet.

It might seem that everyone desires union with herself or that the idea of desiring union with one's self is nonsense. Yet, Stump explains, "A person can be divided against herself. She can lack internal integration in her mind, and the result will be that she is, as we say, double-minded. She can also lack whole-heartedness or integration in the will."[34] The person who wills union with her self desires personal wholeness and integration. Such a person does not want to have conflicting internal desires. She desires to want the things that she wants. In the language used by Frankfurt, she possesses an n+1-order desire for harmonious first-order, second-order, through n-order desires. Implicitly, if someone desires the good for her self and desires personal integration, she desires a wholehearted will for her own good.

While differing cultures attach differing expectations to the same relationship and recognize different types of relationships, some relational models are inherently incompatible with love. For example, the owner-slave relationship is incompatible with love. Desiring the good for another is simply incompatible with owning him as one might own a piece of property. The owner-slave relationship is also incompatible with embracing basic aspects of union with another, such as shared dignity and identification as human, since this relationship reduces another to an inferior with subhuman dignity.

There are also some types of relationships that are not inherently incompatible with love, but that have developed cultural expectations that are incompatible with love. Conceptions of marriage or family that treat spouses or children as chattel are also incompatible with love. So are vocational relationships that are inherently abusive, such as when employers require employees to work unnecessarily dangerous jobs in substandard conditions.[35] In these sorts of relationships, the lover resists the abusive model of the relationship advocated by the culture. The lover also avoids relationships that include union that is too encompassing for the beloved's flourishing, such as when a parent has a smothering relationship with her adult child.

Some types of relationships may be compatible with love for the beloved but incompatible with love for those outside of the relationship. For example, Bonnie and Clyde may be partners in crime who sincerely care for one another, but this type of relationship is incompatible with the virtue of love since criminal activity is unloving to others in society.[36] Similarly, relationships based upon the shared hatred of outsiders, such as those within hate groups or terrorist groups, are incompatible with the virtue of love. Such relationships are based on either rejecting union with other people or desiring harm for other people. Perhaps members of the Ku Klux Klan sincerely care for other Caucasian members of their neighborhood. Yet since Ku Klux Klan philosophy rejects any degree of union with those outside their race, relationships based on their philosophy are incompatible with love.

Relationships are also incompatible with love if they lead to partiality that is incompatible with willing the good for others more broadly. For example, it may be appropriate for a man to save his wife's or child's life instead of a stranger's if he can only save one. Yet a parent who makes no effort to save a neighbor's life because he is preoccupied with playing with his child has a defective conception of a loving parent-child relationship. Similarly, a model of friendship that requires unfair preferential treatment in hiring is incompatible with love for other job applicants.

While this account of love adjudicates between some competing schemas for relationships, it is also flexible. It need not adjudicate among all possible models of relationships. There may be a variety of models for friendship from different cultures, many of which are compatible with the desires of love, but which offer differing models for love between friends. For example, one model of friendship may stress the equality between friends, while another model of friendship may encourage some deference of the younger friend to the older. However, both models of friendship are compatible with willing the good for one another and union with one another and share some family similarities with other models of friendship. The flexibility of this understanding of relationships allows it to accommodate a broad range of relational interactions, expressed in a wide range of cultures at various times. This flexibility is a chief advantage of this account of love.

4.7 LOVE AS RELATIONALLY APPROPRIATE DESIRES

The lover consistently has loving desires toward other persons based on the nature of their relationship. The most basic relationship is that between fellow human beings. This foundational relationship is a sufficient reason for desiring the good for and union with every person. In the lover's closest relationships, love's desires are very strong and require considerable initiative. For example, a parent's love for a young child ought to consist of strong, enduring, multifaceted desires for the good of the child and union with the child. The loving parent desires to provide care, shared time, attention, discipline, physical provision, and guidance. Union between parent and child typically includes shared identification, place of residence, worldview, mutual care and affection, as well as physical and emotional closeness. Other important close relationships exist between spouses, friends, siblings, and other blood relatives. Each of these relationships warrants a different range of desires concerning the beloved.

The lover displays excellence in love when she has loving desires appropriate for the relational role that actually exists. The lover wills union in ways that are appropriate to the relational role that actually exists and does not will union in ways incompatible with that role. In some cases, the lover may desire changes in an existing relationship. The lover may will union in ways that are not yet appropriate in light of his current role in another's life, as when a person desires that a friendship become a romantic relationship or when a person wants to adopt a child.

The nature of the relationship between lover and beloved does not need to be salient in most of their day-to-day interactions. The loving person possesses the appropriate desires of love, but need not undergo an internal process of rationally justifying those desires on the basis of relationships. Furthermore, many relationships are so distant that each other's individual existence is obscured. The individual is merely another person in Iraq, overseas, and so forth. Yet the lover can still care for such people through concern for global trends and events, donation to worthy causes designed to aid the needy, a desire for global justice, and prayer. The lover can desire union with such others based on their shared humanity, even if union including personal attention is not really possible.[37]

Since relationships play a central role in the Neo-Thomistic account of love, it is similar in many ways to Kolodny's account. However, one important difference is that while he claims the lover must hold a belief concerning a relationship's role in justifying love,[38] my account makes no such claim. The lover may hold a different theory of love or no theory at all, so long as she has loving desires toward others. I view Kolodny's account as a deontological conception of love since it requires that the lover hold certain beliefs concerning the proper justification of her love. In contrast, since my account of love construes it as a virtuous excellence of the will, one's beliefs concerning the reasons for love do not play a central role. For example, a loving wife may desire the good for her husband and union with her husband in ways appropriate for their relationship, yet believe that the reason she loves him is his great care for her. On my account, the wife truly loves the husband because she possesses the proper desires of love, but on Kolodny's account, she does not love him because she justifies her love in an incorrect way.

4.8 IMPERSONAL RELATIONSHIPS AND LOVE

Since discussions concerning love are often dominated by in-depth accounts of closer personal relationships, I wish to give special consideration to a distant category of relationships, which I refer to as impersonal relationships. LaFollette offers a useful account of impersonal relationships. He explains,

> A relationship is impersonal if either party relates merely because the other fills a role or satisfies a particular need. Neither party cares who occupies the role or fulfills that need: she is concerned only that someone does, and does it well. I may not care who checks out my groceries; I may care only that someone does it competently.[39]

For LaFollette, what distinguishes impersonal relationships from personal relationships is that impersonal relationships are driven only by a desire to have a particular need satisfied, but the identity of the person who satisfies it is unimportant. Such impersonal relationships are a necessity in contemporary society since the complexities of life frequently require short, impersonal role-related interactions.

There is an ambiguity in LaFollette's definition. In the first sentence, he specifies that a relationship is impersonal if either person merely wants a need fulfilled, but in the second sentence, he specifies that neither party cares who fulfills the role.[40] A relationship is clearly impersonal if both parties relate to one another merely to have a need fulfilled, but there are also cases where the identity of the individual is a salient factor for only one person. For example, a mechanic may simply view a patron as an anonymous customer, while the customer, out of an overdeveloped sense of loyalty, views him as my mechanic and prefers him to other similarly qualified service providers. In this case, it seems that the mechanic has an impersonal relationship with the customer, but the customer has a personal relationship with the mechanic.

I will use LaFollette's account of impersonal relationships, with the qualification that on my account relationships are reciprocal but not necessarily equal. Since relationships are reciprocal, if Hamlet has a relationship with Macbeth, then Macbeth necessarily has a relationship with Hamlet. However, even though relationships are reciprocal, those relationships are not always equal. Hamlet may have a different role in relationship to Macbeth than Macbeth has with Hamlet, as in a parent-child, an employer-employee, or a student-teacher relationship. Therefore, on my account, it is possible for two people to relate so that one person relates personally to the other but the other relates impersonally. This situation is not inherently incompatible with love. For example, if Don Quixote relates to Dulcinea in a personal way, but she has no personal interest in him, love does not require that she develop a personal interest in him. Instead, love requires that she treat him merely with basic human dignity and avoid misleading him concerning her lack of personal interest in him.

One important aspect of love in impersonal relationships is similar to Aquinas's *misercordia*, a care for the well-being of others regardless of relational proximity that expresses itself in times of great need or distress. This aspect of love also has similarities to Martha Nussbaum's account of compassion. She argues that compassion is the basic social emotion which serves as "a central bridge between the individual and the community; it is conceived of as our species' way of hooking the interests of others to our own personal goods."[41] She views compassion as consisting in three beliefs: a belief in the seriousness of another's suffering, a belief that the suffering is not caused by the sufferer's actions, and a belief that the compassionate person could find herself in similar circumstances.[42]

Two aspects of Nussbaum's account of compassion mirror aspects of the Neo-Thomistic account of love. The concern for another's deep suffering, regardless of relationship, is an implication of the lover's desire for the beloved's good. Acknowledging the essential substitutability of lover and sufferer is implicit within desiring unity with the beloved.[43] One difference between Nussbaum's compassion and my account of love is that one can love those who cause their own suffering. The fact that someone causes his own suffering is an important circumstance that may require the lover to act in certain ways, such as providing counsel, or to avoid acting in other ways that encourage the beloved's self-destructive activities, but the sufferer remains an appropriate object for love.

4.9 THE ROLE OF PERSONAL ATTRIBUTES IN LOVE

While the key components of the Neo-Thomistic account of love have been explicated, the role personal attributes play in love still needs to be examined. While the beloved's nonrelational attributes are not reasons for love, the beloved's attributes are still important. First, the lover appreciates the beloved's positive attributes. A father loves *that* his daughter is funny, playful, beautiful, and intelligent, but he does not love her *because* she is funny, playful, beautiful, and intelligent. If his daughter had other attributes, he would still love her and appreciate her other positive attributes. He loves her simply because she is she! If he met another child that was similarly funny, playful, beautiful, and intelligent, he would not love that child in the same way he loves his own. If he discovered another child who was funnier, more playful, more beautiful, and more intelligent, this new child would not replace the daughter in her father's affections.

In our earlier discussion of the goods desired for the beloved, we mentioned that the beloved's attributes influence how love is expressed. A loving parent takes her child's attributes into account when conceiving of the good desired for that child. A person's subjectively valued goals play a role in what constitutes his good. Such goals plays this role either because fulfilled desires are at least partially constitutive of well-being or because achieving goals tends to be pleasurable and pleasure is at least partially constitutive of well-being. The good desired for the beloved also partially depends upon her character qualities. A loving parent might desire increased character for her child, even if it requires temporary physical or emotional hardship.[44] For example, a loving parent still cares for an adult child who has become a violent criminal but may believe the good for him is to be captured by the authorities and rehabilitated.

4.10 AN ARGUMENT FOR THE NEO-THOMISTIC ACCOUNT OF LOVE: THE SHORTCOMINGS OF COMPETING ACCOUNTS

Now that an in-depth explanation of the Neo-Thomistic account of love has been completed, one may ask why it is preferable to the competing accounts in Chapter One. First, each of the conceptions of love in Chapter One has serious flaws, undesirable consequences, or is too limited in its range of applicable loving relationships. Frankfurt's account of love does not allow any possibility of objective excellence regarding the objects of love, is incompatible with viewing love as a virtue, and ignores the possibility of relational reasons for love. Velleman's account of love is unacceptably minimalist and fails to explain important normative experiences of love such as the nonsubstitutability of the beloved and the various types of loving relationships. LaFollette's account applies only to voluntary relationships and vacillates concerning the reasons for love by shifting between specific attributes of the beloved and the lover's shared relational history with the beloved. Kolodny's account has unnecessary requirements concerning the lover's understanding of love, is compatible with pathological love based on incorrect beliefs concerning what kinds of relationships justify love, and does not provide a justification for loving people generally, giving rise to potential partiality-impartiality problems. The Neo-Thomistic account of love avoids these problems.

For example, the Neo-Thomistic account of love avoids problems arising from construing love as the lover's response to the beloved's attributes. If love is primarily based upon particular attributes of the beloved—a sense of humor, attractive physical features, or even virtuous character—this construal implies the lover would be entitled or expected to love anyone with the relevant attributes. This implication is problematic since the beloved in some important relationships is nonsubstitutable. More disturbingly, the lover would be rationally required to cease loving if the relevant attributes of the beloved fade.

Yet the normative experiences of love suggest it is more tenacious than the attributes model permits. Furthermore, the lover would care for anyone with whom he had the relevant relationship. A loving parent would care for any child he had, regardless of the child's attributes. A loving sister may love her siblings in spite of their nonrelational attributes rather than because of these attributes. A loving spouse continues to love, even when attributes that initially motivated the relationship fade.

The Neo-Thomistic account of love also avoids problems arising from Kolodny's view that love is rooted in emotional vulnerability that has historic interactive relationships as its reasons. While Kolodny's construal of love is compatible with relationships that are incompatible with genuine concern for the well-being of the beloved, such as the owner-slave relationship, the relational account of love rejects inherently destructive relationships as loving.

The Neo-Thomistic account escapes the weaknesses of Frankfurt's no-reasons explanation of love. His account was problematic in that it could offer no criteria for evaluating excellence concerning the object of an agent's love. In contrast, this account offers the criterion that all persons should be loved but that love's intensity and form ought to be shaped by the relational connections between lover and beloved.

Velleman's account of love based on the beloved's generic personhood also has undesirable implications: love becomes too minimalist and too uniform in its expression. In contrast, the Neo-Thomistic account of love distinguishes between the many ways love can be expressed in a variety of relationships. It also avoids his minimalist implications of love. In contrast, this account of love's emphasis on the two desires of love has far-reaching implications beyond emotional vulnerability.

4.11 THE NEO-THOMISTIC VIEW AND
THE CRITERIA FOR AN IDEAL ACCOUNT OF LOVE

While my account of love does not have the drawbacks of the leading contemporary alternative accounts of love, it also meets the positive criteria set forward in Chapter One for an attractive conception of love. The four criteria are

(1) The flexibility of the concept of love. It is desirable to have an account of love that can be applied to a broad range of relationships, rather than a very limited subset of relationships. It should also offer some guidance on how the many species of love are distinct from one another.

(2) An adequate account of love must be compatible with the normative psychological phenomena of love. It should be compatible with the considerable range of normative psychological experiences of love, such as the desires of love, the intensity of the desires of love in particular relationships, the uniqueness of the beloved, the irreplaceability of the beloved, and the tenacity of loving relationships.

(3) An account of love should be able to address concerns of partiality and impartiality. An adequate conception of love must be compatible with impartial moral concerns.

(4) Love should be construable as a virtue. An adequate account of love must be compatible with viewing love as a human excellence, an ideal quality. As such, there must be criteria for evaluating a person's loves.

The Neo-Thomistic account fulfills these criteria better than other contemporary conceptions of love. It fulfills the flexibility criterion because it can be used to evaluate excellence in all relationships. Many conceptions of love are not adequately flexible. For example, accounts that claim the reasons for love are the attributes of the beloved typically fail this criterion, such as LaFollette's account. These accounts are primarily applicable to friendships and romantic relationships but have difficulty explaining loving relationships within familial contexts. Velleman's account of love fails the flexibility requirement in a different way, by failing to differentiate between the many modes of love.

In contrast, a chief advantage of the Neo-Thomistic conception of love is that it construes the virtuous disposition in all relationships in terms of two broad, but far-reaching, desires. It emphasizes the essential unity of an agent's character in how she treats strangers, siblings, spouses, parents, friends, and all other persons. The ideal disposition in each relationship can be viewed as a distinct species in the broader genus of love. Excellence in a specific type of love, such as *eros* or *philia,* is a particular expression of the overarching virtue of love.

Furthermore, this account requires the virtuous agent to have a caring disposition toward others generally, fulfilling the moral intuitions behind ethicists who advocate broad benevolence or compassion. The ideal character disposition within both partial relationships and impartial relationships are construed as different expressions of the same desires of love toward other persons. The character quality that makes loving agents excellent at developing relationships transcends any particular relationship. This quality is well expressed by our account of love.

Second, the Neo-Thomistic account has explanatory value concerning the normative psychological experiences of love. The experience of attraction that is typical in partial loving relationships is an expression of the lover's desire for union with the beloved. Furthermore, this account distinguishes between the attraction of inauthentic love based on selfish desires and attraction based on genuine loving desires.

The irreplaceability and uniqueness of the beloved is explained by the uniqueness of union in intimate loving relationships. While the type of union the lover has with the beloved is repeatable with other people, the experience of union itself is unique and unrepeatable due to the uniqueness of both lover and beloved. This fact explains why the loss of a relationship can never be fully replaced by another relationship of the same type. Spouses differ vastly from one another, even if there is similarity in the type of relationship. Children differ from one another, and if a parent loses a child, another one can never replace the first, even if he fulfills a similar role in the parent's life.

The lover's tendency toward certain emotions concerning the beloved is explained as a result of the closeness in intimate relationships. The greater intensity of love's desires is due to the greater closeness and larger scope of these relationships. Therefore, the resulting emotions are strong when these desires are fulfilled or thwarted. It is difficult to compile a complete list of normative psychological experiences associated with love, but most, if not all, of love's typical experiences can be explained by the Neo-Thomistic account.

The Neo-Thomistic account meets the third criterion for an ideal account of love by balancing the ethical requirements of both close personal relationships and impersonal relationships. It accomplishes this balance by requiring love in close relationships to be compatible with impartial love for all. Therefore, my account is impartial in an important sense. However, the distinction between partial and impartial moral theories is ambiguous due to considerable disagreement concerning what makes a moral theory impartial. The *Stanford Encyclopedia of Philosophy* offers a helpful distinction between moral theories exhibiting first-order impartiality and second-order impartiality:

> First-order impartiality is that displayed by an agent in ordinary choice situations—choosing how to spend one's day, who to spend time with, and so forth. Second-order impartiality, by contrast, operates only in a certain, special sort of context: contexts in which the rules, principles and institutions which govern first-order behavior are evaluated and selected. Thus a moral rule granting individuals complete freedom of association, and thus allowing them to display first-order partiality by spending time with whomever they please regardless of whether doing so promotes the greater social good in any particular case, might be given a second-order impartialist justification by demonstrating that such a rule would promote the impersonal good, or that it would be selected by a group of impartial persons who were choosing the moral rules that were to govern society.[45]

My account of love exhibits first-order impartiality in that the lover impartially possesses the same desires of love toward all other people, shaped by the objective criterion of relational and nonrelational circumstances. Admittedly, viewing relational circumstances as a morally relevant reason that shapes one's desires is controversial, and incompatible with some accounts of first-order impartiality. For example, some forms of act utilitarianism would not view my account as possessing genuine first-order impartiality.

My account of love at least possesses a type of second-order impartiality since desires in each relationship must be compatible with love for all persons. This type of impartiality does not require that the lover have equally strong desires toward all others. Instead, an impartial consideration of the needs of all must shape the lover's relationships and desires within them. Like Aquinas's *caritas,* love is impartial in that it involves the same basic desires of the good for and unity with all persons. Furthermore, the desires of love toward all persons modify how love is expressed toward any particular person. Therefore, love in close relationships is expressed in ways compatible with love for all. Relational circumstances never justify indifference toward someone simply because he lacks a close bond with the lover.

While I advocate these principles in the context of a virtue-centered ethical system, it is noteworthy that treating people differently due to relational attributes is compatible with several contemporary ethical systems, including those that hold impartiality as a central value. For example, it is compatible with a rule utilitarian approach to ethics if it can be demonstrated that treating others differently within close relationships tends to maximize the happiness for all. It is also compatible with some interpretations of Kantianism; for example, David Velleman claims that,

> Equal consideration in Kantian ethics consists in considering everyone as having equal access to justifications for acting—which amounts to considering everyone's rights as equal, not everyone's interest. Caring about some people more than others may be perfectly compatible with according everyone equal rights.[46]

If Velleman is correct, and I believe that he is, then even Kantian-style impartiality is arguably compatible with the principle that relational reasons can provide a justifiable basis for treating one person differently than another.

Moral impartiality is valued because it protects against egoism and subjectivism. Yet relational bonds are not always voluntary, and create obligations as well as benefits. Relationships are not mere egoistic or subjective preferences. Aiding a financially troubled sibling may be costly, and listening to a dear friend's personal problems is not necessarily enjoyable. Helping those close to us in hard times may require sacrifices, yet relational closeness puts us in the best position to help these people. Our knowledge of our close relations' troubles and situations is unique. The access we have to them is unparalleled. The nature of aid we can offer is unique to close relationships. Generosity's effects in close relationships differ from the effects of generosity received from distant strangers. Most notably, it builds an ongoing relationship and encourages a cycle of thankfulness and helpfulness within a relationship.

The Neo-Thomistic account of love meets the final criterion for an ideal account by viewing love as a virtue. Unlike accounts of love based on involuntary passions, random attraction, or no reasons at all, the relational account's emphasis on acts of a person's will connects her moral character directly to love. This account of love provides criteria to evaluate an agent's ongoing volitional dispositions toward others, which is arguably the most morally significant aspect of the self. Loving well is a moral excellence, not an involuntary emotion.

4.12 MARTHA NUSSBAUM'S CRITERIA FOR AN ACCEPTABLE ACCOUNT OF LOVE

While the Neo-Thomistic account fulfills my own criteria for an adequate conception of love, it also fulfills the intuitions of other mainstream philosophical thinkers concerning love. For example, in Martha Nussbaum's historical examination of love in *Upheavals of Thought,* she offers three criteria for an acceptable account of love. She believes that an adequate account of love must at least include support for general social compassion, support for mutual reciprocal relationships, and adequate space for individuality. By support for general social compassion, she means that love must include a concern for the serious hardships of all others. Support for mutual reciprocal relationships is present if the account of love encourages a sense of equality within spousal, romantic, or erotic relationships, and protects both people from being treated as a thing for the other's use. Love should also support mutual reciprocal relationships outside of the context of the most intimate relationships. Finally, love has adequate space for individuality if it includes respect for the separateness of each person.[47]

The Neo-Thomistic account does well on all three of Nussbaum's criteria. First, this account provides a strong basis for general social compassion. Love is not merely compatible with goodwill for all persons, but *requires* goodwill toward all. This goodwill includes, and goes beyond, a concern for the serious hardships of others.

Second, while the Neo-Thomistic account does not prescribe all the details of love in intimate spousal and romantic relationships, it is only compatible with desires that are reasonably expected to promote the well-being of the beloved. Models of spousal love that elevate the importance of one member of the relationship are incompatible with love. Similarly, love's desire for union requires a mutual relationship[48] with the beloved. Love is incompatible with the domination of one partner by the other. It is also incompatible with intimate relationships that do not leave adequate room for other reciprocal relationships.

Finally, it might seem that the Neo-Thomistic account might not leave adequate room for each person's individuality due to its emphasis on union. However, this concern is mistaken because this account also places an importance on each person's individuality and autonomy. The beloved's personal traits and desires shape the lover's desires for his flourishing and union. Furthermore, union between persons requires the maintenance of both individual identities. A loss of one individual's personal identity would make union with him impossible. Finally, autonomy is one of the goods desired for the beloved. Even in the parent-child relationship, one of the goods the loving parent desires for his child is eventual autonomy.

4.13 TWO FINAL OBJECTIONS TO THE NEO-THOMISTIC ACCOUNT OF LOVE

One objection to the Neo-Thomistic account of love comes from David Velleman's claim that love does not include a desire to benefit the beloved. He explicitly rejects the claim that love includes a desire to benefit the beloved, labeling the idea a "sentimental fantasy." He explains, "Certainly, love for my children leads me to promote their interests almost daily; yet when I think of other people I love—parents, brothers, friends, former teachers and students—I do not think of myself as an agent of their interests."[49] Note that Velleman's response actually provides evidence for the Neo-Thomistic account's claim that the nature of the loving relationship shapes the lover's desires toward the beloved. He suggests that love for one's children results in different expressions of love than love in other relationships. However, he seems to think that love within many personal relationships does not include a desire to promote the good of the beloved.

Velleman's claim that love does not include a desire to promote the good of the beloved is incorrect. His view of how the lover might promote the good of the beloved is unnecessarily narrow. There are many ways a lover can benefit the beloved without acting as a broad agent of the beloved's interests. The Neo-Thomistic account explains that the nature of the lover's relationship with the beloved shapes his desire for the good of the beloved. For example, a loving teacher does not view himself as a general agent of his students' interests. Rather, he seeks to benefit his students by acting as a thoughtful teacher, helping them develop intellectual virtue, clearly communicating beneficial subject matter, wanting them to succeed academically, and so forth. A loving student benefits her former teachers by appropriately crediting them with their role in the student's success. A loving friend encourages her friends in their pursuit of life's goals and benefits them by being a companion and confidante. Within many types of relationships, the ongoing relationship that the lover seeks with the beloved is itself a benefit to the beloved.

Another objection to the Neo-Thomistic account might claim that goodwill toward others is sufficient for love, that love does not require a desire for union with the beloved. Yet goodwill without a desire for union with others is compatible with many recognizably unloving attitudes. Agents who will the good for other people, but desire no union with them, fail to respond properly to their personhood. For example, it is possible to have an authentic desire for the good of the poor, expressed by voting for governmental redistribution of wealth or donating to charity, while desiring no personal role in their lives. It is also possible to be classist while genuinely desiring the good of the poor. If a parent desires the good for his beloved child but wants no degree of personal union with her, this indifference concerning union indicates a deficiency in love.

It is revealing that similar expressions of goodwill are possible toward nonhuman animals or even inanimate objects. An agent can have goodwill toward nonhuman animals by voting for government-enforced protections of animals or donating to the humane society. An agent can have goodwill toward inanimate objects, such as art, by voting for governmental promotion of art or by donating to a museum. However, persons warrant a response that goes beyond mere goodwill, including a desire for union based upon their shared personhood and humanity. Failure to desire union with another person is a failure to recognize that person's humanity. Thus, it is a failure of love.

ENDNOTES

1. There is also the possibility that one's desires may be overdetermined. I will address this possibility in Chapter 4.4.

2. Ayn Rand, *The Virtue of Selfishness* (New York: The New American Library, 1964), 47.

3. ST II-II.28.1.

4. Rand 1964, 47.

5. Michael Slote, *Morals From Motives* (New York: Oxford University Press, 2001), 29.

6. Christine Swanton, *Virtue Ethics: A Pluralistic View* (New York: Oxford University Press, 2003), 117.

7. Martha Nussbaum, *Upheavals of Thought: The Intelligence of Emotions* (New York: Cambridge University Press, 2001), 31.

8. I address how the love balances impartial concerns for all and partial concerns for those close to the lover in Chapter 4.11.

9. *Cf.* Harry Frankfurt, "Freedom of the Will and the Concept of a Person," *Journal of Philosophy* LXVII (1971): 5–20.

10. *Cf.* Aristotle, *Nicomachean Ethics*, 1105b–1106a.

11. I do not claim that emotions are simply the result of a person's internal desires fulfilled or thwarted by external states of affairs. I merely claim these two factors strongly influence emotions.

12. These claims do not commit me to an objective list theory of well-being. I present the desires of love in this way because people commonly think of the good for humans in terms of many facets such as relationships, health, happiness, success, virtue, and so forth.

13. This view departs from Aquinas's account in an effort to acknowledge the many sincere disputes about the nature of the good in philosophy and society more generally.

14. Of course there are some important vocations that necessarily have an unusually large scope, such as soldier, police officer, and perhaps doctor. Yet a job in sales should not require a sixty-hour workweek.

15. While both of these examples describe situations in which the beloved's character is the reason union with the beloved is no longer good for him, it is possible there are other types of circumstances that would have a similar result. I focus on character-related examples because these are the least controversial.

16. Raz also discusses attachments with nonpersonal entities, but I focus exclusively on his discussion of personal attachments since only they are relevant to this discussion.

17. Joseph Raz, *Value, Respect, and Attachment* (New York: Cambridge University Press, 2001), 12.

18. Raz 2001, 15–22.

19. Raz 2001, 15–22.

20. Raz 2001, 17.

21. Richard Lucas and Portia Dyrenforth, "Does the Existence of Social Relationships Matter for Subjective Well-Being?" in *Self and Relationships*, eds. Kathleen D. Vohs and Eli J. Finkel (New York: The Guildford Press, 2006), 256.

22. This second account of relationships seems to be the least compelling of the three. If interactions between persons in general do not establish a relationship between them, the most likely explanation for this fact would be that simple interactions don't necessarily include significant interpersonal awareness. Yet increasing the frequency of interactions also does not guarantee significant interpersonal awareness. Therefore, I judge both the first and the third accounts of relationships to be more attractive.

23. Niko Kolodny, "Love as Valuing a Relationship," *The Philosophical Review* 112 (2003): 147–148.

24. Kolodny 2003, 148.

25. Kolodny 2003, 148.

26. Kolodny 2003, 148.

27. It might seem that a corporate entity would qualify as a particular participant in love. However, this possibility is ruled out since Kolodny stipulates that love is always between two persons, and corporate entities do not seem to be persons in any way relevant to love.

28. Kolodny 2003, 148.

29. Kolodny 2003, 148.

30. Robert Kraut, "Love *De Re*," *Midwest Studies in Philosophy* 10 (1986): 426.

31. A person also has a relationship with himself. However, this relationship departs slightly from this definition since there is no "other" in this relationship. This relationship concerns the proper role one plays in his own life.

32. Of course, sometimes the ethnic, religious, or socioeconomic identity of one's neighbors is salient in choosing a residence. Such actions are vicious and unloving when motivated by a desire for distance from others people based only on their ethnic, religious, or socioeconomic status.

33. Similarly, Aquinas claims that we ought to have charity toward our selves. *Cf.* ST II-II.25.4.

34. Stump 2006, 33.

35. Of course, some jobs are both necessary and dangerous, such as those in law enforcement. There is nothing inherently unloving about employing another in these situations.

36. There may be unusual circumstances in which criminal activity is not unloving to society in general, as in civil disobedience to unjust laws. However, when I refer to "partners in crime," I refer to violent criminals who break just laws.

37. Of course, the types of union one believes to be possible vary depending on his metaphysical beliefs. As already noted, Aquinas believes a kind of union is possible for all in the afterlife. Other worldviews may allow different kinds of desires for union with all humanity.

38. Kolodny 2003, 146.

39. Hugh LaFollette, *Personal Relationships* (Cambridge, MA: Blackwell Publishers, 1996), 4.

40. This ambiguity in LaFollette's definition continues beyond this short quotation because his discussion shifts between examples using singular pronouns such as, "she is concerned" and "I may not care," and plural pronouns "it is impersonal because we interact." The examples using singular pronouns seem to imply that a relationship is impersonal if either person is motivated by impersonal concerns, while the examples using plural pronouns seem to suggest that both people must be motivated by impersonal concerns.

41. Martha Nussbaum, "Compassion: The Basic Social Emotion," *Social Philosophy and Policy* 13 (1996): 28.

42. Nussbaum 1996, 31.

43. Of course, there are some specific ills to which the lover might not be vulnerable. Obviously, men are not vulnerable to the pains women suffer in labor. Yet union with the beloved leads the lover to identity with the suffering of the beloved more

generally. Even if the lover could not be harmed in the specific way that the beloved is harmed, he is vulnerable to pain, disease, and suffering.

44. Whether or not a virtue is actually a constituent of well-being, it is frequently viewed as such. I suggest that there is enough evidence to view desiring virtue for the beloved as an authentic desire of love.

45. Troy Jollimore, "Impartiality," in *Stanford Encyclopedia of Philosophy*, April 18, 2006, http://plato.stanford.edu/entries/impartiality/ (accessed 19 Sept. 2007).

46. David Velleman, "Love as a Moral Emotion," *Ethics* 109 (1999): 340.

47. Nussbaum 2001, 479–481.

48. I exclude love in relationships such as the parent-child relationship because Nussbaum is not concerned with inequality within these relationships.

49. Velleman 1999, 353.

Chapter 5

The Benefits of Love

What are the benefits of possessing the virtue of love? In previous chapters I defended the view that love is *a disposition towards relationally appropriate acts of the will consisting of disinterested desires for the good of the beloved and unity with the beloved held as final ends*. This chapter argues that love provides final ends that motivate enjoyable and beneficial activities, brings about psychic integration, motivates self-improvement, increases the lover's epistemic goods, and makes relationships more harmonious, enjoyable, and tenacious. This chapter shows how each distinct benefit of love results in pleasure, fulfilled desires, or both. Through these five benefits, love necessarily benefits the lover and typically increases the lover's overall well-being.

These claims are opposed by thinkers who suggest there is no necessary connection between a person's well-being and love or similar virtues like benevolence or compassion. Even when the beneficial nature of love is not explicitly rejected, it is typically under recognized or vaguely endorsed. For example, Michael Slote's claim that an *eudaimonistic* account of virtue cannot support virtues like love implies there is no necessary connection between love and the lover's well-being.[1] David Velleman does not say whether love benefits the lover, but since his conception of love is modeled upon Kantian respect he likely shares Kant's belief that virtue and love make no necessary contribution to the virtuous person's well-being.[2] Niko Kolodny also does not explore the role of love in the agent's well-being.[3]

In contrast, Harry Frankfurt seems aware that love contributes to the lover's well-being, and his writings influence my account of two benefits of love: the lover's necessarily increased psychic integration and love's role in providing final ends.[4] Hugh LaFollette acknowledges that relationships are valuable and claims that they generally increase one's happiness, elevate one's sense of self-worth, promote self-knowledge, and develop character.[5] Yet LaFollette only analyzes the benefits of relationships rather than the benefits of love itself. While I do not dispute the value of relationships, some of love's benefits are independent of relationships. In the contemporary discussion of love, the role love plays in advancing the lover's well-being has been underdeveloped when it has not been completely denied.

5.1 THE KANTIAN OBJECTION TO CONNECTING VIRTUE AND WELL-BEING

One historical objection against connecting love and well-being that deserves special consideration is offered by Immanuel Kant. In Chapter One, we noted his claim that the only ways virtue and happiness could have a necessary connection would be if either the motive for pursuing virtue were a desire for happiness, or virtue necessarily caused happiness.[6] He claims that neither option is really possible. Since he views duty as the only morally appropriate motive, he claims that seeking virtue in order to attain happiness is vicious. Therefore, virtue and happiness cannot coincide in that way. He also argues that attaining happiness is based upon one's practical skill for achieving desires[7] rather than one's degree of virtue, which makes the second option impossible. Since he believes that possessing a virtue like love guarantees no increase in the lover's practical ability for fulfilling desires, Kant concludes that there can be no necessary connection between virtue and well-being.

However, Kant's second strategy for establishing a necessary connection between virtue and happiness deserves further investigation. While practical skills rather than moral motivations undoubtedly aid in attaining pleasure and satisfying desires, some virtues necessarily increase the agent's practical skill. For example, the virtue of courage necessarily increases an agent's practical skills for attaining desires. On the traditional Aristotelian account,[8] courage requires controlling one's fear in proportion to danger.[9] Courage has an intrinsic prudential benefit since experiencing the appropriate amount of fear warranted by a situation ensures the courageous person does not irrationally abandon goals based on unmerited fears. Conversely, the courageous person does not underestimate the dangers of particular situations and goals. Therefore, courage increases a person's ability to fulfill desires since it increases a person's ability to take calculated risks in pursuit of desired goals.

While love does not directly increase practical skills, there are other ways that virtue might increase a person's happiness. Another way virtue might increase a person's happiness is by shaping the virtuous person's desires in particular ways. The quantity of desires fulfilled by an agent and their relative importance to the agent depend not only upon the agent's practical skills, but also upon what an agent desires. Having unrealistic or impossible desires guarantee the agent will be unable to fulfill them regardless of her practical skills. Since the lover necessarily has a specific set of relatively important desires for the good of and union with other persons in relationally appropriate ways, it may increase her well-being by shaping her desires. If these desires are more easily fulfilled than others would have been, if they are more enjoyable when fulfilled, or if they tend to stay fulfilled longer, then this virtue necessarily benefits the lover in ways Kant did not consider.

Virtue could also increase the virtuous person's well-being without increasing his practical skills if virtue necessarily provided goods that are instrumentally useful for attaining desires. For example, industriousness might be viewed as a virtue that motivates an appropriate level of hard work. While industriousness guarantees no increase in practical skills, the industrious person will typically have more resources for achieving his desires. The industrious person will likely obtain more money or status than a lazy person, and these goods can be used in pursuit of his own desires. Admittedly, this fact does not establish a necessary connection between industriousness and well-being since someone who is completely inept at fulfilling desires may fail to fulfill them despite an increase in resources. Yet it does show an additional way that virtue could make fulfilled desires significantly more likely. Similarly, the lover may not have more practical skill than an unloving person, but might gain epistemic goods and relationships that the unloving person does not have. If the lover typically has a greater epistemic base and a larger number of higher quality relationships that are instrumentally useful in attaining her desires, then her desires are more likely to be fulfilled.

Another way to reject Kant's views would be to reject his desire satisfaction account of well-being. There are other ways virtue might benefit the virtuous according to other accounts of well-being. Obviously, a *eudaimonist* would view virtue itself as a constituent of well-being, and reject Kant's view. It is also possible that virtue would increase well-being according to hedonistic theories in ways Kant did not consider. For example, it is possible that being a loving person is inherently more pleasurable than being a vicious person. If loving others is inherently more pleasurable than being apathetic or hateful to them, then love is beneficial according to hedonistic accounts of well-being regardless of the lover's practical skills. While I will not argue for an alternative account of well-being, this strategy would also be an effective way to respond to Kant's objection.

Before this chapter proceeds by examining various benefits of love, we need to revisit the criterion for recognizing a benefit of love. Chapter One observed that the four major views of well-being are hedonistic theories, desire fulfillment theories, *eudaimonistic* theories and objective list theories. These theories differ concerning what they identify as basic constituents of well-being.

Since *eudaimonistic* theories view virtue itself as a constituent of well-being, they require the least attention in this discussion. Obviously, possessing the virtue of love necessarily contributes to well-being according to these theories. An additional way that the virtue of love contributes to well-being on strict *eudaimonistic* theories will be its role in motivating self-improvement and self-perfection. In the discussion of this benefit of love, it is obvious that *eudaimonistic* theories would view love as providing an additional instrumental contribution to well-being since it results in a strong motivation for developing additional virtues.

Similarly, objective list theories will not require much attention since they typically view virtue, pleasure, and/or desire fulfillment as constituents of well-being. Therefore, this chapter seeks to demonstrate that the virtue of love results in an increase in pleasure that contributes to well-being according to hedonistic theories, an increase in desire satisfaction that contributes to well-being according to desire satisfaction theories, or both. However, an ambiguity still remains in the criterion for a benefit of love. Must the benefit of love necessarily result in all circumstances, or is it enough that the benefit be a likely result of love? In the sections that follow, I will distinguish between benefits that necessarily result and benefits that are only a likely result. *Therefore, the following sections will enumerate distinct ways that possessing love necessarily or likely improves well-being through an increase in pleasure and/or desire satisfaction.*

While the benefits of love are distinct from one another, there is a degree of overlap among them. For example, both an increase in epistemic goods and an increase in the number and quality of personal relationships result from love. However, some epistemic benefits of love are insights offered from friends within relationships made possible by love. These benefits will be addressed separately since not all epistemic benefits of love come through relationships, and because the relationships made possible by love also contribute to well-being in ways other than providing epistemic goods.

5.2 LOVE'S NECESSARY BENEFIT OF FINAL ENDS

One benefit of possessing the virtue of love is that it necessarily provides the lover with final ends. Since the lover desires the good of other persons and union with them as final ends she necessarily gains numerous final ends, desired for their own sake. Frankfurt argues that final ends are necessarily beneficial to human beings. He explains:

> We are creatures who cannot avoid being active. Therefore, we will still be active even if we have no aims; but we will be active without purpose. Now being without purpose does not entail having no preferences concerning the possible outcomes of behavior, nor does it entail being invulnerable to harm. Someone who has no goals may be fully susceptible to suffering and to benefiting from his conduct. He may also be quite capable of recognizing the value of its effects upon him. This means that regardless of how empty we are of intent, what we do may nonetheless be important to us. It may serve our interests, or defeat them, even though our interests do not guide it.[10]

The first benefit of final ends is that they guide an agent's efforts to reflect her preferences, thereby, making it more likely that her desires will be fulfilled. Consider Frankfurt's implicit distinction between goals and preferences. Goals are ends that are always preferences, but preferences are not necessarily held as personal goals. Preferences are merely states of affairs preferred by a person. For example, an agent may prefer that one candidate win an election rather than another, but it is possible that this theoretical preference will never be pursued by any action. In contrast, an agent's ends are desired states of affairs that are integrated into her motivational structure and shape her actions. Someone who takes the election of a particular candidate as an end will have at least some tendency to act to help bring about that goal.

For a person without final ends no activity or state of affairs is valued as an ultimate goal. Furthermore, without final ends no activity or state of affairs is instrumentally valuable, since instrumental value relies upon the value of the final goal promoted by the instrumental activity. If a person holds nothing to be valuable as either an end or a means then no activity has meaning for that person. A person whose life is devoid of meaningful activities will inevitably be characterized by boredom, emptiness, and purposelessness.[11] Such a person experiences less pleasure and achieves fewer preferences than one guided by final ends, which integrate the person's preferences into his motivational structure. A person without final ends typically satisfies fewer preferences because his actions are not guided by goals that help him fulfill his preferences.

Consider the difference between an agent with a mere theoretical preference for health and one who wholeheartedly embraces health as a final end. Poor health inevitably decreases well-being because it results in a more painful existence that limits the activities a person can engage in, thereby narrowing the scope of achievable desires. A person without final ends is not consistently motivated to pursue the activities necessary for maintaining health. Such a person will choose daily activities based on habit or momentary whim without considering whether or not they advance his health or other preferences. Unsurprisingly, some lives without final ends become marked by sedentary entertainment and pursuit of short-term whims without an interest in health guiding activities. This purposeless existence typically results in a shorter and less pleasant life span.

While the beneficial nature of final ends is established by Frankfurt's argument, it may seem that the benefits of love's ends are no greater than any other ends. This feature of love may seem as if it only provides a benefit over the relatively rare person with no final ends. Any person who takes typical human desires for vocational success, an exciting romantic life, a long life span, or economic success as final ends seems to be just as well off as the loving person because they both have final ends.

However, there is a second aspect of the virtue of love that gives the lover a prudential advantage over many who take ordinary goals as final ends. Since love is a virtue that requires a high degree of consistency concerning the pursuit of loving desires, it gives an advantage over any disposition that is half-hearted or less consistent in its commitment to its final ends. For example, many people desire vocational success as a final end. This end does guide some of their actions. Yet, their disposition toward pursing this end may not be as consistent or wholehearted as the disposition possessed by the loving person. Such a person may desire success, but be easily distracted by short-term desires or lack the willpower to pursue these goals in less than optimal conditions. Since the virtue of love entails consistency in love's pursuits, the lover's actions are guided by her ends more consistently than agents with halfhearted commitments to their ends. This consistency increases the likelihood that the lover's desires will be fulfilled.

This advantage of the virtue of love as a final end would be shared by any similarly well-developed disposition that resulted in consistent pursuit of one's final ends. Other virtues might be similar in this respect. Some vices that are sufficiently well-integrated in their consistent pursuit of vicious final ends might be equally beneficial in this way. Some dispositions entailing the wholehearted pursuit of morally neutral final ends might offer an equal advantage. Yet, any half-hearted or inconsistent disposition would be prudentially inferior. And while few people completely lack final ends there are many more who are half-hearted and inconsistent in pursuing their ends.

While possessing the virtue of love is one of many ways to gain final ends, some final ends are more beneficial than others. For example, not every final end requires a sufficient amount of complex activity to endow life with ongoing meaning. Frankfurt explains,

> Any rational decision concerning the adoption of final ends must be made partly on the basis of an evaluation of the kinds of activities by which the various prospective ends would be pursued. It requires a consideration not only of the value that is inherent in these activities taken by themselves, but also of the terminal value they possess as contributors of meaning to life.[12]

The activities necessary for pursuing final ends vary greatly in type, quantity, and variety. Even a worthwhile final end might be achieved too easily. If a person in a technologically advanced society has the single end of protecting her children from polio this worthwhile goal can be achieved with little meaningful activity. A final end is also less beneficial if the actions required for pursuing it are dull, repetitive, or boring. For example, helping build the most advanced automobile might be a worthwhile final end. Yet if the sole action one can contribute to this goal is installing a single bolt to a car door on an assembly line every thirty seconds, this end will provide little complex and enjoyable activity.

Some final ends might require a sufficient amount and variety of activities to fill life with meaning, yet require inherently unpleasant activities in their pursuit. Goals that continually put one into conflict with others may hinder well-being because the required activities are unpleasant or undermine a person's other preferences. If one wants to become the head of a mafia family as a final end, he may need to harm or betray those close to himself to achieve this goal. He may never feel truly safe, and may need extraordinary vigilance to protect himself and those close to him. These activities are typically viewed as unpleasant and will likely undermine other common preferences in a person's life such as a desire for close relationships marked by trust.

Another reason that some final ends are less beneficial than others is that some final ends might be extremely difficult to achieve and result in frustration and disappointment rather than pleasure and achievement.[13] Becoming a world-class marathon runner may be a worthwhile goal requiring a variety of interesting activities, but it is an extraordinarily difficult goal to achieve. Even runners who dedicate years of hard work are more likely to fail than to succeed. Therefore, the achievability of one's final ends also effects how much they contribute to one's well-being.

The best final ends require a considerable amount of pleasant, complex, and meaningful activities in pursuit of a valuable goal, yet the ultimate goal itself will be relatively attainable. How do the ends of love fare on these considerations? First, it should be noted that the activities promoted by love are numerous and complex. Since a loving person seeks the good of others she must understand what constitutes the distinctive human goods needed by humans generally and the particular desires of specific beloved people. Persons are complex entities whose good is multifaceted. The good for humans includes physical, mental, social, emotional, and perhaps spiritual well-being. Loving parents are excellent examples of people who seek to understand the multifaceted good of their children. They typically investigate how to engender their children's physical well-being: through proper nutrition, exercise, and medical care. They learn how to promote children's mental and emotional development through personal interaction, shared learning activities, communicating basic life skills, and so forth. While learning how to promote their children's well-being, parents are involved in a variety of complex activities that also provide tools for achieving their own interests through information they have gained that can be used to improve their own physical, mental, and emotional health.

In close relationships, love motivates a considerable variety of everyday activities, such as ongoing attentiveness to the beloved, careful continued development of relationships, shared time, attempts to meet the needs and desires of the beloved, and so forth. Furthermore, the loving person seeks to understand the individuals she loves to support them in attaining those goods. While some goods contribute to the well-being of any person, other goods will only contribute to the well-being of particular persons. In less intimate relationships of love, a desire for the beloved's good can also lead to numerous activities, including philanthropic activities for general charitable causes, aid to particular others in need, donations, volunteer work, social action, and so forth.

Attaining and maintaining union with persons requires a variety of ongoing activities. Union with other persons cannot be obtained without an awareness of the many facets of the beloved. This goal requires ongoing effort including shared time and experiences in a variety of circumstances. Persons are not static beings, but are continually changing. Therefore, maintaining and deepening union with a beloved person is a complex, ongoing task. Since humans are relational beings, the interaction needed for promoting the good of others and union with them is enjoyable. Furthermore, love engenders activity within a variety of relational contexts, which leads to even further diversity in the activities required for achieving love's desires. A person acting out of love of his parents is involved in different activities than the same person in his relationships with his friends, children, or spouse.

More distant relationships of love, such as those with fellow citizens, co-workers, and members of a shared faith, also lead to a wide variety of enjoyable civic, vocational, and religious activities. Working for the greater good of others in these groups imbues these activities with meaning and purpose they would not otherwise possess. In these relationships love leads one to become more involved with, attuned to, and connected to these broader communities.

The desires of love require a considerable variety of complex, interesting, and ultimately self-beneficial activities. Furthermore, the final value most people attribute to relational goals is quite high. Persons and relationships with persons are frequently viewed among the most intrinsically valuable goods in existence.

Many, but certainly not all, of the activities promoted by love are typically judged to be pleasant rather than painful or distasteful. Interacting with other people, communicating with them, sharing time and attention with them, and seeking to promote their good are fundamentally pleasant activities. Of course, there are unpleasant activities that are sometimes required by love, such as nursing a sick child or spouse, and boring, repetitive tasks such as housecleaning. Yet even these tasks are not completely unpleasant since aiding close relatives in hard times fosters a deeper sense of connection with them. Repetitive tasks of daily life typically have beneficial results for ourselves as well as those we care for, such as a clean and functional home, which might even be desired by an unloving person.

How attainable are the goals of love? Answering this question is difficult because it relies upon particular circumstances, as well as one's views concerning which goods need to be promoted in the beloved's life. In any case, love's goals are always contingent on factors outside of the lover's control. One cannot ensure anyone's good, and union with others is contingent upon the beloved's responsiveness. Therefore, there are barriers to accomplishing love's goals and achieving them cannot be assured. While these facts are unfortunate, there are few final ends that have no risk of failure, except perhaps those concerning an agent's own motives and desires.[14] Since there are few or no final ends that do not have such drawbacks, these considerations do not make the final ends of love significantly less beneficial. A more troubling problem is that if physical health is needed for the good of the beloved, then the beloved's well-being will inevitably deteriorate with age.

However, the goals of love are also more attainable than many ends. First, the goals of love rarely lead to direct zero-sum competition with goals held by other people. The lover's desires for the good of the beloved and union with the beloved in relationally appropriate ways rarely undermine anyone else's good or thwart the desires of others.[15] The goals of love typically avoid competition with the goals of others and usually have no one seeking to thwart them. In contrast, goals centered on vocational success or obtaining financial goods frequently put the agent in direct conflict with other people.

These goals often lead to situations in which only one person can receive a particular promotion, prize, or honor.

Second, achieving love's goals does not require unusual skills or training that is inaccessible to the average person. One need not have unusual academic or physical talents to attain love's goals. One must simply respond well to others and their distinct relationships with the lover. Therefore, the ends of love are more easily achieved than many goals one could pursue.

While possessing the virtue of love is sufficient to provide final ends that fill a lifetime with meaningful and enjoyable activities, it might seem that many other ends would serve equally well. While there may be other final ends that are equally beneficial to the agent, ends that give meaning to a lifetime of activity are relatively rare. For example, hobbies typically fail in this regard. Consider the activities encouraged by a hobby such as amassing the world's largest, most diverse collection of bottle caps. Acquiring such a collection requires gathering a limited amount of information and a considerable amount of activity in order to obtain the bottle caps, as well as social interaction needed to obtain them. While these activities can be time-consuming, they are relatively limited in meaningfulness, complexity, and overall ability to engage a person's entire self. Even worse, achieving the final end is likely to be disappointing since most people would judge that the efforts required by the goal are disproportionate to its value.

Similarly, vocational goals often fail to provide deeply beneficial and meaningful final ends. The degree to which vocational goals are beneficial as final ends varies from vocation to vocation and partially depends on the individual's motivations for engaging in that vocation. Some people do not engage in vocational goals as final ends at all, but only as a means of acquiring resources needed for life or other goals. In these situations, vocational goals do not provide any benefits as final ends. Another problem is that many jobs do not offer much variety or complexity of activities, such as assembly line jobs, call center jobs, middle management, and customer service related jobs. These jobs are limited in their ability to engage the whole self. There are also jobs that involve interesting activities, but are typically judged to have limited ultimate value when pursued as a final end. For example, some jobs in marketing and advertising require considerable creativity carried out through interesting, complex activities. Yet a person may judge that increasing a relatively useless product's name recognition through clever advertising has little or no final value.

Furthermore, the amount of final value most people attribute to typical jobs in society is limited. It is almost cliché that no one at the end of his life wishes he had spent more time at the office. The kinds of jobs most often attributed the greatest final value by an agent are typically those closely connected to benefiting and relating to people. Many jobs in medicine, education, ministry, and counseling offer these sorts of opportunities. If this observation is correct, then the activities that are most likely to provide a life full of meaning and purpose are those most intimately involved with other persons, which explains why the virtue of love is so helpful in providing a life of meaningful activity. Just as the jobs that are associated with benefiting and relating to persons are frequently judged to have great final value, the virtue of love leads to activities with great final value because these activities involve benefiting and relating to people.

Finally, the ends of love are beneficial because they make the instrumental activities needed to pursue them more enjoyable and meaningful. The virtue of love can imbue otherwise boring and repetitive activities with greater meaning. A loving person may work for decades in a relatively tedious job such as an assembly line, but the job's role in benefiting family members, the community, and society can make the work more meaningful and enjoyable.

Frankfurt explains that ends covey meaning to the instrumental activities necessary for attaining them:

In evaluating a prospective final end, accordingly, it is essential to consider how much terminal value that end would convey to the means by which it would have to be pursued. In this sense, final ends must be judged on the basis of their usefulness. From one point of view, the activities in which we pursue our terminally valuable final ends have only the instrumental value that is characteristic of means. From another point of view, however, these activities are themselves terminally valuable, and they imbue with instrumental value the final ends for the sake of which they are undertaken.[16]

Not all ends add equal value to the means necessary for their pursuit. Some final ends, such as those of love, can make the means necessary for attaining those ends more enjoyable by imbuing them with meaning and purpose. Working a tedious job with the end of "paying the bills so I can live" may be less enjoyable and meaningful than working the same job with the end of "providing for my beloved family." Identical activities performed with different ends in view can be experience differently. Therefore, love also benefits the lover by making the activities used in the pursuit of love more enjoyable.

For each of these reasons the ends associated with love are among the most beneficial goals. Neera Badhwar similarly reports,

Nothing calls for the investment of self in valued objects and activities as love does, an investment that shapes the contours of our identities and creates a self worth loving. In short, love is the fuel that feeds our lives, and the primary source of identity and meaning and, thus, of happiness. A particular love may not be a net good, of course, since it may bring grief.... But, as the primary affective bond "to persons, things, or ideals that have value and importance for us" (Singer 1994:2), love is an indispensable part of a meaningful life.[17]

While Badhwar is discussing a slightly different conception of love since the Neo-Thomistic account applies only to persons rather than things and ideals, her comments are noteworthy. She claims love is not merely *a* source of meaning and happiness in life, but *the* source, and thus connects it to the best type of final ends. Her commentary reinforces my argument that love benefits the lover through enabling him to obtain a meaningful life by providing highly beneficial final ends.

While Badhwar claims that love for persons, things, or ideals all act similarly in this respect, most final ends based in inanimate things are unlikely to provide a benefit comparable to those based in love of persons. Since objects tend to be simpler than persons, they tend to require a lower number of interesting and complex activities to attain and maintain union with them. While things can be valuable in themselves, such as the Grand Canyon, most things are sought after because of their influence on people and on improving their lot.

I am more optimistic that final ends based in ideals could offer benefits similar to the ends of love. Yet many final ends based in ideals are closely connected with ends based in the love of persons. Ideals like justice, the common good, equality, freedom, and peace have a close kinship with love. Love entails a commitment to many such ideals. Therefore, any benefit offered by commitments to these ideals is also entailed by love.

Similarly, Joseph Raz claims that personal attachments benefit a person in ways similar to final ends. Attachments, like final ends, give meaning to life's activities. Raz explains,

> Personal meaning does indeed depend on attachments: we live for our relations with people we love, for the goals we pursue, be they professional, political, social, or other, and for those aspects of the world which have come to have special meaning for us.... If you doubt that, try and revive the spirits of a depressed or suicidal person by pointing out how much of value there is in the world: mention the beauty of nature, treasures of supreme art filling the museums, the wealth of sublime music, the great number of lovers, etc. One is more likely to drive such a person further into gloom. Their problem is not the absence of value in the world but the absence of meaning in their lives. Personal meaning ... derives from attachments.[18]

While it is obvious that the goals we pursue provide our lives with meaning and meaningful activities by providing final ends, whether Raz's claim that we live for our relations with people we love also entails final ends is less obvious. However, in last chapter's discussion of union, I claimed that a desire for union in close relationships entails a desire for an attachment to that person as a final end. [19] Therefore, the claim that we live for our relationships with people we love also entails the value of final ends gained from love. Our relationships lack meaning and depth to the degree that those relationship lack love. Love enables one to recognize the value of a relationship and imbues it with subjective meaning. Without love, relationships are merely instruments to pursue one's own ends.

However, the virtue of love is more beneficial than any one of Raz's personal attachments. The person with the full virtue of love is better off than one with a single loving relationship that provides a small number of final ends that might be lost. Death can eliminate the possibility of achieving the final ends associated with any particular relationship, thus preventing those ends from providing meaningful activity. Furthermore, any particular relationship may fail for reasons outside of the individual's control. If a person only has final ends from a single loving relationship, losing it can empty an entire life of meaning. In contrast, a loving person has many relationships that provide final ends including those with parents, children, spouses, friends, neighbors, co-workers, members of a shared faith, and fellow citizens. This large supply of relationships continually provides final ends, ensuring the lover always has ends to guide meaningful activity.

Since final ends are integral to a person's flourishing it is unsurprising that empirical psychologists such as Robert Emmons have concluded that "people's values and goals are potent contributors to their overall levels of happiness."[20] While it seems self-evident that goals contribute to a person's happiness, a more subtle question concerns which goals are likely to contribute the most to a person's happiness. Psychological research demonstrates that goals associated with love are correlated with measurably higher amounts of reported happiness. Emmons demonstrates that at least two types of goals, or strivings, associated with the virtue of love have a direct correlation with an increase in reported happiness. He explains,

> In a number of different samples, we have found that the proportion of intimacy strivings in a person's striving system predicts greater levels of positive well-being.... Intimacy strivings reflect a concern for establishing deep and mutually gratifying relationships.... Generativity strivings, defined as those strivings that involve creating, giving of oneself to others, and having an influence on future generations also relate to higher levels of life satisfaction and to measures of positive affectivity.[21]

While Emmons's categories of strivings are not identical to the types of desires we have been associating with love, "intimacy strivings" certainly include the lover's desire for union with the beloved, and "generativity strivings" include the lover's desire for the good of the beloved. While these findings from empirical psychology support my central argument, they merely reinforce the general claim that love benefits the lover. The more important and difficult question is the one that we've been exploring, how does love advance the lover's well-being?

Finally, an examination of Martha Nussbaum's discussion of love as a *eudaimonistic* emotion is relevant to this discussion of final ends. She argues that emotions like love have a direct connection to one's personal conception of *eudaimonia*. She claims,

> A conception of eudaimonia is taken to be inclusive of all to which the agent ascribes intrinsic value: if one can show someone that she has omitted some-thing without which she would not think her life complete, then it is a sufficient argument for the addition of the item in question.[22]

There is an interesting connection between Nussbaum's account of *eudaimonia* and Frankfurt's account of personal preferences. First, in suggesting that *eudaimonia* includes everything an agent views with intrinsic value, Nussbaum implies that *eudaimonia* consists of everything a person views as a worthwhile final end. To have no conception of *eudaimonia* entails that one has no final ends.

It is also noteworthy that her description of *eudaimonia* entails that its constituents include all of one's personal preferences whether the individual believes they have objective value for all or merely subjective value for the self. She explains,

> But so far we have left out, or so it seems, the most important thing of all, something that lies deep in ancient eudaimonism but that is never explicitly recognized. Emotions contain an ineliminable reference to *me*, to the fact that it is *my* scheme of goals and projects.[23]

It is this reference to the self that requires subjective desires to be included in one's conception of *eudaimonia*. For example, the person who believes that attaining a successful career in botany is a central constituent in her personal good life has botany as part of her *eudaimonia*.

While there are a number of obstacles that everyone faces in their pursuit of *eudaimonia* the most interesting barriers are created by the individual himself. Some accounts of *eudaimonia* are internally conflicted, cannot really be attained, or are not integrated into the person's motivational structure. Nussbaum explains,

> In short, the ancient eudaimonist framework will be a good one for thinking about the emotional life only when we acknowledge that people's sense of what

is important and valuable is often messy, disorderly, and not in line with their reflective ethical beliefs.[24]

One's view of *eudaimonia* can be merely disorderly or deeply incoherent. Someone may hold values that are incompatible with one another, such as ethical values that are irreconcilable with her other goals. While any view of *eudaimonia* provides goals for an agent to pursue; when integrated into her motivational structure as ends, some views of *eudaimonia* are more orderly, coherent, and integrated than others. These accounts of *eudaimonia* will provide more beneficial final ends, because they are more easily pursued and have no internal barriers to their fulfillment.

Possessing the virtue of love ensures that an important central constituent of a person's view of *eudaimonia* is well-ordered, coherent, and integrated. Since love requires that the agent loves all persons in relationally appropriate ways, and since loving in each relationship must be compatible with love in every other relationship,[25] possessing the virtue of love ensures a significant amount of order to one's final ends. This orderliness ensures that the agent's goals that stem from love are compatible with each other. Furthermore, as discussed in the next section, the lover's goals are well-integrated into her motivational structure, ensuring that her psyche has a significant degree of integration.

In this section, we established that possessing the virtue of love necessarily provides the lover with final ends that motivate a significant variety of interesting, complex, and generally pleasurable activities in pursuit of goals that are relatively attainable. We also found that ends meeting these criteria are relatively difficult to obtain. Therefore, the lover experiences more pleasure and more fulfilled desires than someone without such final ends. Furthermore, since love is constituted by a wide range of desires, the lover always has an ongoing supply of final ends and desires to be pursued. Someone with no desires, or with only unattainable desires, is in a worse situation since he possesses no desires that can be fulfilled. Finally, the ends of love benefit the lover by adding meaning and purpose to the activities needed to accomplish them.

5.3 THE NECESSARY BENEFIT OF PSYCHIC INTEGRATION

As mentioned in the previous section, possessing the virtue of love requires the lover to integrate her psyche. An agent does not have the virtue of love if her desires toward others are deeply conflicted, or if they are mere theoretical preferences that are not integrated into the will. It is not possible for an agent to pursue consistently the good of others or union with others if her desires toward them are mixed or not prioritized.

Much of the contemporary philosophical discussion on the nature of the psyche stems from Harry Frankfurt's influential article "Free Will and The Concept of a Person." He presents a model for discussing the psyche that allows for competing and even contradictory desires, as well as a hierarchy of desires. Furthermore, he introduces a conception of second-order desires that are concerned with which first-order desires a person wants to cultivate.[26] He also distinguishes between second-order desires intended to move first-order desires, which he calls second-order volitions, and second-order desires that are not intended to shape first-order desires.[27] He claims that second-order volitions are essential for personhood.[28] Frankfurt views the ability to bring one's first-order desires in line with one's second-order desires as a necessary and sufficient condition for possessing free will.[29]

Frankfurt demonstrates that the psyche is complex and some agents' psyches are not well integrated. To possess the virtue of love, a person must have both first-order desires and second-order volitions of love toward people in general. However, it is possible that she may have comparatively weak first-order desires that are counter to love, since love does not require that someone have a perfectly integrated psyche. Love also does not require that the psyche be integrated concerning absolutely all desires; however, there are a significant number of desires relevant to love, including a person's desires toward all other persons. Furthermore, excellence in love requires that the lover's desires concerning a wide variety of other topics be compatible with the desires of love. For example, someone may have both loving desires and a first-order desire for pleasure. While there is no direct conflict between loving desires and a first-order desire for one's own pleasure, the desire for pleasure must be integrated into the psyche in a way that does not conflict with love.

The person with a disunified psyche has a larger amount of unorganized or even mutually exclusive desires coexisting within the psyche. The unified psyche required by love aids an agent in accomplishing her preferences and leads to a more pleasant life than possessing a disunified psyche. These claims are not only philosophically intuitive, but have been reinforced by the findings of empirical psychology.

Emmons also offers a description of psychic disunification, which he describes as goal conflict. He reports,

> [Goal] Conflicts are problem situations that involve two competing and mutually exclusive alternative resolutions (McReynolds, 1990). A good all-purpose definition is provided by Heitler (1990): Conflict is a situation in which seemingly incompatible elements exert force in opposing or divergent directions"

(p.5). Conflicts have a discernible grammar—they are expressed as oppositional statements ("I want to write this book but I also want to play golf").[30]

Of course, many competing goals are not truly incompatible. Emmons's conflicting first-order desires to write his book and to play golf are only truly incommensurable if he wants to do them both within a specific time frame. He cannot both write his book and play golf at noon on a particular day, but he certainly can play golf today and write his book tomorrow. He can even accomplish both goals in a single day by golfing in the morning and writing his book in the afternoon.

At least two distinct types of psychic unintegration are incompatible with love. In simple unintegrated psyches, the agent's desires form a set of potentially compatible but unordered desires. An agent's desires for high income, entertainment, relationships, success, and pleasure are not necessarily incompatible with one another. Many people achieve similar sets of goals. Yet without a well-ordered psychological structure prioritizing some desires over others, the individual may be unable to attain any desire if he is continually distracted by equally strong competing desires with no criteria for choosing among them. Such an agent lacks proper bonds to his goals since he is too easily distracted by other desires, and may suddenly abandon pursuit of one desire for another.

The dilemma of someone who is unable to choose between similarly attractive preferences is illustrated in the story of Buridan's ass, a fictional creature placed equidistant from two identical stacks of hay. The animal could eat from either stack of hay if it had some criterion for choosing between its desires, even if it were an arbitrary criterion such as flipping a coin (or whatever the equivalent is for quadrupeds), but without such a criterion he may fail to eat from either haystack. According to the traditional illustration, Buridan's ass will starve because it has no rational reason for choosing to eat from one stack of hay rather than the other.[31]

Like this fictional creature, a person with an unintegrated psyche has no firm criterion established for choosing between competing desires and is therefore less likely to achieve any of them. Even if he is not paralyzed by indecision and a lack of comprehensive prioritization between his goals, he will likely pursue his goals inconsistently. Even though the desires of an agent with simple psychic unintegration are compatible with one another, he is less likely to achieve any of his goals. Humans are finite beings with finite resources, and the lack of bondedness to goals experienced by those with unintegrated psyches causes them to use those resources inefficiently. Therefore, those who lack well-ordered psyches are less likely to accomplish their goals and preferences than are agents with integrated psyches. This experience also tends to be less pleasant.

Young children often have unintegrated psyches. A child may enter his room in search of a shirt to keep warm, but come out with his favorite toy car instead. The toy may then be abandoned if he notices cookies left out on the counter. By this time, the child may have forgotten the original reason he entered his room, but he still suffers from the cold since he never found his shirt. In young children, an unintegrated psyche is less harmful since adult supervision ensures they will get most of their important needs met. An adult with an unintegrated psyche is in a more undesirable position since no one ensures her needs will be met.

A well-ordered psyche does not merely prioritize desires in a simple rank order. An agent with a well-integrated psyche who values relationships over money does not choose relationship-building activities over money-making activities in absolutely every circumstance, but instead structures life as a whole to reflect his priorities. Such a person structures life's activities based on which ends he considers worthy of pursuit. Someone with a well-integrated psyche may sometimes exchange the pursuit of one desire for the pursuit of a desire with higher priority. A person with an integrated psyche may even temporarily postpone the pursuit of a more important ultimate goal for a less important, but more urgent goal. A religious person may value time in prayer over grocery shopping, but shopping for food may be more urgent if the refrigerator is empty. What makes grocery shopping more urgent is not its relative importance, but the fact that attaining the good grocery shopping helps achieve, relieved physical hunger, requires acting within a shorter time span. Yet such choices are in accordance with the agent's integrated priorities and do not reflect impulsiveness or internal psychic disorder.

A second type of unintegrated psyche is a deeply divided psyche with mutually exclusive highly valued desires. Someone may have first-order desires to lose weight and to consume inordinate amounts of fattening foods, or a woman may desire to marry two different men. As illustrated by Emmons's account of goal conflict, extremely disunified psyches not only lack prioritization and integration of desires, but also possess desires that are inherently incompatible with one another. Accomplishing one valued desire necessarily thwarts another valued desire. In these cases, the divided psyche may completely paralyze the agent and prevent him from pursuing goals altogether. This case is not like the simple case of Buridan's ass, which can accomplish both desires by eating from one stack of hay after eating from the other. Instead, achieving one goal necessarily undermines the second goal.

Another potential effect of an extremely disunified psyche is that an agent may alternate between pursuing each of the incompatible goals, thereby undermining both goals. In some decisions, ambivalence between two attractive options can result in the loss of both opportunities. For example, a person may alienate two potential romantic partners through his inability to choose between them.

A particularly painful type of deeply divided psyche occurs when the internal conflict is between first-order desires and second-order volitions, rather than only between two first-order desires. In this case, the person is alienated from his own desires. He does not want to desire the things he desires. Frankfurt illustrates this psyche with the example of the unwilling addict, who desires drugs but does not wish to desire drugs.[32]

Experiencing a deeply disunified psyche can be heart-wrenching because a person who is unable to choose between two deeply valued goals will either become paralyzed in indecision or undermine at least one treasured goal. Such a person is less likely to achieve desires and her fulfilled desires will be less pleasurable than if goal attainment did not entail frustrating competing goals. Therefore, it is unsurprising that empirical psychology identifies goal conflict as a major source of pain and frustration. Emmons connects the internal goal conflict that accompanies psychic unintegration with painful emotional turmoil and physical illness:

> Goal conflicts are part of the human experience. When there are choices to be made or decisions to be reached, competing desires are frequently involved. We desire many things in life—we want affection from loved ones, recognition from our peers, a comfortable lifestyle. Other desires may keep us from achieving all that we want. We want to maintain our independence from others, we want to avoid calling attention to ourselves, we want to live a simple and frugal life. We wish to spend time with our family, but we wish to advance in our career. We want to take risks, but we want to be secure.... Research has confirmed that conflict is a major source of suffering and misery in people's lives. Conflicting motive systems are a source of self-regulatory failure. Poorly handled, chronic conflicts are at the root of many physical illnesses and poor mental and emotional health. Depression, anxiety, ulcers, and heart disease have all been associated with the inner turmoil that surrounds unresolved conflicts.[33]

Psychic integration is a hallmark of emotional health and successful self-regulation of the internal person. Unresolved conflicting desires are destructive to both mental and physical health. The stress of mental conflict can express itself in observable physical consequences. An integrated psyche avoids this stress and ensures that there are no internal psychic barriers to goal accomplishment. A famous example of a radically disunified psyche is found in Augustine's *Confessions*. In Book VIII, leading up to his conversion, he describes himself as tortured and paralyzed due to his radically divided psyche. He portrays himself as deeply divided. He desires the worldly sexual delights of his past as well as spiritual pleasures that are incompatible with reckless sexual indulgence. This divided will paralyzes him in the frustrating pain of indecision. Augustine describes this experience:

> From where did this monstrous state come? And how did it come here? Mind commands body, and it immediately obeys; but when mind commands itself it is resisted. Mind commands the hand to move, and the hand's readiness is so great that it is difficult to distinguish command from obedience. And mind is mind, while hand is body. Mind commands itself to will, but it does not obey. From where did this monstrous state come? And how did it get here? I say that will commands itself to will something: it would not order if it were unwilling, and yet it disobeys that command.[34]

Augustine found the experience of the divided psyche to be frustrating, painful, and even monstrous. His psyche held two incompatible goals and was at war with itself. Only when his will became integrated could he find peace. While this example illustrates the negative effects of experiencing a deeply divided psyche for a short time, a life-long divided psyche would inevitably lead to ongoing displeasure as any course of action would result in pain and goal frustration.

The virtue of love requires considerable integration of the psyche since someone who both desires union with a person and desires distance from that same person does not love him well. The lover must also desire his own flourishing in a way that is compatible with the flourishing of all others. The lover must integrate his psyche so that the desires for union with the beloved and the beloved's good are compatible with other competing desires, and conflicting desires are subordinated or eliminated. Furthermore, since the loving person has such desires toward other persons in general, his desires in all relationships must have a high degree of integration.

The integration required by love benefits the loving agent. A person with a deeply divided psyche is in an undesirable predicament, since attaining one desire entails frustrating another strong desire. Furthermore, an agent with a deeply divided psyche is less likely to fulfill any of her desires since competing desires consistently undermine each other's pursuit. A self that is unable to integrate is left with mutually incompatible goals.

On any account of well-being that views desire fulfillment as a constituent of well-being, agents with integrated psyches have tremendous advantages over agents with disunified psyches. If a person's psyche is disunified due to mutually incompatible goals, then any activity which might advance his well-being by fulfilling one desire will simultaneously undermine his well-being by frustrating a competing desire. Only when the self integrates around some desires rather than others will the agent successfully prioritize some desires over others, thereby increasing the opportunity for desire fulfillment without simultaneous desire frustration. Furthermore, living with an integrated psyche is more pleasurable than living with a disunified psyche, since fulfilling desires without frustrating other desires is more enjoyable than the alternatives.

Laura Ekstrom summarizes the benefits of psychic integration in terms of an increase in autonomy, which results in a more satisfying and self-directed life.

> The thought is, the more self-directed one's life is, the more satisfying that life will be, as the less one will be pulled in different directions by external forces and unconscious drives and the less one will be plagued by inner tension, by confusion over what to do, and by alienation from certain of one's decisions and actions.[35]

She cites inner tension and conflict between conscious goals and unconscious drives as threats that undermine personal autonomy and personal well-being. Accordingly, the wholeheartedness love entails in one's desires toward other people increases autonomy in this wide ranging area of life.

One interesting question is whether humans can integrate their psyches saround absolutely any goal, or whether there are only certain goals around which they can fully integrate their psyches. For example, Kant held that the will cannot integrate around desires that it recognizes as necessarily incompatible with personal well-being. He claims that an individual's psyche must view the practical rationality concerning one's well-being and moral duty as potentially compatible, and that no one could carry out moral imperatives that were assured to destroy the individual's happiness. If practical rationality concerning personal well-being clearly conflicts with the demands of morality then the person cannot integrate her psyche since desires for both personal well-being and to fulfill the moral law are necessary features of rational beings. This psychological theory is behind his famous argument for postulating the existence of God and the immortality of the soul. Kant explains,

> The ideas of *God* and *immortality*, however, are not conditions of the moral law but only conditions of the necessary object of a will determined by this law, that is, of the mere practical use of our pure reason.... But they are nevertheless, conditions of applying the morally determined will to its object given to it a priori (the highest good). Consequently their possibility in this practical relation can and must be *assumed*.... And this need is not a hypothetical one for some *discretionary* purpose of speculation ... but rather *a need having the force of law*, to assume something without which that cannot happen which one *ought* to set unfailingly as the aim of one's conduct.[36]

Kant's claim is that one must believe in the possibility of God and immortality in order to live by the moral law, because the human psyche cannot integrate its will around desires it recognizes as necessarily destructive to personal well-being. Therefore, one must postulate any belief needed to view moral behavior as compatible with prudential concerns.

Similarly, Aquinas holds that a person can only integrate his psyche around certain things.[37] Due to a natural inclination toward the good, humanity is unable to quench fully good desires regardless of personal viciousness. Therefore, he argues that true personal peace can only be achieved when a person's desires are directed toward that which is truly good. He explains,

> Peace is constituted by calm and unified appetite. Just as appetite may incline towards what is good simply or good apparently, peace may also be either real or apparent. Indeed, real peace is not possible unless the appetite desires what is truly good. Since, all evil still has many defects which cause the appetite to remain restless and troubled, even if an evil goal is apparently good and satisfies part of the appetite. Therefore, real peace cannot exist except within good men who desire good things.[38]

Aquinas believes that humanity's natural appetite for the good cannot be completely satisfied elsewhere. If someone tries to satisfy the appetite by acquiring something that is not unqualifiedly good—say pleasure that comes at the cost of virtue or relationships—he cannot truly integrate the psyche around these goods and be at peace with himself. Someone who attempts to reject the good necessarily experiences a degree of psychic disintegration.[39] Some part of the will continually desires that which is truly good.

Love can integrate the psyche on both Kant's and Aquinas's accounts. It can integrate the psyche on Kant's account because love is compatible with practical rationality concerning one's own good. Since love necessarily includes a desire for one's own good the will can integrate around love's desires according to his psychological views. Love can also integrate the psyche on Aquinas's account because a loving response to persons would express humanity's natural inclination toward the good, if such an inclination exists. While love benefits the lover by integrating her psyche whether or not Kant's and Aquinas's accounts are accurate, these accounts raise the additional possibility that love may be one of the few things that is capable of integrating the psyche.

To illustrate how love benefits a person through psychic integration, consider the case of an alcoholic named "Ted," a twenty-five year old married man and father of a young child. He desires to quit drinking in order to be a more helpful husband, a good father, and a responsible provider, but he also desires to continue drinking in order to enjoy the pleasure of alcohol and the social atmosphere at his local pub. If he holds these desires with relatively equivalent strengths, fulfilling either desire will not increase Ted's well-being. When either desire is fulfilled, Ted is no better off. He is in a hopeless state since fulfilling either desire entails frustrating an equally strong desire. The virtue of love would enable him to integrate his psyche around a desire for the good of and union with his beloved family, which entails that he would subordinate his desires to frequent the pub. However, without such integration he may continually struggle with his competing desires, frustrating both goals. Even as he enjoys drinking at the local pub he may experience guilt at the neglect of his family. Yet, while he is with his family he may be emotionally absent, wishing he were at the local pub.

In this section, we have seen that love requires the lover to integrate her psyche around the desires of love. Love requires a significant degree of psychic integration since the desires of love must be held toward all persons. Someone who does not consistently hold the desires of love or whose psyche holds strong conflicting desires does not possess the full virtue of love. To the degree that a person has the virtue of love, her psyche must be integrated around loving desires. An integrated psyche advances a person's well-being, because she is better able to achieve a larger number of desires. Furthermore, wholeheartedness toward one's desires is more pleasurable than ongoing internal conflict.

5.4 THE NECESSARY BENEFIT OF MOTIVATING SELF-IMPROVEMENT

Possessing the virtue of love benefits the lover by serving as a motivation for self-improvement. The idea of an interconnection or a unity of the virtues has existed since ancient times. While I am sympathetic to the idea that all genuine virtues have a necessary connection with love,[40] I will not argue for this position. Instead, I merely argue that possessing the virtue of love entails a desire to possess some other virtues as well. Last section's example of "Ted the alcoholic" also illustrates this benefit of the virtue of love. When one wills the good for others and wills union with others, these desires provide a strong motive for self-improvement and even self-perfection. When a person desires the good for others, he desires that the beloved's life be filled by whatever goods he can imagine. If the lover also desires union with the beloved marked by closeness, shared experience, and perhaps even shared identity, the combination of these two desires implies that the lover needs to become a good that improves the beloved's life. The lover wants unity with the beloved to be unambiguously good for her.

Immanuel Kant makes a similar observation about moral duty in general. He observes that one's moral duty, which includes promoting the happiness of others, [41] requires a person to improve himself and cultivate personal talents. He explains,

> A third [person] finds in himself a talent whose cultivation would make him a useful man for all sorts of purposes. But he sees himself in comfortable circumstances, and he prefers to give himself up to pleasure rather than to bother about increasing and improving his fortunate natural aptitudes. Yet he asks himself further "Does my maxim of neglecting my natural gifts, besides agreeing in itself with my tendency to indulgence, agree also with what is called duty?" ... Only he cannot possibly will that this should become a universal law of nature or should be implanted in us as such a law by a natural instinct. For as a rational being he necessarily wills that all his powers should be developed, since they serve him, and are given him, for all sorts of possible ends. [42]

Kant's observation is that promoting the good of others requires a degree of self-improvement. His concluding sentence implies that developing one's own abilities improves one's pursuit of all ends. Just as Kant claims that promoting the happiness of others requires that the agent improve himself, love requires the lover to improve himself.

Love provides the lover with varying degrees of motivation for self-improvement from relationship to relationship. The closer the union required by love within a particular relationship, the stronger the motive for self-perfection that love provides. Love for a distant cousin is unlikely to generate much motive for self-improvement. In contrast, love for one's parents, spouse, or child offers a tremendous motive for self-improvement. Children can be motivated by a desire to make their parents proud. This desire can help a child stay out of trouble to avoid embarrassing his parents, develop positive habits, and accomplish goals that please his parents. In romantic relationships, lovers and spouses are sometimes motivated to change for the better. They often face innumerable challenges to be together and such challenges often require self-improvement. Of course, this example may be problematic since these changes are sometimes short-lived and may be motivated by selfish desires. Yet possessing the virtue of love provides a greater motivation for self-improvement than any one loving relationship does. The loving person is aware that a wide range of people in a range of relationships will benefit from his own self-improvement.

The paradigm example of love providing a motive for self-improvement is a parent's love for a newborn child. It is not unusual for a new parent to change her life for the sake of her child. A parent who wills the good for her child understands that one of the most beneficial goods for her child is an ideal parent. The parent's will for union with the child transforms a desire that some adult be a good parent for her child into a desire that she herself become an ideal parent for him. Such a parent is motivated to make significant lifestyle and character changes. A parent may change her eating habits, reject addictive substances, reprioritize spending habits, and make other wide-ranging changes in order to serve her child well. An undisciplined parent may develop more orderly habits. A lazy person may seek a career to ensure that her child has long-term financial provision.

Raz makes a related claim by distinguishing goals that require personal participation from those that do not. He argues that goals requiring the agent's personal participation are particularly powerful in their motivational effectiveness. His paradigm example takes place within the close relationship between a parent and his children. He says,

> It may be thought that all goals which will suffer from my absence, or where the goal itself essentially requires my presence, are suitable goals for me to live for. For example, if the goal is to look after my children to maturity then (as we normally understand what is good for children) it is vital that I—their parent—will look after them, not merely that someone will, and therefore it is reasonable that my goal will not be conditional on my survival. My goal is to survive to look after my children, not merely to look after them so long as I survive.[43]

Raz is correct that some goals require the agent's personal presence and involvement, though few to the degree required by the goals of love in close relationships. Furthermore, these goals entail instrumental self-beneficial desires intended to attain nonselfish ends. A loving parent wants not merely to enjoy and raise his children while he lives, but also to survive in order to continue this parental role. The lover's ongoing union with others requires personal presence, involvement, and commitment. If the lover's union with the beloved is going to benefit the beloved, a range of virtues may also be needed. Some virtues will be necessary to benefit the beloved in every relationship, while others may only be required in certain relationships.

Rosalind McDougall gives an account of distinctive virtues needed for virtuous parenting. She claims parenting requires at least the three virtues of acceptingness, committedness, and a future-agent-focus. She explains,

> Just as Hursthouse suggests that the virtues emerge when we consider the question, "How am I to live well?" in the context of facts about human life, I will argue that (at least) acceptingness, committedness, and future-agent-focus emerge as parental virtues when we consider the question "how is one to parent well?" in the context of the relevant facts and a primary aim of flourishing children.[44]

Since a loving parent wants to be a good parent for her child she develops traits that are conducive to her child's well-being. McDougall describes three virtues that are needed to parent well. First, a deep unconditional acceptingness of the child in spite of current or future attributes is a critical parental virtue.[45] The second virtue is a wholehearted committedness to the raising of the child. This virtue is necessary for the ongoing sacrifices involved in rearing a child from the early extremely dependent stages to flourishing adulthood.[46] Finally, good parents need future-agent-focus, a habitual future orientation that keeps the child's future role as a moral agent in mind. This virtue leads both to the development of virtue in the child for future interaction with society and to developing the child's potential as an independent agent.[47]

Each of these three virtues can also increase the parent's long-term pleasure and ability to attain her own desires. Acceptingness can improve the quality of one's relationships and increases one's happiness, since one is not preoccupied with trying to change another person. Committedness can increase the goals a parent views as viable. Before developing the long-term committedness required by raising a child, a four- or five-year goal may seem insurmountable; however the wholehearted long-term commitments involved in good parenting make other previously unattainable goals seem attainable. The longer-term perspective encouraged by committedness enables the parent to pursue and attain a wider range of goals. Finally, the ability to maintain a habitual future focus includes very useful skills for predicting the long-term results of current actions. These skills are easily used in other areas of life to obtain desired results and increase long-term pleasure and happiness.

McDougall's model could be extended to other important relationships. There are dispositions needed to be an ideal friend, child, spouse, employee, and so forth. In each relationship one may ask "What traits are needed to love well in this relationship?" The traits needed in each relationship may have some similarities to one another, but will also be distinctive.

Alasdair MacIntyre has also observed that specific roles and relationships can require specific skills. He explains, "Teachers in general then—parents, other family members, those who instruct apprentices in crafts—have to have in significant measure the habits that they try to inculcate."[48] If MacIntyre is correct, then the parent-child relationship also causes the loving parent to develop virtue, because she realizes that the virtues the parent wants the child to possess must be modeled. McDougall already emphasizes the importance of raising a virtuous child. MacIntyre similarly notes that a parent who desires the good of her child recognizes that he needs a wide range of intellectual and moral virtues to face life's challenges. Yet character is not taught in a purely theoretical way. The everyday hypocrisy of claiming to value virtue while living viciously is not an effective strategy for developing virtue in a child. Instead, the parent must actually possess and model the virtues he seeks to instill in the child.

MacIntyre emphasizes the general interdependence of human community and claims that humans require two sets of virtues in order to flourish, the virtues of independent practical reasoning and the virtues of acknowledged dependence. The first set of virtues includes the traditional virtues emphasizing an individual's intellectual and moral excellence such as, "justice, temperateness, truthfulness, courage, and the like."[49] The virtues of acknowledged dependence are those needed to relate properly to others in light of our interdependence with them including just-generosity, uncalculated giving, hospitality, and *misericordia*.[50] MacIntyre argues that humans need these virtues in order to flourish. These virtues aid in relationships and in developing ourselves in a way needed to benefit from relationships. Someone who is inhospitable undermines important relationships. A person who is unable to give without calculating the benefits for himself enjoys relationships less. Someone who is unable to bond with others by sharing their grief is likely to experience long-term loneliness. Each of these virtues ultimately benefits the virtuous person.

I similarly argue that in the wide variety of relationships love benefits its possessor by motivating the development of other virtues, which benefit both lover and beloved. For example, love requires at least some degree of supporting virtues like courage, self-control, and self-knowledge. Love also requires rejecting vices like laziness, envy, and hatred. These virtues offer benefits of their own. A person with the virtue of self-control is more likely to attain goals in life. The courage the lover gains while developing love also enables her to pursue other goals more effectively.

It may not be obvious that love requires some of these virtues, such as courage. Yet the Aristotelian tradition views courage as a disposition to experience fear in proportion to the actual risk or danger. Someone whose life is dominated by fear will not love well. Having desires results in the risk that those desires might go unfulfilled and irrational fear can prevent people from loving. For example, the lover may fear rejection by the beloved, which would prevent the desire for union with the beloved from being fulfilled. Or the lover may fear that the good of the beloved might not be attained. By caring for another person, the lover risks pain that could be avoided. There may even be circumstances where the good of the beloved requires the lover to take physical risks.

Furthermore, fearful persons sometimes have difficulty loving because they realize that making commitments to love particular persons now may undermine future opportunities to love more attractive persons later. The lover needs courage in order to prevent fear from extinguishing the desires of love. Courage is also a better trait to aid in expressing love than foolhardiness, which causes a person to underestimate dangers. If the lover underestimates risks in pursuing love, he might take unnecessary risks, act imprudently, and alienate the beloved. For example, in the early stages of romantic love a foolhardy person may pursue the relationship too aggressively and alienate the beloved.

Self-control is also needed to advance the good of the beloved when the lover is offered immediate pleasures that may undermine the good of the beloved or undermine the lover's unity with the beloved. The lover must not allow the appetite to dominate his actions and undermine the good of the beloved. However, while a degree of various moral and intellectual virtues is needed to develop love, possessing the virtue of love does not require possessing every virtue in its fullest form.

Possessing virtues in more perfect degrees enables a person to love better, while vices typically undermine a person's ability to love. Consider the tragedy of *Othello*. While Othello initially seems sincere in his love for his wife Desdemona, he is gullible, untrusting, imprudent, and jealous. These vices eventually destroy both their lives when he murders her for her imagined unfaithfulness and then commits suicide.[51] Possessing the virtue of love helps avoid such tragedies since these vices are incompatible with love. A fully loving person seeks to eliminate such traits.

This section's claim that the virtues benefit their possessor suffers from the same ambiguity that faces my entire project. Rosalind Hursthouse identifies the ambiguity of this question:

> It can mean "Does doing what is virtuous, being virtuous on a particular occasion, always benefit the agent?" (Call this "the particular question.") Or it can mean "Does possession and exercise of the virtues benefit the one who has them over all?" (Call this "the general question.")[52]

Hursthouse answers these questions by suggesting that possessing virtue is generally beneficial to most people in most situations, while there are particular tragic situations where virtuous actions undermine one's well-being. She compares her claims about the generally beneficial nature of the virtues to a doctor's advice to exercise, limit one's drinking, and avoid smoking.[53] Neither set of claims guarantees desirable results for a particular person in a particular situation. Yet Hursthouse maintains that virtue is "the only reliable bet"[54] for flourishing. In at least one way, I make a stronger claim concerning the virtue of love's connection with well-being than Hursthouse makes for virtue in general, since I claim that some benefits of love necessarily occur for all people, regardless of circumstances. However, I do not deny Hursthouse's claim that there are tragic dilemmas in which loving actions may end poorly for the virtuous or the lover.

The mere possession of virtues only contributes to well-being according to *eudaimonistic* accounts or objective list accounts that view virtue as a constituent of well-being. However, possessing additional virtues also helps the lover accomplish preferences and attain pleasure in all areas of life. The courageous person is courageous in her pursuit of goals generally. She will neither abandon goals too easily due to fear nor underestimate the risks involved in her actions. The courageous person avoids the unnecessary pain of fear that the coward experiences. The temperate person controls her appetites and can use that self-control in the pursuit of other goods such as bodily health. Temperance tends to bring about greater long-term pleasure by ensuring that short-term uncontrolled appetites do not undercut long-term pleasure. As Hursthouse suggests, possessing these virtues does not guarantee that all will go well in life. Yet for most people in most situations at most times, these virtues will benefit the lover, resulting in an increase in pleasure and desire satisfaction.

Someone might object that it is possible for someone to be genuinely benevolent, but so unreflective that he does not realize that his role in the beloved's flourishing requires self-improvement. Therefore, it might seem that love does not necessarily provide a motivation for self-improvement. However love, like all Aristotelian virtues, is a character excellence that includes at least a degree of practical wisdom. A person with such vicious unreflectiveness would not really possess the full virtue of love. Love does not require that a person's practical judgment be infallible, but merely that the lover possess some minimal amount of practical wisdom. The need for practical wisdom was also seen in last chapter's discussion of the goods the lover wills for the beloved, where I similarly concluded that the lover must be reasonably warranted in viewing the goods he desires for the lover as genuine goods.

5.5 LOVE'S BENEFICIAL ROLE IN RELATIONSHIPS

Love's role in improving the lover's relationships is its best-known benefit. From Aristotle, Aquinas, and Kant to LaFollette, MacIntyre, and contemporary social psychology, the lover's improved relationships are widely recognized as a benefit of love. There are a number of ways that love improves the lover's relationships. First, there are desirable kinds of relationships that a person cannot possess without love. A significant degree of the virtue of love is a necessary condition for attaining and maintaining certain desirable relationships that benefit both lover and beloved. While loving and unloving people have the same categories of relationships such as friends, spouses, children, parents, and co-workers, love fundamentally changes the nature of these relationships.

These desirable relationships are described differently by various thinkers. Aristotle refers to these relationships as friendships based on virtue.[55] He emphasizes the unique good these relationships provide for those involved in them. These friendships are beneficial in numerous ways. Aristotle views a friend as the greatest external good,[56] a source of consolation in pain,[57] and one who helps the agent grow in virtue.[58] These relationships are more permanent than other relationships,[59] are unqualifiedly pleasant,[60] are useful,[61] are resistant to slander,[62] share possessions in common,[63] are more harmonious than other relationships,[64] and involve sharing in life's pains and pleasures.[65] He also describes a more intimate degree of interpersonal union that is only possible in virtue-based friendships. He explains,

> But it is impossible for people of low character to be like-minded except to a small extent, in the same way that it is impossible for them to be friends, since they aim at having more in the way of benefits and come up short in work and public services; and each of them, though he wants these things for himself, watches his neighbor closely to hinder him, since if they are not constantly on guard, the common good is destroyed.[66]

The virtue of both friends makes possible a unique kind of relationship and unity, which Aristotle believes cannot be found in other relationships. Vice and self-centeredness undermine union in other relationships. As vicious people in friendships seek their own good without regard to the friend's good, the friendship is undermined as trust is eroded.

In contrast, friendships of virtue allow for a type of trust and care not found elsewhere. These relationships are a unique context where both friends receive the best kinds of benefits from one another. Love for one's virtuous friend brings him closer to something uniquely beneficial to one's self, a virtuous person who cares similarly for the lover. Aristotle explains,

> And by loving the friend, they love what is good for themselves, for when a good person becomes a friend, he becomes good for the one to whom he is a friend. So each of them loves what is good for himself, and also gives back an equal amount in return in wishing as well as in what is pleasant.[67]

As one grows in closer unity with one's virtuous friend, the friendship increasingly benefits him. Other relationships are less beneficial because growing closer to someone who is not virtuous is less beneficial than growing closer to one who is virtuous. Furthermore, if the agent is not virtuous himself then his own lack of virtue undermines some of the relationship's good.

Another in-depth account of how love transforms relationships is found in Alasdair MacIntyre's discussion of the relationships of mutual giving and receiving in his book *Dependent Rational Animals*. He emphasizes the importance of these relationships in times of vulnerability and dependence.

During times of dependency, it is beneficial to have others committed to the agent within mutually loving relationships. When one is vulnerable, having others who are committed to him can ease the challenge of times of dependency. The natural life cycle has times of great dependency, especially during sickness, injury, and the latter years of life. Even when the lover is not in a time of physical dependency, the typical human life has periods of economic and emotional need that is best filled by someone committed to the lover in a relationship of mutual giving and receiving. Some emotional needs may only be fulfilled within these relationships. Emotional needs in times of mourning, disappointment, and struggle are most fully met by others in mutual loving relationships with the lover. Even periods of life where flourishing adults are the most independent are greatly improved by these relationships.[68] These relationships are uniquely enjoyable because they involve loving someone who loves you. Mutual relationships of unconditional love are free from much of the mental stress, emotional instability, and relational strife that accompany many relationships.

A second way that love benefits the lover through relationships is that it makes beneficial relationships more likely. While there are unique relationships that are not possible without love, other beneficial relationships do not require love, but are still more likely to be attained by the loving person. These relationships are categorized by Aristotle as friendships of utility or friendships of pleasure.[69]

Love makes positive relationships more likely for a number of reasons. First, since the lover wills union with others he is more likely to have closer and longer-lasting relationships. The lover's desire for union with others makes him more likely to initiate, pursue, deepen, maintain, and restore relationships. The lover's relationships are improved by the presence of mercy. Since the lover has a disposition toward desiring union with the beloved, she is willing to sustain a relationship through the wrongs and misunderstandings that accompany the day-to-day life of close relationships. Mercy enables an agent to forgive and reconcile with the beloved when a wrong has been committed. Relationships without mercy are undermined as long-term grudges develop and destructive relationship cycles ensue. Unmerciful people undermine relationships as they act out of anger or withdraw from one another instead of reconciling. The lover's merciful and forgiving attitude even benefits her when she is in a relationship with someone who is unmerciful. The lover's mercy can still prevent or minimize damage to the relationship as she seeks to protect the relationship out of love. Furthermore, mercy allows an agent to avoid long-term pain caused by an unnecessary focus on past painful events. Love also gives the lover more reason for contrition when she commits wrongs or makes mistakes within relationships. Since she values union within relationships, she is more likely to seek reconciliation, request forgiveness, and make peace with those around her. While contrition may be temporarily unpleasant, the long-term relational benefits of contrition outweigh any short-term unpleasantness.

While it is intuitive that relationships are generally beneficial, the value of relationships has also been empirically confirmed in recent years. For example, LaFollette cites psychologist Steve Duck to establish the wide-ranging benefits experienced from good relationships. He claims,

> People with fewer friends are more prone to tonsillitis and cancer; while people who are in the process of divorcing actually stand an increased risk of heart disease, injury in traffic accidents, and being attacked by muggers.... People who are poor at making friends have been shown to have worse teeth and to get more serious illnesses.... Some researchers are starting to claim a direct connection between friendship problems and breakdown of the body's defenses against invasion by viruses. So it is not merely for reasons of enjoyment and satisfaction that we need to keep our friendships in good repair and try to let them help us; we need friends for life (Duck 1983:7–8).[70]

Relationships are directly or indirectly related to an increase in a person's health and safety. While they may require an investment of time and other resources, Duck identifies a wide range of benefits beyond the direct enjoyment of the relationship itself. While these claims are interesting and somewhat intuitive, this research does not explain why or how friendship is related to these benefits. It is even possible that the causal relationship is backwards in some of these cases. Rather than friendship and good relationships causing some of these benefits such as a lower incidence of serious illness or the possession of better teeth, perhaps these benefits makes friendship more likely. For example, it is possible that suffering from a serious illness diminishes one's social opportunities if he is bedridden and accordingly lowers his opportunities to establish new friendships. While Duck may overstate the causal power of relationships in connection to some of these benefits, it is likely that there is at least some validity to his claims.

There is also a less ambitious claim made by psychologists such as Grainne Fitzsimons, who identifies high-quality social relationships as a central feature of personal psychological health. She explains,

> The maintenance of positive social relationships is at the core of psychological well-being. Thus assessing the quality of these relationships is important for mental health (Leary, 2004; Leary & Downs, 1995). There is no shortage of dimensions on which people can judge the quality of their social relationships; studied dimensions have ranged from the partner's trustworthiness, loyalty, and supportiveness, to balance of power, equity, and similarity within the relationship (See Berscheid & Reis, 1998).[71]

Since high-quality social relationships marked by trust, loyalty, supportiveness, and equality are central to psychological well-being, love will contribute to well-being to the degree that it makes these relationships more likely. So, how does the virtue of love encourage such relationships?

First, love makes the lover's relationships more harmonious and peaceful. Since the loving person considers the good of others as part of his own good, destructive interpersonal habits such as competitiveness and envy are less likely to arise within these relationships. Many problems within relationships occur when one seeks his own good at the other's expense, but love alleviates this problem since the lover does not seek his own good at the beloved's expense.

Second, the beloved is likely to respond to the lover differently than he would if he were unloving. Since the lover does not seek to take advantage of others and seeks to benefit them, others are more likely to respond to his initiative in relationships than they would be if he were not benevolent. When someone sincerely desires another's good, the object of that desire typically becomes more emotionally open, more trusting, and more appreciative of the lover. The lover's willingness to be merciful or contrite in appropriate circumstances makes it easier for the beloved to trust him. The beloved has less reason to be hostile to the lover than he would if he were selfish and unloving. Similarly, the lover's desire for relationally appropriate union typically makes the beloved more responsive to the lover. Relationships with those who will an appropriate type of union are more attractive than relationships with those who are too apathetic, too smothering, or otherwise inappropriate in their desires.

Not only does love make relationships more likely, it also causes the lover to enjoy his relationships more since attaining union within these relationships satisfies a valued desire. Desiring union in ways appropriate to a relationship is a relatively attainable goal that results in greater enjoyment of relationships. Fulfilling desires for friendship and relationships is generally pleasant. The activities required to bring about closeness in relationships, such as shared time, attention, and communication also tend to be pleasant and enjoyable activities.

It is possible to receive some benefits from relationships with friends, parents, spouses, children, and others without the virtue of love. Furthermore, some benefits depend on the choices of others in these relationships, rather than the agent himself. The lover may be surrounded by vicious individuals who do not respond to love. Yet love makes benefits from relationships more likely. Unloving individuals undermine relationships and place even the limited benefits of these relationships at risk. People who do not will the good of others risk alienating them and losing relational benefits from them. People who do not will union with others risk losing relational benefits since many relational benefits are contingent upon maintaining a degree of union in relationships. Failing to will union in a relationship increases distance in that relationship, undermining both the relationship and the benefits gained from the relationship. Furthermore, relationships are inherently less pleasant for the unloving person, since union attained in these relationships does not fulfill a desire for union.

Another way that love improves relationships for the lover is that while some kinds of relationships can be maintained without love, the unloving person inevitably loses some benefits within those relationships. Some benefits from relationships with friends, spouses, parents, or children cannot be attained at all by an agent who does not will union within these relationships. The pleasant closeness of emotional union within relationships is not possible if such union is not desired. Emotional union within relationships results in relieved loneliness and an expanded sense of self. Loneliness results from unfulfilled preferences for emotional proximity and shared attention. Relational attention and emotional proximity fill a widely experienced need for intimacy with other people. This benefit of relationships is lost in proportion to the degree a person fails to will union.

Andrea Veltman identifies a related Kantian claim that portrays the self-disclosure allowed by union in close friendships as a beneficial aspect of the best relationships. She claims,

> Kant similarly characterizes the highest friendship as one that allows friends to jointly know each other, but instead of identifying a benefit of self-knowledge in the activity of mutual knowing, Kant notes that the highest friendship permits an intrinsically valuable self-disclosure unachievable through any other venue. In revealing themselves to a trusted friend, people in the highest friendships become known by another person, thereby connected to another person, and no longer remain alone.[72]

The activity of self-revelation is required for union with others. Self-revelation results in a deeper connection with other people and relieved loneliness. Inasmuch as love makes these sorts of relationships more likely, it is beneficial to the lover.

Union with others also expands the agent's sense of self. A person who is united with others counts the well-being of others as part of her own well-being. A benefit to the beloved is a benefit to the lover as well. Since the lover also desires the good of others, she desires something that simultaneously advances her own good. Having an expanded sense of self provides the lover with a larger amount of desires to attend to, thus reducing the importance of her other desires. This benefits the lover by distracting her from her own disappointments and encourages an outward focus on others.

In contrast to the outward attention that accompanies union with others, too much self-reflection can be detrimental. For example, LaFollette argues that too much self-reflection can lead to conceit and diminish one's strengths. He claims,

> A conceited person is not merely aware of her strengths and successes (real or imaginary); she thinks about, relishes, and focuses on them. Conversely, she ignores her weaknesses. But, as I noted in the previous chapter, constant self-reflection often diminishes those strengths we do have. If, for example, we are unduly proud of our oratorical skills, we will likely be less effective as orators; we will become more concerned with our *having* the skills, and less concerned with *using* them.[73]

While LaFollette overstates his point since only an extreme case of conceit would lead someone to so much self-reflection that his gifts diminish from neglect, we could bolster his critique by emphasizing that the conceited person also loses epistemic goods. Someone with too much conceit or self-reflection fails to draw upon the objectivity of others. Furthermore, conceit and too much self-reflection undermine relationships by encouraging the agent to overvalue his self. While most people want their friends to prosper, few people enjoy friends who constantly focus on themselves. However, it is important to acknowledge that not all self-reflection leads to conceit. The motivation for one's self-reflection significantly influences whether or not it leads to conceit. For example, self-reflection motivated by love, a desire to serve others better, or out of a desire for self-improvement, is unlikely to lead to conceit.

While LaFollette is correct that even focusing on positive things like one's strengths and successes can be detrimental to well-being, his critique can be expanded. Focusing on negative attributes like failures, weaknesses, or thwarted desires can have drawbacks similar to those of conceit. This focus takes attention away from using and developing one's talents. It distances us from others and the objectivity they can provide. Furthermore, negative self-reflection is a painful activity, which undermines confidence and discourages one from pursuing desires. Therefore, an expanded sense of self that takes one's attention from the self benefits the lover.

In conclusion, possessing the virtue of love makes a higher number of higher-quality relationships more likely for the lover. It makes these relationships more pleasant and enjoyable. Since the lover desires these relationships, they contribute to her well-being by fulfilling her desire for them. These relationships are also instrumentally useful for attaining other important desires held by the lover. While the lover desires these relationships as ends in themselves, people in relationship with the lover will often seek to fulfill her desires and promote her good as well.

However, possessing love does not guarantee any relational benefits. Having the virtue of love does not guarantee that others will respond to the agent's love. Even if the beloved responds to the lover, the quality of that response may be inferior and the lover may reap minimal benefits at a high cost within that particular relationship. Yet without the virtue of love, true mutual relationships of giving and receiving are impossible. And while some benefits of loving relationships can be received by being the beneficiary of another's love, an unloving person is less likely to obtain these benefits. Furthermore, even when physical or financial benefits are replicated, the intrinsic emotional benefits of a relationship cannot be gained in other ways because the loving actions of both members of the relationship directly constitute the benefit.

5.6 THE NECESSARY BENEFIT OF EPISTEMIC GOODS

A final benefit of love is that possessing the virtue of love increases the lover's epistemic goods. These goods can typically be used to help increase the lover's pleasure and accomplish the lover's desires. Love increases the lover's epistemic goods in a number of ways including knowledge gained through close relationships with others, an increase in self-knowledge, knowledge gained through empathy, and knowledge concerning what benefits humans.

F. M. Berenson explains that relationships provide a unique opportunity to gain knowledge that is not obtainable through other methods including scientific methodology. He explains,

> It is only in reciprocal personal relationships that subjective aspects of a person's life have a chance of spontaneously and fully manifesting themselves. Attitudes and reciprocal responses are of crucial importance—these are lacking in cases of scientific knowledge.[74]

One distinct benefit of the reciprocal relationships love engenders is that they give the lover access to epistemic goods that are only available in such relationships. Knowledge of another person revealed through spontaneous, free, and uncalculated reactions is gained in reciprocal relationships. Reciprocal relationships marked by love have the additional advantage that the beloved is likely to reveal more of her true self to the lover since her responses need not be shaped by self-protective motives and fear.

Loving relationships provide opportunities to gain important knowledge. For example, as an agent loves her own children well she is better able to understand, acknowledge, and appreciate the role her own parents played in her life. Acknowledging and understanding the reality of human interdependence relieves unrealistic and unhealthy expectations encouraged by some individuals and cultures. As the lover seeks the good for others, she becomes better informed concerning the kinds of goods that typically benefit humans. As a parent learns about the healthy diet needed by his children, he also gains useful knowledge for advancing his own health.

In contrast, knowledge gained through a fairly nonrelational and nonloving structure such as a job interview provides much less reliable information. In a job interview there is little freedom for either party to respond spontaneously to the other. There is a considerable motive to guard one's true reactions and tailor them in an attempt to impress the other. Since job interviews are guided by the limited types of knowledge sought, information concerning each party lacks larger context and will be less complete and accurate.

The closeness with others gained through relationships also expands the lover's experience base. The lover has access to the experiences of other types of people and those in differing circumstances. Since not everyone has the same experiences, others' experiences allow access to a broader base of knowledge. For example, those who are brought up in a wealthy culture benefit when caring for those of different backgrounds, and by learning to understand and empathize with their experiences. Caring for someone who comes from a less wealthy culture can help the lover become more thankful for the opportunities she has, more generous toward others, and less bonded to material wealth. Such thankfulness is also inherently pleasant since it involves reflecting upon the positive aspects of one's life.

Possessing the virtue of love also increases the lover's self-knowledge. First, the lover must develop a significant degree of self-knowledge to unite with the beloved. Someone who is ignorant of herself cannot unite or share herself with the beloved. As the lover seeks union with the beloved through self-revelation, she becomes more self-aware in the process. While some degree of self-knowledge is needed to carry out the desires of love, the loving relationships that result from love also increase a person's self-knowledge. The lover's sharing of herself as she draws nearer to the beloved brings her own attributes to her own attention, resulting in a deeper self-awareness. As she seeks to unite with the beloved in his goals that partially constitute his good, she is led to examine her own goals. As she seeks to advance the good of others, she becomes more aware of her own talents.

Furthermore, as the lover reveals herself to the beloved he can add his insights to deepen the lover's self-knowledge. Since the lover desires union with the beloved, she reveals herself more fully and honestly than if she did not love. Without such openness the lover cannot truly unite with the beloved.

This openness allows the beloved to know the lover better. Since the beloved knows the lover in this intimate way, he is able to share insights about the lover that others would not possess.

The idea that relationships can increase one's knowledge goes back at least as far as Aristotle. Veltman describes the connection between friendship and knowledge in Aristotle. She explains,

> Inventively, Aristotle argues that knowing another person in friendship enables friends of like virtue to know themselves. By knowing another person who resembles ourselves, we are able to overcome the difficulties normally involved in self-perception and, in effect, see ourselves in seeing someone whose character mirrors our own.[75]

Accordingly, Aristotle claims that friends offer an epistemic benefit by mirroring each other's character.[76] Since Aristotle argues that the purest form of friendship is a relationship between two virtuous people, this type of friendship enables one to observe a similar person while avoiding the loss of objectivity typically experienced when considering the self. Such friendship enables one to observe someone else's similar traits from an external perspective.

It might seem that Aristotle's benefit of increased self-knowledge through friendship is not a benefit of love since love does not appear in his catalogue of virtues. However, as I've interpreted the virtue of love it is a necessary condition for cultivating the closest types of friendships. The genuinely other-centered reciprocal friendship Aristotle describes is not possible without a desire for union with one's friend. And Aristotle repeatedly mentions that friends wish good to each other.[77]

In close relationships, the lover experiences herself as a subject of the beloved's perception. A desire for union in relationships often results in shared attention, which can also increase the lover's self-knowledge. As the lover is attentive to the beloved while the beloved perceives and responds to her, she experiences a view of herself from another perspective. This relational dynamic is not isolated to adult friendships. As a parent interacts with her baby, the child's reactions can increase the parent's self-knowledge. The child may cower as the parent unintentionally raises her voice, smile in response to the parent's touch, look bewildered in response to a parent's new hairstyle, or laugh in response to some unexpected trait or action by the parent. Each of these reactions to the lover, which are within the capacities of even young infants, draws the loving parent's attention to the attribute or action causing the child's reaction. The parent's attention is drawn to a feature of herself that she might not otherwise notice. As the child ages, she can increase the parent's self-knowledge through verbal interaction. Young children are very inquisitive and may ask about things adults may not notice, or may be too polite to point out.

A related way that love results in an increase in epistemic goods is by developing empathy. As the lover becomes closer to the beloved and desires his good, she develops empathy for him and is able to see how he perceives her. Empathy consists of a type of emotional union between lover and beloved.

Berenson offers an account of empathy, but admits that an ambiguity exists. Berenson says that empathy is either, "the power of projecting one's personality into, and so fully understanding, the object of contemplation,"[78] or "the power of entering into another's personality and imaginatively experiencing his experiences."[79] The first definition suggests that the essence of empathy lies in understanding how the lover would feel in the beloved's situation, while the second definition requires understanding how the beloved experiences his own situation. Berenson identifies problematic aspects of both interpretations of empathy. The first account is problematic because one's own reaction to a situation may differ from the beloved's reaction. Yet the second interpretation of empathy requires too much of the empathetic person, since few people know another so well as to know her precise reaction to each situation.[80]

I suggest that the empathy engendered by the virtue of love requires aspects of both interpretations of empathy. First, the empathetic person must understand his own reaction to the beloved's situation, particularly how he views the situation's effect on the beloved's good. Yet if one desires another's good and union with her, then developing an awareness of how she views her own circumstances is also necessary since attaining her own desires will typically contribute to her well-being. One must know how the beloved views the situation herself, and what goods the beloved views as promoted or threatened. In response to Berenson's concern that this type of empathy is too demanding on the empathetic person, I acknowledge that the lover is not always completely successful in his attempt to understand the beloved's circumstances from her own viewpoint. However, the lover at least seeks to understand how the beloved views the situation and its likely consequences. Empathy increases the lover's epistemic goods by increasing his awareness of others' circumstances and of how they view those circumstances.

Developing empathy toward others more generally also increases the lover's epistemic goods. When one is empathetic toward others she learns that her own experiences and emotions have important similarities to the experiences and emotions of others. This experience reassures the lover that her experience is not isolated, and provides a basis for increased community with others.

When one is empathetic toward others she is better able to accomplish her own preferences because she better understands the motivations and experiences of others. When one is empathetic, the knowledge she gains makes her better able to discern the true character of others, less likely to be taken advantage of by others, and less likely to fear others without good reason.

The epistemic goods gained through the virtue of love can be instrumentally beneficial to the lover because increased knowledge helps one obtain preferences and pleasure.[81] Both self-knowledge and the knowledge of others gained through empathy are particularly useful in this way. Understanding one's self and other people makes fulfilling desires much easier and leads to reduced conflict in life. A person who gains such knowledge will likely have a more pleasurable and easier life.

5.7 IS LOVE INHERENTLY PLEASURABLE?

A final possible benefit of love is that love itself might be pleasurable. Neera Badhwar offers this type of argument suggesting that love is an inherently pleasurable activity. She says,

> Love is necessarily a good to the lover because it is an inherently pleasurable affirmation of value. But this is only one aspect of the benefit of love. Love is also a good to the lover because to love someone is necessarily to experience the loved object as good for oneself.... Finally, love is a good to oneself because it involves self-expression and self-creation.[82]

Badhwar makes several claims trying to support her conclusion that love is beneficial to the lover. First, she claims that love is beneficial because it is an inherently pleasant affirmation of value. This claim is somewhat ambiguous. Is love inherently pleasant because it is an affirmation of value or is love simply one type of affirmation of value that happens to be inherently pleasant? A charitable interpretation requires rejecting the first reading of Badhwar's claim since some affirmations of value are simply not pleasurable. For example, when one affirms the instrumental value of a trip to the dentist to relieve a toothache such affirmation is not undividedly pleasurable. Some people do not even judge this affirmation to be pleasurable on the whole and choose to live with ongoing dental pain rather than endure the temporary pain associated with dental work. Other affirmations of value may be unpleasant because they involve moral judgments resulting in guilt. When a former racist repents his racism and affirms the value of people of all races, the guilt involved is unpleasant. One may also affirm the value of the punishment of the guilty, without finding pleasure in it.

While these facts suggest the first interpretation of Badhwar's claim would be incorrect, even the second reading of her claim may be difficult to support. Is every act of love an unqualifiedly pleasant affirmation of value? It does not seem to be the case. For example, grieving a lost loved one includes significant psychological pain even if it simultaneously affirms the value of the deceased.

Badhwar also claims that love is an inherently pleasurable activity because the lover experiences the beloved as a good for herself. If true, this fact would make the virtue of love very valuable since it would increase the frequency of the lover's pleasurable experiences. This claim about love is more plausible than her first claim. The lover necessarily desires the good for and union with the beloved as ends in themselves. Implicitly, the lover desires both the beloved as a good for himself and the beloved's good as a good for himself. Even though the lover views union with the beloved as a good for himself, it might seem that it is not inherently pleasurable to experience something as a good for one's self, especially if that good cannot be attained. Yet, comprehending a good for one's self is pleasurable, even if it is not yet, nor will ever be obtained. Merely knowing that such a good exists is pleasurable and seeking it even more so. Yet again, love is not unqualified in its pleasantness. Experiencing another as good for one's self is simultaneously painful if the beloved is distant.

Finally, Badhwar claims that love involves self-creation and self-expression, which are inherently good for the lover. While she does not use the language of psychic integration or final ends, her claim that love benefits the lover through self-creation and self-expression has similar implications. By defining and creating one's self in terms of choosing final ends, love has the benefits described in the earlier section on final ends. If the person creates himself by wholeheartedly endorsing the goals of love, this self-creation entails that he has psychic unity with himself. As argued in the earlier sections of this chapter, the final ends and psychic integration from love are inherently beneficial and result in increased pleasure. However, any pleasure gained in this way has already been accounted for in the earlier sections of this chapter.

5.8 LOVE IN TRAGIC CIRCUMSTANCES

What is the upshot of this chapter? First, there is a necessary connection between the virtue of love and well-being in the ways described in the previous sections. Second, the net overall effects of love are typically beneficial to the lover. In this section, I add a third *eudaimonistic* claim that, on the relevant matters, love is the only advisable disposition. The risks present in love are less serious than the harms inherent in unloving dispositions. However, there are some overly optimistic *eudaimonistic* claims that I do not endorse.

First, I do not claim that possessing the virtue of love guarantees a life of overall well-being. For example, Plato held that virtue was synonymous with well-being.[83] I make no such claim. Without arguing that virtue is the only or most important constituent of well-being, this position is untenable.[84] As long as our account of well-being focuses on the importance of pleasure or fulfilled desires, it is difficult to see how any virtue could *guarantee* the agent's well-being. The lover is still vulnerable to all sorts of tragedies. For example, possessing the virtue of love provides no guarantee against painful disease, acts of nature, or the evil actions of other people. At best, it might make such tragedies less likely or less harmful when they occur.

Similarly, Bernard Williams acknowledges that since the time of the ancient Stoics, "The idea that one's whole life can in some such way be rendered immune to luck has perhaps rarely prevailed since (it did not prevail, for instance, in mainstream Christianity)."[85] Therefore, it is unsurprising that the loving person's life is vulnerable to some unfortunate circumstances. Even Aquinas does not claim that the virtue of love guarantees well-being in this lifetime, but only that it is necessary for eternal happiness after this lifetime.[86] Therefore, it is unsurprising that we will be able to identify circumstances where things go badly for the lover.

A second *eudaimonistic* claim that I do not endorse is that the net effects of love itself are always beneficial to the agent. The claim that the net effects of a virtue in a particularly unlucky person's life can be harmful is compatible with the claim that the virtue has several substantial beneficial effects, that it is typically beneficial overall, and that it is the only prudent disposition to develop. For example, courage is a virtue that has many benefits and is typically beneficial overall, but few would claim that courage entails no risks for the courageous person. Undoubtedly, there are situations in which the courageous person dies while the coward survives by fleeing.

The prudence of love is also similar to the prudence of temperance. Temperance expressed in a healthy lifestyle including a nutritious diet, exercise, and avoidance of smoking necessarily benefits an individual with improved health. Furthermore, it typically increases one's overall well-being over the course of a lifetime. Yet, there are circumstances where the costs of temperance actually result in a net decrease in an agent's overall pleasure over a lifetime. Consider the temperate, healthy person who dies by being hit by a bus at the age of forty-five. If he had pursued a more indulgent lifestyle, then he would have experienced more pleasure during his forty-five years, but would not have lived long enough to experience the serious negative health consequences that accompany such a lifestyle. Therefore, temperance has an overall negative effect on his well-being. Yet, temperance was the only prudent way to live his life. He was unlucky, but the risks inherent in an indulgent lifestyle were far greater. Similarly, love is the only prudent way to live despite its risks. In the next chapter, we will consider various vicious alternatives to love and demonstrate that they are imprudent approaches to life. Accordingly, Christine Swanton concedes,

> The claim that a trait cannot be a virtue unless it characteristically benefits the agent is consistent with a claim that exercise of a virtue does not guarantee agent-flourishing. As Aristotle emphasizes, the truths of ethics are truths for the most part. This leaves room for the eudaemonist to concede that in responding appropriately to various values, bonds, and so on, there is no guarantee that an agent will lead a life that is good for her.... Just as healthy living does not guarantee health, so being virtuous does not guarantee happiness. However, one should cultivate the virtues because that is "the only reliable bet" for one's flourishing, "though ... I might be unlucky and, because of my virtue, wind up on the rack."[87]

In some ways, my claim for the *eudaimonistic* nature of love is stronger than Swanton's claim for *eudaimonism* more generally. For I do not merely claim that love characteristically benefits the agent, but also that it necessarily has certain beneficial aspects. The danger is that the benefits of love might be outweighed by its risks in certain unlucky circumstances. Therefore, we will consider how the lover fares in tragic circumstances.

First, consider circumstances where disease threatens the beloved's well-being. Specifically, consider the tragedy of terminal childhood cancer. A loving mother cares for a child who dies after a painful and costly two-year struggle with cancer. The lover's desire for the beloved's well-being is threatened. The beloved will not flourish long-term. The lover's care for the beloved will sap considerable time, energy, and resources. Furthermore, ongoing desires for union with the beloved will not be fulfilled in this lifetime.

It might seem that an apathetic disposition would be a more effective strategy for maximizing the mother's well-being. After all, the mother's long-term desire for the child's well-being will not be fulfilled. Caring in this relationship requires the expenditure of limited resources. Moreover, the child will not flourish enough to offer care for the mother in her own times of infirmity or old age. Love will result in an emotionally exhausting two years, a considerable expenditure of time, energy, and finances, and a lifetime of wishing the child had flourished.

Would love make someone worse off in this circumstance? One barrier to answering this question is that these circumstances would be tragic for anyone, and not just for the lover. In losing a child, even an apathetic person loses a costly, instrumentally valuable relationship that could have been helpful in later times of financial, emotional, or physical crisis. Furthermore, even the indifferent parent has already invested considerable time, energy, and resources into the dying child. The relevant question is not whether losing a child is a difficult circumstance that results in less pleasure and fulfilled desires than ordinary circumstances, but whether the lover is worse off than the nonlover in this situation.

A second barrier to answering this question is that even if the lover is worse off in this particular relationship it does not follow that she is necessarily worse off overall. Since we are examining the overall effects of the loving disposition on one's life, we must keep the entirety of the agent's life in view. Love helps the lover in numerous ways and affects all of her relationships. The net benefits of love elsewhere in the lover's life might outweigh its painful effects in a single relationship. Therefore, even if the effects of love have an overall negative effect on well-being within one relationship, the lover is not necessarily worse off in terms of love's total effect on her life.

In what ways does love benefit the mother despite this tragedy? The final ends and psychic unity entailed by love still benefit the mother. She still has the advantage of well-integrated final ends that result in consistent and meaningful behaviors that are likely to bring about the fulfillment of some of her desires. The daily tasks needed to care for an ailing child need not be entirely unpleasant. Filling a sick child's days with love, joy, and as much comfort as possible will fulfill some of the lover's shorter-term desires. The benefit of final ends continues even after the child passes away.[88] For example, Aristotle talks about the possibility of one's happiness being influenced by events after his death.[89] Therefore, the parent may try to benefit the departed child by fulfilling desires expressed when he was alive, honoring him, or taking other actions she believes influence his well-being. She may give an appropriate funeral that honors him and expresses the joy of their relationship. She may pray for his eternal condition. She may serve others with similar problems to honor her son. In some worldviews, she may even look forward to being reunited with him after this life. Moreover, since the mother has the full virtue of love she has other final ends from other relationships that ensure her life does not lack meaning or purpose after the child dies. She will have ongoing and painful unfulfilled desires concerning her lost son, but eventually her love for herself and others will help her engage in a meaningful life once again.

Love's benefit of an integrated psyche is helpful regardless of one's circumstances. Developing an internal structure that prioritizes one's desires appropriately and minimizes internal conflict among them is always beneficial. If the mother had internally conflicted desires toward her son, and vacillated between caring about him and being detached in order to protect herself, then she would accomplish neither goal. She would cause herself guilt over caring poorly for her son while failing to love well and failing to enjoy the time she had with him. She would also fail to detach herself enough to protect herself from the painful loss. Most importantly, since the virtue of love integrates one's desires concerning all people, her love toward herself and others will not be permanently destroyed by her loss. She will continue to love people in a nonambivalent and consistent way long-term. Therefore, her well-integrated loving desires toward others will help her recover and continue to pursue a positive relational life despite this painful loss.

Love's benefit of additional virtues is also helpful for the bereaved mother. If she has loved well in the past, she may have already developed virtues that aid her in this current crisis. Love may have already taught her how to endure in difficult times for the sake of the beloved. Furthermore, the virtue she develops here will be useful in facing future crises including her own eventual death. Hardships in life will come whether or not she is a loving mother, but the virtues that love engenders will aid her in facing these hardships.

Love's benefit of close relationships might be particularly important for the bereaved mother. Without love, it is impossible to form the close relational bonds that constitute relationships of mutual giving and receiving. The relationships that love has improved can help her in this time of grief. The same type of bond that causes this loss to be so painful simultaneously enables her to benefit from other close relationships both now and in the future. Furthermore, caring for the sick child together with other family members strengthens their long term-relationships. The same virtue that causes pain at one's child's death may help her form a closer life-long bond with a second child.

Love benefits the loving mother in these ways. None of these benefits is entailed by the apathetic mother's disposition. Yet the unloving mother might obtain at least some of these benefits in other ways. Love is not the only way to obtain final ends. It may be possible to integrate the psyche without love. The virtues engendered by love might be attainable without love.[90] Yet, the relational benefits of love could not be obtained in other ways. The loving mother enjoyed a unique attachment to her son that the indifferent mother never enjoyed. The loving mother is capable of forming and enjoying a type of relational attachment with others that the indifferent mother cannot possess. The relationships she has are capable of more depth, more pleasure, and are more enduring.

While love benefits the mother in some ways, it also results in additional pain. The loving mother has lost someone who is irreplaceable to her. She still desires some type of union with her lost son. She at least wishes their earthly relationship could continue. She is left with a painful unfulfilled desire because that close relationship cannot continue. Yet even grief requires a simultaneous acknowledgement of the goodness of the lost relationship. Consider Nicholas Wolterstorff's commentary on his departed son, "If he was worth loving, he is worth grieving over. Grief is existential testimony to the worth of the one loved. That worth abides."[91] Grief involves experiencing both the pleasure of affirming the value of the relationship as well as the pain of its loss. Yet, the pain of grief outweighs the pleasure. Wolterstorff also asks, "How can I be thankful, in his gone-ness, for what he was? I find that I am. But the pain of the *no more* outweighs the gratitude of the *once was*. Will it always be so?"[92]

Does love result in a net gain or loss to well-being in the context of the mother's relationship with her lost son? During the child's life, the loving parent enjoyed the relationship more deeply. The parent had joy that the apathetic parent never experienced within the relationship. Before, during, and after the child's life, the loving parent can have better, closer, and more helpful relationships with others than the unloving person. The unloving person is fundamentally alone in the world. While it is difficult to quantify the pleasure the parent gains during the child's life, the pain experienced at the child's death, or the pain of her ongoing grief, since the child only lived a few years the parent is likely to grieve far longer than she enjoyed the child. Overall, it seems likely that the pain outweighs the pleasure love causes within the relationship.[93]

While the loving mother has lost something unique and irreplaceable, the apathetic mother would have merely lost a costly investment of time and energy in the child that did not produce much in return. For the apathetic mother the child truly is replaceable with another child. The death of a beloved child is more painful to the lover precisely because she lost something that the nonlover never had. She lost a close, uniquely enjoyable relationship with her son. The apathetic mother's self-willed indifference toward others prevents her from enjoying any of her relationships as ends in themselves, but also insulates her from the loss of such relationships. The indifferent person *never* enjoyed her relationship with her son as an end. His flourishing or closeness to her never fulfilled a desire. She could only hope that the investment she made into his life would result in an instrumentally useful long-term relationship, which it did not. Therefore, the apathetic mother loses her total, but smaller, investment of time and energy into the relationship.[94] The loving mother loses more because she invested more into the relationship and enjoyed it more.

In conclusion, the loving mother does endure more pain in this tragedy than the apathetic mother does. Yet the overall benefits of the virtue of love throughout her lifetime are still likely to outweigh the pain the loving mother feels within this one relationship. She is still likely to have a life that is better on the whole as a result of love. The global benefits of love throughout her life will typically be large enough to outweigh the local harms from the pain love causes within a particular tragic relationship. She still benefits from love's final ends, integrated psyche, motive for self-improvement, improved relationships, and epistemic goods. Furthermore, love was the only advisable disposition to develop toward her children and elsewhere in life. Indifference has its own far more serious risks, which we will investigate in the next chapter.

Let us consider, although more briefly, the other major type of relational tragedy. A second set of tragic circumstances arises where the beloved rejects the lover's desire for union. Rejection by one you love in a close relationship is among life's most painful experiences. Most people are fortunate enough to experience enough acceptance from others to make the occasional rejection tolerable. Yet some people live in worse than average circumstances. How does the lover fare when she experiences rejection from those she loves?

Consider the situation of Helga Schneider, whose mother abandoned her at the age of four to become a guard at a concentration camp. After being abandoned, she saw her mother exactly twice. She saw that her mother expressed no particular regret for her actions or for destroying their lost relationship. She reflects upon her receipt of the letter that gave her the opportunity to see her ailing eighty-seven-year-old mother for the second and final time.

> I'm becoming more and more convinced that I should have ignored the letter. I would have been unsettled for several days, and then I would gradually have buried it along with the rest, slipping once more towards some semblance of tranquility. And yet I didn't. I allowed myself to be overwhelmed by the news.[95]

Many of us would share Helga's opinion that she would have been better off being indifferent toward such a mother. Desiring union with such a person causes plenty of pain. When looking at the total effects of her love over a lifetime would she have been better off loving her mother or being indifferent toward her?[96]

As in the previous scenario, it is important to separate the tragedy of the circumstances from any harm stemming specifically from love. Helga is in a terrible situation regardless of her character. Even if she is indifferent to her mother, she has lost a relationship with much instrumental value. Yet there is an additional harm stemming from love. Much pain from her mother's initial and ongoing abandonment could have been avoided if she had been thoroughly indifferent toward her. This pain stems from the lover's unfulfilled desire for union, and would be reduced if she were indifferent toward her mother.

Yet it is possible to overestimate the pain we attribute to Helga in this situation. It is important to remember that love does not mandate that she ruin her life over her mother's rejection. It only requires that she have appropriately strong loving desires concerning her. In fact, if she lets herself become relationally debilitated by this rejection, she likely does not have the virtue of love. The virtue of love requires that she love not only her mother, but also herself, her brother, her father, her friends, and others in a way that is compatible with love for every one of them. Someone who lets a single painful relationship destroy her life is not loving well in her other relationships. Furthermore, love is compatible with the possibility that Helga would realize that her beloved mother's character is so vicious that union with her is not possible.[97] In this case, she would desire union with her mother in the sense that she wishes it were possible, but she would not desire it in the sense of actively pursuing it under current circumstances. In fact, she expresses a similar sentiment as she writes, "I look at you, Mother, and I feel a terrible lacerating rift within me: between the instinctive attraction for my own blood and the irrevocable rejection of what you have been, of what you still are."[98] Love does not require that the lover continually pursue someone who has become this thoroughly vicious.

While these considerations reduce the amount of pain we might assign to Helga as the result of her love for her mother, there is little doubt that love causes her considerable pain within the relationship. While Helga's love for her mother results in pain within that relationship, what benefits does it offer her? As in the previous scenario, the final ends and integrated psyche that love provides concerning all people are extraordinarily helpful. Since Helga has well-integrated loving desires toward all people, the pain caused within a single important relationship is somewhat muted by her ends within a wide variety of other relationships. Love leads her to pursue a vibrant relational life with other people while preventing her from forming a pathologically strong attachment to her vicious mother. Love also entails love toward herself ensuring that she continue to care for her own well-being.

Helga's possession of the virtue of love would also be helpful in her other relationships. It would be easy for anyone who experienced such a painful rejection to become apathetic toward union with others or even seek distance from them in all of her relationships. Yet the virtue of love ensures that her mother's rejection does not undermine her other relationships as well. The improved relationships allowed by love enable her to survive such a rejection and form relatively healthy attachments to other people.

The higher quality relationships that love allows would also enable her to obtain important self-knowledge. Therefore, she could experience healthy relationships that would enable her to see that it was nothing about herself that caused her mother's rejection. Yet if she were indifferent toward all others then she would have no such opportunity for these relationships. Obviously, no rational person would blame a four year old for her mother's abandonment of her. If Helga were thoroughly indifferent toward union with others, she would cut herself off from healthy relational experiences that demonstrate that others view her as valuable. Her mother was defective, not herself. Furthermore, her willingness to see her mother years later reminds her that the broken relationship was never her own fault. Her mother continued to live as an unrepentant Nazi. This knowledge is certainly painful, but it also affirms that Helga did nothing to deserve this rejection.

Like the loving bereaved mother, Helga would experience a net harm to her well-being from love within this relationship. However, the overall benefits of love within her life outweigh this harm. And love was the only prudent attitude to take. Love might have enabled her to reconcile with her mother if she had been repentant. Furthermore, it was necessary for other positive relationships in her life.

There are circumstances in which the virtue of love would result in an overall loss of well-being in a person's life. Yet neither of these situations is an obvious example of such a case. Given that love's benefits come from the overall effects of love throughout all of a person's relationships, the most likely source of overall harm from love would come from tragic circumstances in numerous close relationships. Love is unlikely to have an overall harmful effect when a single beloved person dies prematurely or rejects the lover. Love is only likely to have a net harmful effect when the lover loses many close relationships through disease, rejection, or other tragedy.

Is the fact that love might result in overall harm in such situations surprising? I think not. Both Aristotle and Aquinas acknowledge the need for close relationships with others for well-being in this life. Aristotle affirms that friendship is "an absolute necessity in life. No one would choose to live without friends, even if he had all the other goods."[99] Similarly, Aquinas affirms that happiness in this lifetime requires friends.[100] Since neither claims that a virtuous disposition ensures the friendly response of others, it is ultimately unsurprising that the lover is vulnerable in this way.

ENDNOTES

1. Michael Slote, *Morals From Motives* (New York: Oxford University Press, 2001), 21.
2. For a discussion of Velleman's views see Chapter 2.2.

3. For a discussion of Kolodny's views see Chapter 2.4.

4. For a discussion of Frankfurt's views on love see Chapter 2.1. For a discussion of the implications of Frankfurt's views concerning the prudential value of love see Chapters 5.2–5.3.

5. Hugh LaFollette, *Personal Relationships* (Cambridge, MA: Blackwell Publishers, 1996), 85–89.

6. *Cf.* Immanuel Kant, *Critique of Practical Reason*, trans. and ed. Mary Gregor (New York: Cambridge University Press, 1997), 5:114.

7. Elsewhere Kant defines happiness in terms of satisfying one's inclinations, committing him to a desire fulfillment account of well-being. *Cf.* Kant 1997, 5:73.

8. Kant's rejection of a necessary connection between virtue and well-being stems in part from his narrower construal of virtue. Yet it is worth demonstrating that many traditional accounts of virtue do allow for such a connection.

9. Aristotle, *Nicomachean Ethics*, trans. Joe Sachs (Newburyport, MA: Focus Publishing, 2002), 1107b.

10. Harry Frankfurt, *Necessity, Volition, and Love* (Cambridge: Cambridge University Press, 1999), 84.

11. Frankfurt 1999, 84–87.

12. Frankfurt 1999, 91.

13. Frankfurt 1999, 85.

14. Even these types of goals may not be solely dependent on one's own choices. Someone who fails to experience the freedom of the will would not be able to choose their desires. *Cf.* Harry Frankfurt, "Freedom of the Will and the Concept of a Person," *The Journal of Philosophy* 68 (1971): 5–20.

15. There are occasional exceptions to this claim. Obviously, marrying someone and pursuing the goals of love in the context of marriage thwarts the goals of other potential suitors. However, the competitive dynamics of this situation are relatively rare when examined in the lifelong context of loving goals. An adult child's attempt to gain autonomy might also seem to be a counterexample, but it is not. A parent using practical wisdom will accept and encourage appropriate steps toward autonomy.

16. Frankfurt 1999, 91.

17. Neera K. Badhwar, "Love," in *The Oxford Handbook of Practical Ethics*, ed. Hugh LaFollette (New York: Oxford University Press, 2003), 53.

18. Joseph Raz, *Value, Respect, and Attachment* (Cambridge: Cambridge University Press, 2001), 19.

19. *Cf. The Prudence of Love*, Chapter 4.4.

20. Robert Emmons, *Psychology of Ultimate Concern* (New York: Guilford Press, 1999), 43.

21. Emmons 1999, 48.

22. Martha Nussbaum, *Upheavals of Thought: The Intelligence of Emotions* (New York: Cambridge University Press, 2001), 32.

23. Nussbaum 2001, 52.

24. Nussbaum 2001, 52.

25. *Cf. The Prudence of Love*, Chapter 4.6.

26. Harry Frankfurt, "Freedom of the Will and the Concept of a Person," *Journal of Philosophy* 68 (1971): 8–9.

27. Frankfurt 1971, 10.

28. Frankfurt 1971, 10–11.

29. Frankfurt 1971, 14.

30. Emmons 1999, 69.

31. The story of Buridan's ass actually predates the philosophy of John Buridan, with whom the story is typically associated. Versions of the story appear as early as Aristotle's *De Caelo* 295b32. *Cf.* Jack Zupko, "John Buridan," *The Stanford Encyclopedia of Philosophy*, July 10, 2006. http://plato.stanford.edu/entries/buridan/ (accessed 5 Dec. 2007).

32. Frankfurt 1971, 12.

33. Emmons 1999, 67–68.

34. Augustine, *The Confessions of St. Augustine*, 8.9.21. I consulted the translations of Jack Ryan and Edward Bouverie Pusey and found the Ryan translation to be helpful.

35. Laura Ekstrom, "Autonomy and Personal Integration," in *Personal Autonomy*, ed. James Stacey Taylor (New York: Cambridge University Press, 2005), 158.

36. Immanuel Kant 1997, *Critique of Practical Reason*, 5:4–5.

37. *Cf.* Eleonore Stump, "Love, By All Accounts," *Proceedings and Addresses of the American Philosophical Association* 80 (2006): 33–34.

38. ST II-II.29.2 ad 3.

39. Aristotle similarly claims that vicious people are unable to integrate their psyches. He claims, "Such people do not even feel joy or pleasure along with themselves, since the soul within them is in a state of civil war, and one part, on account of vice, is pained at refraining from certain things when another part is pleased; one part drags them here and the other part there, as if tearing them apart." Aristotle, *Nicomachean Ethics*, 1166b.

40. Aquinas also held the view that all virtue has a necessary connection to love. *Cf.* ST I-II.65.

41. *Cf.* Immanuel Kant, *Metaphysics of Morals*, trans. Mary Gregor (New York: Cambridge University Press, 1996), 6:345.

42. Immanuel Kant, *Groundwork of the Metaphysics of Morals*, trans. H.J. Paton (New York: Harper and Row Publishers, Inc., 1964), 5:422–3.

43. Raz 2001, 108.

44. Rosalind McDougall, "Parental Virtue: A New Way of Thinking about the Morality of Reproductive Actions," *Bioethics* 21 (2007): 185.

45. McDougall 2007, 185.

46. McDougall 2007, 186.

47. McDougall 2007, 186.

48. Alasdair MacIntyre, *Dependent Rational Animals: Why Human Beings Need the Virtues* (Chicago: Open Court Publishing Company, 2002), 89.

49. MacIntyre 2002, 120.

50. MacIntyre 2002, 119–125.

51. *Cf.* William Shakespeare, *Othello* (Naperville, IL: Sourcebooks, 2005).

52. Rosalind Hursthouse, *On Virtue Ethics* (New York: Oxford University Press, 1999), 171.

53. Hursthouse 1999, 172.

54. Hursthouse 1999, 172.

55. Aristotle, *Nicomachean Ethics*, 1156b.

56. Aristotle, *Nicomachean Ethics*, 1169b.

57. Aristotle, *Nicomachean Ethics*, 1171b.

58. Aristotle, *Nicomachean Ethics*, 1171a.

59. Aristotle, *Nicomachean Ethics*, 1156b.

60. Aristotle, *Nicomachean Ethics*, 1156b.

61. Aristotle, *Nicomachean Ethics*, 1157a.

62. Aristotle, *Nicomachean Ethics*, 1157a.

63. Aristotle, *Nicomachean Ethics*, 1159b.

64. Aristotle, *Nicomachean Ethics*, 1162b.

65. Aristotle, *Nicomachean Ethics*, 1166a.

66. Aristotle, *Nicomachean Ethics*, 1167b.

67. Aristotle, *Nicomachean Ethics*, 1157b.

68. MacIntyre 2002, 119–129.

69. Aristotle, *Nicomachean Ethics*, 1156a.

70. LaFollette 1996, 85.

71. Grainne Fitzsimons, "Pursuing Goals and Perceiving Others: A Self-Regulatory Perspective on Interpersonal Relationships," in *Self and Relationships*, eds. Kathleen D. Vohs and Eli J. Finkel (New York: Guilford Press, 2006), 36.

72. Andrea Veltman, "Aristotle and Kant on Self-Disclosure in Friendship," *Journal of Value Inquiry* 38 (2004): 225.

73. LaFollette 1996, 86.

74. F. M. Berenson, *Understanding Persons: Personal and Impersonal Relationships* (New York: St. Martin's Press, 1981), 105.

75. Veltman 2004, 225.

76. *Cf.* Aristotle, *Magna Moralia*, *The Metaphysics*, 2 vols., trans. Hugh Tredennick and G. Cyril Armstrong (Cambridge, Massachusetts: Harvard University Press, 1977–1980), 1213a.

77. *Cf.* Aristotle, *Nicomachean Ethics*, 1157b.

78. Berenson 1981, 109.

79. Berenson 1981, 109.

80. Berenson 1981, 110.

81. Some researchers claim that successful relationships depend in part on positive illusions concerning the beloved. (*Cf.* Sandra L. Murray, "A Leap of Faith? Positive Illusions in Romantic Relationships," *Personality and Social Psychology Bulletin* 23 (1997): 586–604.) While I do not endorse their claims, if true, this observation might seem to demonstrate that love results in a loss of some epistemic goods. There are three reasons this possibility does not detract from my claim that love causes an increase in well-being by providing instrumentally beneficial epistemic goods. First,

even if such illusions are common in successful relationships, nothing in my account of love requires the lover to hold positive illusions about the beloved. While mild degrees of such illusions may be correlated with positive relationships, desiring the good for and union with the beloved does not require these illusions. Second, even if caring for other people tends to cause such illusions, it is unclear that they detract from well-being. It is possible that they make relationships more enjoyable without leading to pain or undermining other important desires. Finally, the claim that love typically results in a net increase in well-being by increasing the lover's epistemic goods is perfectly compatible with the claim that the love causes a small loss in other epistemic goods.

82. Neera Badhwar, "Love," in *The Oxford Handbook of Practical Ethics*, ed. Hugh LaFollette (New York: Oxford University Press, 2003), 53.

83. *Cf.* Plato, *Apology*, in *Plato: Five Dialogues*, 2d ed., trans. G. M. A. Grube (Indianapolis, IN: Hackett Publishing Company, Inc., 2002), 41c–d.

84. I am not necessarily opposed to arguments that claim virtue and well-being are synonymous, but I do not want my arguments here to depend upon such controversial claims.

85. Bernard Williams, *Moral Luck: Philosophical Papers* (New York: Cambridge University Press, 1981), 20.

86. *Cf.* ST I-II.4.4. and ST I-II.5.3.

87. Christine Swanton, *Virtue Ethics: A Pluralistic View* (New York: Oxford University Press, 2003), 78.

88. Whether love provides final ends after the beloved dies depends upon what the lover believes contributes to the beloved's well-being and whether she believes some sort of union is still possible with the beloved. This fact is implied by Chapter 4.4's claim that the lover desires whatever he believes will contribute to the beloved's well-being. Depending upon one's worldview, continuing to fulfill the beloved's desires, praying for him, or honoring him in some way may continue to be "good" for him. To serve as a beneficial final end, the individual need not be correct in his belief that these activities benefit the beloved.

89. *Cf.* Aristotle, *Nicomachean Ethics*, 1101b.

90. Aquinas and I would not think that the other virtues are truly attainable apart from love, but I have not argued for this viewpoint. *Cf. The Prudence of Love*, Chapter 3.1.

91. Nicholas Wolterstorff, *Lament for a Son* (Grand Rapids, MI: William B. Eerdmans Publishing Company, 1987), 5.

92. Wolterstorff 1987, 13.

93. While I will not argue for this position in this book, this scenario has convinced me that there is something deeply inadequate within both the hedonistic and desire fulfillment accounts of well-being. It seems that most bereaved parents experience a loss of well-being in terms of hedonistic value and fulfilled desires. Yet they would be indignant if someone were to suggest that they would have been better off being indifferent toward the child or if the child had never been born. This tendency is evidence that most people view properly attached relationships as a direct constitu-

ent of well-being even if they do not result in an increase in pleasure. Furthermore, it implies that they view properly attached relationships as a more important constituent of well-being than pleasure or fulfilled desire.

94. In at least one sense, the apathetic mother's tragedy is worse than the loving mother's tragedy. The apathetic mother suffers a complete loss of her investment into the relationship with her child. While the loving mother suffers more pain than the apathetic mother does, she also experiences more joys in the relationship than the apathetic mother does.

95. Helga Schneider, *Let Me Go*, trans. Shaun Whiteside (New York: Walker Publishing Company, Inc., 2001), 5.

96. My intention is to use Schneider's tragic circumstances to illustrate how love might affect someone in a similar situation. I do not intend to make any claims concerning Schneider's moral character.

97. *Cf. The Prudence of Love*, Chapter 4.4.

98. Schneider 2001, 82.

99. Aristotle, *Nicomachean Ethics*, 1155a.

100. *Cf.* ST I-II.4.8.

Chapter 6

Unloving Agents

While love benefits the lover in numerous ways which contribute to the lover's well-being by increasing the lover's pleasure, allowing the lover to fulfill more desires, or both, unloving dispositions have harmful consequences. Some consequences of these dispositions are likely to occur while others will necessarily occur. Furthermore, these vices will typically lower the vicious agent's overall well-being. The consequences are most destructive when the vices exist in their fullest form. Gabriele Taylor makes a similar observation in her book on the *Deadly Vices*, the destructiveness of the vice is clearest when the vice exists most fully. She explains that the destructiveness of the vices is most obvious "where the person is presented as if e.g. pride or envy were her sole characteristic, as if she personified pride or envy. It is in these paradigmatic cases that the vices in question are wholly destructive of the person whose vices they are; that is their nature."[1] Therefore, this chapter focuses upon paradigmatic examples of nonloving dispositions.

There are several distinct ways a person can fail to love. First, it is possible to hate by having desires that are diametrically opposed to love. Second, it is possible to be apathetic by having neither desire of love or the desires of hatred. Third, it is possible to have relationally inappropriate desires for union with people. Finally, it is possible to love incompletely by possessing only one of love's desires.[2]

Since love benefits the agent, we should expect vicious dispositions that embody the opposite of love to be most harmful to the agent. Therefore, hate should be more destructive than apathy since it includes the opposite of both of love's desires. Apathy should be more destructive than incomplete love since it includes neither of love's desires while incomplete love includes one of love's desires. The damage from these dispositions will be most evident in the agent's most intimate relationships. So, these dispositions will be most destructive in their effects on the relationships the agent has with himself, his spouse, his children, his parents, and his friends.

Just as Chapter Five focused upon the benefits of love in terms of increased pleasure and desire fulfillment, this chapter focuses upon the effects nonloving dispositions have on attaining pleasure and fulfilling desires. It is unsurprising that a viciously unloving agent is harmed by her disposition according to views that construe virtue as a constituent of well-being. Therefore, this chapter does not focus on these accounts. It also avoids focusing on list theories of well-being since most lists include pleasure, fulfilled desires, or virtue as constituents of well-being. If we demonstrate that vicious, unloving dispositions result in less overall pleasure and fewer fulfilled desires, then we also succeed in demonstrating that it is harmful on most list theories.

This chapter proceeds by analyzing the harmful nature of several nonloving dispositions. It begins with the dispositions least similar to love and proceeds to those more similar to love. Therefore, we will examine hate, apathy, inappropriately bonded love, and several expressions of incomplete love. Then we will continue by critiquing the two most promising strategies for avoiding the harms of unloving dispositions: caring for others as a means to the agent's own flourishing and deception. Finally, we will conclude by examining the rare conditions necessary for a vicious person to benefit from her vices.

6.1 AGENTS OF HATRED: DESIRING THE HARM FOR AND DISUNITY WITH PERSONS

Since it is traditional[3] to describe hatred as the opposite of love I portray hatred as a disposition toward desiring the harm for and distance[4] from people held as final ends. In Chapter 4.4, we concluded that the lover's desire for the good of the beloved entails that he desire that the beloved possess everything the lover is warranted in viewing as necessary for a fully flourishing life, such as health, pleasure, happiness, knowledge, achievement, virtue, friendship, and fulfilled desires. Conversely, the hater desires that the hated not possess these goods, and possess their opposites instead. The hater desires harm for the hated such as infirmity, pain, sorrow, ignorance, failure, loneliness, and unsatisfied desires.[5]

The hater also desires distance from the hated. In Chapter 4.4, we also discussed several types of relationally appropriate forms of union including intimate forms of union like shared life, family identification, personal attention, affection, and sexual intimacy, as well as less intimate forms like shared human identification, dignity, and the recognition of value or status.

In contrast, the hater does not desire union with people and seeks distance from them instead.

The desires of hatred are held as final ends. Therefore, hate is not intended to accomplish anything for the hater. For example, a desire to kill a romantic rival in order to eliminate competition is not hateful because hatred's desires are not intended to be instrumental in accomplishing further goals. Of course, overdetermination of hateful desires and actions is possible. It is possible to hate someone who happens to be a barrier to one's goals. The perception that someone is a barrier to the agent's goals can even be the source of one's hatred toward him. Yet a desire to harm others or a desire for distance from them does not express hatred unless it is held as a final end.

Hatred toward distant or unknown people can be expressed in xenophobia, racism, and classism. The hater desires harm for distant others and continued distance from them. No unity or intimacy is desired with them. The hater also desires harm for the hated and feels joy when the hated is harmed. It is also possible to hate specific others. A hater often hates those closest to him. If a hater despises a person within a close relationship, he may deliberately withhold loving behavior appropriate for such a relationship. Instead of caring for aging parents, a hateful child may intentionally neglect them. Instead of celebrating a spouse's birthday, a hateful spouse may be intentionally distant and self-indulgent on the occasion. Obviously, there are also more aggressive ways to express hatred such as emotional manipulation, verbal abuse, and physical violence.

While it is possible to hate one particular person or one particular group of people, our focus is upon the broad disposition of hatred. Someone who hates a particular person does not necessarily possess a broad disposition of hatred. Even someone who is a racist may not have a broad disposition of hatred. Someone with the fully developed, paradigmatic disposition of hatred tends to hate everyone.

This account of hatred is controversial. For example, Frances Berenson denies that hatred is the opposite of love. She argues,

> Hate is usually taken as the opposite of love. This view is wrong because in order to hate someone I must already care deeply, in some way, about him. I cannot hate anything that does not matter to me greatly. For this reason I see love and hate as intense, powerful and related emotions; they are not negations of each other, as is often supposed.[6]

I reject Berenson's construal of love and hate as emotions for reasons explained in Chapter Four.[7] However, she raises an interesting point. Hatred is often rooted in caring intensely about something. This pattern is often evident in unhealthy relationships. Someone desires a relationship with another person a great deal, but becomes deeply hateful when she is rejected, or he consistently disappoints her, or cheats on her, for example. Yet this pattern does not explain every instance of hatred. It is possible to hate something or someone that does not matter at all to you if it harms or threatens something you care about. For example, it is possible to hate a murderer you have never met because he killed someone you loved. It is even possible to hate a stranger simply for enjoying life or something in life that you find yourself unable to enjoy. Therefore, I reject Berenson's position and present hatred as the opposite of love.

My view of hatred is closer to Aurel Kolnai's account. He suggests,

> Prototypically, the movement proper to hatred is directed to the destruction of its object; or at least to an impact on the object stopping short of destruction but aligned with it and consonant to its spirit or symbolic of destruction in one essential respect (humiliation, insult, expulsion, etc.)[8]

While it might seem that Kolnai's account reflects a desire for harm for the hated but not a desire for distance from the hated, a close examination reveals that both desires are present. Obviously, a desire for the hated's destruction is similar to a desire for harm for the hated. Yet, Kolnai also lists expulsion among the symbolic modes of destruction. Expulsion in and of itself may or may not be destructive to an individual. Expulsion from the school of one's dreams is probably destructive to a person's long-term well-being, expulsion from a wine tasting club is probably trivial to one's well-being, and expulsion from a casino where one has become a compulsive gambler may aid a person's well-being. While expulsion differs from harm or destruction, a desire that a person be expelled from one's presence or community is better understood as an expression of hatred's desire for distance from that person. A desire that a person be expelled is hateful when motivated by a desire for distance from that person. Accordingly, I view hatred as including both a desire for harm for the hated and a desire for distance from the hated.

6.2 THE HARM OF SELF-HATRED

The most damaging aspect of hatred is that someone with the full disposition of hatred will hate all persons including herself. As discussed in Chapter 4.6, the relationship one has with the self is one's most intimate relationship. It is also the relationship in which the benefits and harms of various dispositions have their most drastic affects. Since the fully hateful person desires harm for herself, she acts in self-destructive ways that are intended to harm herself and destroy goods in her life. She seeks to undermine her own health, pleasure, happiness, knowledge, achievement, virtue, friendship, and fulfillment of desires. Instead, she seeks to fill her life with infirmity, pain, sorrow, ignorance, failure, loneliness, and frustration. Self-hatred is especially harmful because the hater is in a unique position to inflict great harm upon the hated. Obviously, such a life will be full of pain rather than pleasure since the self-hating person desires harm for herself and is able to inflict it.[9]

The desire fulfillment model of well-being raises interesting questions concerning the self-hater's well-being. While it may be counterintuitive, many desire fulfillment models allow that accomplishing self-hating desires would contribute to the agent's well-being. Therefore, it might seem that self-hatred would result in considerable prudential value since its desires are easy to accomplish. However, a serious problem for the self-hater is that fulfilled desires are among the goods that the hater does not want the hated to obtain. Therefore, any fulfilled self-hating desire simultaneously thwarts the agent's desire that she not have fulfilled desires.

Moreover, this dynamic affects all of the self-hater's desires. Anytime she fulfills a desire she simultaneously thwarts a self-hateful desire that she fail to have the good of fulfilled desires. Therefore, in addition to its other harms, self-hatred entails systematic psychic disharmony. This disharmony necessarily results in considerable pain by ensuring that many of the hater's desires will always be unfilled.[10]

The hater's psychic disunity is also an expression of his rejection of unity with himself. Since the self-hater rejects union with himself, it is unsurprising that this disposition results in a disharmonious psyche. The self-hater does not bond with his own desires. He simultaneously desires and does not desire the same states of affairs. Furthermore, he desires not to be identified with his desires. Someone who is thoroughly estranged from himself may not even know which of his conflicting desires to identify with.

Eleonore Stump suggests that when one is radically divided against himself it is unclear which set of desires the self should be identified with. She examines the dilemma one encounters when evaluating a person with a divided psyche. She observes that some investigators make an unwarranted assumption that the "real" self is the self that seeks the help of counselors.

If this identification were not presupposed, in what sense would it be true that the counselor is close to the troubled person who seeks his help? The locution 'the troubled person' suggests that there is just one true self in that person, namely, the self which is seeking help. But when a person is divided against himself, it is hard to know what to count as his true self. On the contrary, there seems not to be *one* self in such cases; rather, there seem to be at least *two*, and two which are in conflict with each other. When we say of a person alienated from himself that *he* is close to his counselor, we are supposing that the part of his internally divided psyche which wants healing and help is to be identified with his true self. But why should we suppose that? Why should we think that the self which seeks closeness with the counselor is the true self? How is the true self to be identified?[11]

Obviously, such a person is in a terrible self-imposed predicament. As long as this fractured psyche continues, it will be impossible for him to satisfy most of his desires or have a very pleasurable life. Only through self-willed harmony can such a psyche be repaired. The agent must successfully will union with himself and reject self-hatred if he is to ever advance his well-being much at all.

6.3 THE HARM OF HATRED TOWARD OTHERS

Since few people will be so thoroughly hateful that they will even hate themselves, let us turn our attention to the agent who hates others but cares for himself. Since this hater cares for himself we will assume that he wants goods like health, pleasure, fulfillment of desires, success, and relationships for himself. In contrast, he will desire harm such as infirmity, pain, sorrow, ignorance, failure, loneliness, and unsatisfied desires for others. He also wants disunity with others.

The most obvious harm from hatred of others occurs in the relational area of life. Just as high quality relationships benefit the lover, the absence of such relationships harms the hater. There is considerable research establishing a connection between positive close relationships and well-being. For example, Richard Lucas and Portia Dyrenforth report:

> Among those factors that people can control, social relationships seem to matter most [to their subjective well-being].... Argyle (2001) stated that "social relationships have a powerful effect on happiness and other aspects of well-being, and are perhaps its greatest single cause (p.71). Myers called the link between friendship and well-being a "deep truth" (1992, p.154) and stated that although "age, gender, and income ... give little clue to someone's happiness ... better clues come from knowing ... whether [people] enjoy a supportive network of close relationships" (2000, p. 65).[12]

While a connection between relationships and well-being is intuitive these claims go even further. Consider the claims: that relationships matter most to one's subjective well-being of all the factors within one's control, that relationships are the greatest single cause of happiness, and that relationships provide a better prediction of happiness than age, gender, and income. Whether or not all of these claims are true, their agreement concerning the connection between high quality relationships and well-being is noteworthy. Such claims from social psychologists give reason to believe that dispositions encouraging or improving relationships will typically contribute to well-being while dispositions that detract from or destroy relationships will undercut well-being. Furthermore, these claims suggest that even if the hater gains instrumentally valuable resources such as time, energy, or money, these gains are unlikely to make up for the loss of relational benefits.

It might seem that relationships are only important to those who desire them and that the hater might somehow be immune to the harm from a lack of relationships. Undoubtedly, at least some of the ways relationships benefit individuals involve the agents' desire for relationships. Since the hater desires distance from others he seems to lack this desire, and therefore be immune from the harm of having it go unfulfilled. However, it is unclear whether this inference is correct. While the hater desires distance from others, if he cares for his own well-being and wants the goods traditionally associated with well-being he will simultaneously desire close relationships. Accordingly, Aristotle claims, "No one would choose to live without friends, even if he had all the other goods."[13] Therefore, there is reason to think that hatred of others but love of self entails psychic disharmony in that such a person wants distance from others while desiring close friendships. However, there is no need to belabor this point. Even if the hater unambivalently desires distance from others, relationships are instrumentally beneficial. Even someone who does not want relationships will be harmed if he completely loses access to their important, instrumental benefits.

Accordingly, Lucas and Dyrenforth report, "Each individual has limited skills, intelligence, information, strength, and energy. Pooling resources can often lead to non-zero-sum outcomes that benefit all."[14] Even the most gifted and resourceful individual can benefit from the resources of others. Others have physical resources the individual does not have and cannot manufacture on his own: clothing, medicine, shelter, food, technology, currency, and so forth. Others also have epistemic goods that the individual lacks: medical, technological, economic, nutritional, and so forth. Relationships are helpful to everyone because others' physical and intellectual resources broaden the range of experiences that are possible in life. They provide practical remedies for pains and practical resources to pursue pleasures and desires. Anyone who completely cuts himself off from such resources severely limits ways to pursue his well-being.

How does hatred affect relationships? As with all nonloving dispositions, the hater cannot have the best kinds of relationships. In Chapter 5.5 we described these relationships in Aristotle's terminology of friendships of virtue and in Alasdair MacIntyre's terminology of relationships of mutual giving and receiving. These relationships are impossible without love because they are partially constituted by mutual goodwill and desire for union. These relationships tend to be pleasurable in themselves since the participants enjoy one another's company. Furthermore, these relationships are instrumentally useful for fulfilling other desires and attaining pleasure since the participants are deeply committed to one another and help each other in good times and hard times. Friendships of virtue also provide superior relational security for both individuals. The history of the relationship, the on-going experience of mutual goodwill, and the knowledge that common values are the foundation of the relationship provide a basis for security that minimizes fear and uncertainty.

The hater and other nonloving people can only have inferior relationships based on other things, such as the shared utility of the relationship or the pleasant nature of the relationship. Aristotle noted,

> These friendships, then, are also incidental, since the person is loved not in so far as he is who he is, but in so far as he provides some good or pleasure. Such friendships are thus easily dissolved, when the parties to them do not remain unchanged; for if one party is no longer pleasant or useful, the other stops loving him.[15]

The hater can only have relationships with a less stable basis than virtue. Pleasantness and usefulness in relationships are more likely to fluctuate, thereby providing a less stable foundation for long-term relationships.

While the best kinds of relationships are not available to the hater, her relationships are burdened by additional problems. The hater does not enjoy unity in relationships because she desires distance from others. Any amount of unity that occurs within relationships actually thwarts her desires. She will not enjoy these relationships in themselves, but can only enjoy them for their instrumental value in advancing her other desires. While the hater may still live in physical proximity to others, her relationships are marked by self-willed emotional distance. The hater's relationships are not harmonious because her hate introduces instability into them. If others recognize the hater's true disposition, they will typically respond in negative and self-protective ways.[16]

An equally serious problem for the hater is that, by harming others, he may indirectly inflict harm upon himself. Charles Hartshorne has suggested,

> There is of course partial agreement between the aim at future well-being for oneself and the aim at the good of others.... A great deal of self-interested action is self-defeating, and there are often great rewards for bringing genuine good to others.[17]

Hartshorne raises a serious problem for the hater. If his own well-being is intertwined with the well-being of others around him, then harming others can undermine his own good. While self-interested actions can be self-defeating, hateful actions are even more likely to have self-harmful effects. Hatred toward one's spouse, children, parents, neighbors, and friends threatens to destroy those who provide important resources to the hater. Success in destroying their well-being can have serious consequences for the hater. Perhaps, a particularly shrewd or lucky hater could navigate this challenge successfully, but harming these people at least eliminates useful resources for the hater.

While hatred undermines the hater's opportunities to benefit from close personal relationships, it also undermines the cohesion of the surrounding community. Love has implications for one's disposition toward both close relationships and others more generally. MacIntyre claims not only that a person is affected by dyadic relationships, but also that relationships take place within a communal network. He explains,

> We find ourselves placed at some particular point within a network of relationships of giving and receiving, in which, generally and characteristically, what and how far we are able to give depends in part on what and how far we received.... We receive from parents and other family elders, from teachers and those to whom we are apprenticed, and from those who care for us when we are sick, injured, weakened by aging, or otherwise incapacitated. Later on others, children, students, those who are in various ways incapacitated, and others in gross and urgent need have to rely on us to give.[18]

An additional danger for the hater is that successful harm of those around him can undermine the stability of communities that contribute to his well-being. Harm to these communal structures can ultimately harm the hater as well.

Imagine the effect a single hater might have on an academic department of four or five faculty. His malevolence toward others harms everyone in the department, including himself. He benefits less from the other faculty's vocational skills since they are alienated from him to varying degrees. They are less willing to work with him on joint projects, comment on his papers, or share their skill in teaching or interacting with administration. The hostility the hater injects into the department creates a distraction for everyone, undermines his own productivity, and makes his work less enjoyable. Furthermore, such a department is less likely to attract and keep good colleagues. Accomplished colleagues may leave for friendlier departments. The best new prospects will be deterred from joining if they hear of the department's negative reputation or notice the department's dysfunctional dynamics during the interview process. Ultimately, the hater enjoys his work less and accomplishes fewer vocational desires. As he acts upon his hatred for those around him, he harms people and communities that promote his own well-being.

An additional problem for the hater is that the desires of hatred are difficult to accomplish without negative consequences. His desire to harm the hated will typically be resisted. Many expressions of hatred have social or legal consequences. The hater risks being ostracized, losing his job, being sued, or even imprisoned. Of course, most haters are sensible enough to avoid actions that engender the most negative responses. The more prudent hater will avoid expressing hatred in the most overt and socially unacceptable ways since these actions have easily foreseeable negative consequences that threaten his well-being.

These realities cause an additional harm for the hater by introducing disunity into her psyche. She can either benefit from the instrumentally valuable people around her, or she can harm them and risk losing potential benefits from them. Similarly, she can pursue hateful desires in straightforward ways or avoid the consequences of overt and socially unacceptable ways of expressing hatred, but not both. In each situation, she must weigh the potential possibilities for fulfilling hateful desires, social risks, and the risks of undermining relationships and communities that her well-being depends upon. The hater's competing priorities consistently pull her in different and incompatible directions.

John Ingen considers the mental strain and general difficulty of a slightly different, but similarly damaging disposition of thorough egoism. Like our hateful agent, the egoist cares for no one's well-being except his own, but unlike the hater the egoist does not necessarily desire to harm others:

> The first human cost or practical consideration for a normative agent like Edgar Egoist is that such a life is simply a hard or difficult life. How difficult a life will depend upon Edgar's particular set of prioritized wants. But the difficulty is systematically far reaching because of Edgar's need to simultaneously juggle (a) society's norms and social consequences, (b) Edgar's own egoistic program, and (c) the normative guidance of proximate resource persons like son Egbert under a careful disguise of intentions. I say that Edgar's life is systematically more difficult because the careful application of his egoistic system requires the continual application of this three-step evaluation process. Now what is more difficult about Edgar's evaluation program as compared with that of Mike Moralist is (1) the need for secrecy of agency identification and (2) the fact that for Edgar (a), (b), and (c) evaluation needs above are always active and never nearly reducible to one another.[19]

Ingen identifies one of the internal challenges for the hater. Like the egoist, he needs to balance his radically discordant goals. Both the hater and the egoist need to navigate the conflict between the accepted norms and social consequences of actions, the need for deceptive interactions with others who might be instrumentally useful, and his own personal goals. Like the egoist, the hater must frequently rely upon secrecy if he is to accomplish his desires. Unlike the egoist, the hater's goals are so antithetical to relationships and society that the social risks to himself are considerably more severe. Furthermore, while the egoist might simply pursue materialistic goals within society's rules, the hater's agenda of harming others forces him to be in continual direct conflict with others. The hater cannot consistently fulfill his desires within the rules of society.

It might seem that the hater is not always in such a negative predicament. It might seem that only societies like our own present such a challenging environment for the hater, because of the relational and social consequences of expressing hatred in our society. In contrast, it seems that many hateful people flourish in unusual societies such as Nazi Germany or the racist communities of the Old South. However, this appearance is incorrect. It is important to distinguish someone who is thoroughly hateful from someone who is only disposed to hate some people. Racist attitudes, as expressed in Nazi Germany, are certainly part of the fully hateful disposition. Yet, many such people are not fully hateful and actually care for many other persons. While the Nazi who cares for his friends and family is hardly a moral ideal, he does not have the full-fledged disposition of hatred. A Nazi who was thoroughly hateful would also hate other Nazis, his friends, his Führer, and his family. If this Nazi's hatred became known, he would experience negative relational and social consequences at least as severe as those in our own society. Societies like Nazi Germany are an easier setting for the hater only in that expressing *some* of his hateful desires will not bring severe social consequences.[20]

Obviously, there is a differing range of relational and social risks faced by the hater. Some haters in some circumstances face less risk than others. The specific ways the hater expresses hatred, his degree of cleverness, the degree to which societal norms restrict actions expressing hatred, and how individuals choose to respond to the hater all influence the risks he faces. Yet expressing hatred even in socially acceptable ways entails serious risks. A slave owner may be legally permitted and socially expected to beat his slaves. However, society's acceptance of this practice provides no guarantee against a slave's vengeance in the middle of the night. Similarly, the hater may lower his risks by identifying individuals who display an ongoing willingness to accept his hatred. Yet, even the careful choice of victims cannot ensure the hater's safety. In one famous example, Francine Hughes tolerated her husband's violent abuse for over a decade before killing him in his sleep one opportune night.[21]

In conclusion, hatred is harmful to the agent. This damage is most evident and severe in the case of self-hatred. However, even if he only hates others, the hater still gets less pleasure from relationships than nonhaters do, undermines instrumentally useful relationships, undermines communities that his well-being depends upon, risks social consequences in the pursuit of difficult ends, and puts considerable strain on his psyche as he pursues goals that put him into continual conflict with others and societal norms.

6.4 APATHETIC AGENTS: APATHY TOWARD SELF

Apathetic agents lack both desires of love but do not have the opposite desires constituting hatred. This person's character is marked by total indifference toward persons' well-being and unity with them. While the apathetic person is indifferent concerning the well-being of persons, she may have desires in other areas of life.

Apathetic agents typically fail to flourish in many ways. Just as hatred entails self-hatred, the fully apathetic person is even apathetic toward her own well-being. Apathy toward one's own well-being entails that apathetic agents do not pursue things like pleasure, health, achievement, relationships, knowledge, virtue, friendship, and fulfilled desires as constituents of their well-being. He may pursue these goods for other reasons, but not because they contribute to his well-being. This tendency is damaging to the apathetic person because his decision-making process does not consider whether his goals, actions, and desires ultimately advance or undercut his well-being. Like a reckless adolescent, the apathetic person pursues whatever desires happen to interest him without weighing their effects on long-term well-being. If he wants the pleasure of cigarettes and fatty foods, he indulges in them without considering their long-term effects on his health. If he wants to indulge in high-risk sex, start destructive fires, or steal from others, he does so without considering the consequences to his well-being.

In contrast, people who care about their own well-being desire to promote their well-being. This entails having a higher-order volition that attempts to shape lower-order desires so that they tend to advance the agent's well-being. For example, if someone who cares about her own well-being realizes that a lower-desire is harmful to her, she will attempt to modify that desire. She may be successful or unsuccessful in this effort and she may make considerable efforts or smaller efforts, but some consideration for her own well-being is an integral part of her psyche's self-regulatory process. Richard Kraut says,

We rightly assume that direct self-love should become part of our psychological equipment at some stage in our development. A child who is brought up properly must be taught how to take care of herself, and it is good for her to have a direct interest in her own well-being. She must learn to see that, in appropriate circumstances, "That is good for me" can serve on its own as a powerful reason for action.[22]

Kraut emphasizes that learning to act to advance one's own well-being is an important part of human development that is compatible with moral norms. An individual's long-term flourishing is largely dependent upon possession of an effective internal self-regulatory process that evaluates desires in terms of their effects on well-being.

The apathetic person lacks this self-regulatory feature. Therefore, whether or not her desires advance her well-being is left entirely to chance. She may be fortunate and desire things that promote her well-being like the taste of healthy food and the invigorating pleasure of exercise. She may be unlucky and desire things that undermine her well-being like the taste of fatty foods, the pleasure of smoking, and a sedentary lifestyle. If she cared about her well-being then her internal self-regulatory process would challenge her desires for these things and try to eliminate them and reduce their harmful effects. Since she is apathetic toward her well-being, her higher-order desires make no such efforts. The long-term result of this disposition typically decreases one's total amount of pleasure, undermines one's health, and lowers the number of fulfilled desires.

Her apathy toward union with herself also harms her well-being. It is difficult to outline all that is entailed by union with the self, but union with the self at least includes some sort of bondedness the agent has with her desires. Therefore, apathy toward union with one's self has at least two harmful results.

First, someone with no desire for union with herself lacks a desire for internal unity among her desires. She does not have a higher-order volition that her lower-order desires form a unified harmonious self of any kind. She fails to participate in this important aspect of self-formation. With no psychic structure that attempts to form a coherent self the agent finds herself pulled in many conflicting directions. She is still an agent, but her desires are completely disordered. Consider these insights on the importance of internal self-regulation by psychologist Grainne Fitzsimons:

Via self-regulation, individuals come to realize their dreams and desires—to turn their visions of the future into graspable realities, whether those visions be learning a new language, becoming a better parent, or being the first person in the family to graduate from college. Self-regulation is greatly important because it helps people create the self and the social world in which they want to live.

Not surprisingly, given its importance, the process of self-regulation is thought to shape many other psychological constructs.[23]

Fitzsimons identifies self-regulation as a psychological process that shapes the self. While the apathetic person may have other self-regulatory constructs, she has no internal process that seeks self unity. She makes no effort to resolve conflicts between her desires. Unsurprisingly, her psyche will include competing, contradictory, and unordered desires. Such a psyche creates considerable internal barriers to fulfilling desires and having a pleasurable life.[24]

A second harmful implication of failing to will unity with one's self is that the agent does not care whether or not her desires have long-term stability. While someone who wills union with herself may have differing desires over time, she exerts at least some effort to connect her most important current desires to her future desires. She will identify some of her desires as important to the self and protect them over time. For example, she may be bonded to desires concerning her own character or desires concerning important people in her life such as her husband, friends, and children. She will not let these desires simply disappear or be threatened by newer desires. If she recognizes such a threat, she attempts to eliminate it. If she is committed to her spouse, but becomes attracted to another person, she tries to eliminate this new desire or address it in a way that does not threaten her commitment to her husband.

In contrast, the apathetic disposition allows complete instability in the self. Since the agent is not appropriately bonded with her own desires she allows new desires to enter her psyche without considering their compatibility with already existent desires. Her character and interests may change suddenly in ways that are incompatible with her previous interests. Therefore, efforts exerted in the pursuit of today's desires may not advance the desires she has tomorrow. This creates a serious problem for the pursuit of long-term projects of any kind. For example, today's interest in becoming a doctor too easily gives way to other interests even if significant resources have already been expended in the pursuit of a medical degree. Christine Swanton offers this example of someone who is not appropriately bonded to her own projects and desires:

There are virtues such as loyalty and perseverance which focus on demands of bonding to institutions and projects, as well as people…. Consider a student who begins her university studies doing philosophy. In her second year she decides that though she enjoys philosophy a great deal she would do more good in the world being a lawyer. So she switches to a law degree. After two years there, she realizes that being a doctor is even more useful. She enrolls in Medical School. There she discovers that she is better at the pure sciences than she had thought and realizes that if she works hard she would do more good in the world as a research biochemist. She changes to a Bachelor of Science degree. Let us say that each of these value judgements is absolutely correct. Yet we feel there is something wrong, especially if failure to stick with projects is a form of escape characteristic of lack of self-love. There is a lack of bonding with her own projects that should see her through those projects.[25]

While Swanton discusses this vice as a lack of perseverance evident in one's failing to bond with one's projects, she also insightfully draws a connection between a lack of bondedness with one's projects and a lack of self-love. It is easy to see how this disposition would detract from one's well-being since it entails such internal instability that it allows considerable resources to be expended toward projects or desires that are abandoned far too quickly.

Laura Ekstrom comments on a central insight she finds in Frankfurt's work on personhood that explains the importance of internal self-regulation.

What matters for autonomy is what we take to have been implicit in the formation of a higher-level attitude, namely, the activity of reflective endorsement. The reason this matters is that our ability mentally to draw away from our own mental states and to subject them to critical evaluation enables us to ensure that our desires do not automatically move us to act, making us the passive vehicles through which the strongest impulses hold sway. Our critical engagement with reasons, our evaluation of desires and courses of action with respect to worth, and our endorsement of some of these—these activities constitute the participation of the self.[26]

On Ekstrom's analysis, one of Frankfurt's contributions to the analysis of autonomy is his insight into how one participates in the self. Yet, the apathetic person fails to participate in the self in many important ways. He does not evaluate his own desires, reasons, and motivations with regard to his own well-being, whether they add to or detract from self-unity, or whether they extend or abandon the values of the current self. The apathetic person is too passive on these matters. He becomes susceptible to whatever strong desire dominates his personality today, even if it only holds sway for today and dissipates tomorrow. Obviously, this lack of participation in the psyche lowers one's number of fulfilled desires since the agent does not regulate her desires to ensure that desires are likely to advance the agent's well-being, that they are relatively harmonious with one another, and that today's efforts are not wasted in pursuit of desires that will be abandoned tomorrow.

6.5 APATHY TOWARD OTHERS

Thus far, our discussion of the apathetic person has focused on the paradigmatic apathetic person who does not even care for her own well-being. We will now consider apathy's effects on someone who cares at least minimally for herself, but is thoroughly apathetic toward other people. Apathy concerning the good of others may sound relatively harmless compared to the active hatred of others. Yet total apathy toward others' well-being and union with them is harmful to both the apathetic agent and those around him. The apathetic agent pursues his own desires without considering their effects on other people. Consider this description of Adolf Eichmann's apathy toward others from Hannah Arendt's writings.

> Except for an extraordinary degree of diligence in looking out for his personal advancement, he had no motives at all.... He merely, to put the matter colloquially, *never realized what he was doing.* It was precisely this lack of imagination which enabled him to sit there for months on end facing a German Jew who was conducting the police interrogation.... It was sheer thoughtlessness—something by no means identical with stupidity—that predisposed him to become one of the greatest criminals of that period.... [S]uch remoteness from reality and such thoughtlessness can wreak more havoc than all the evil instincts taken together. (Arendt 1964 p.287)[27]

Christine McKinnon cites this example to portray the vice of thoughtlessness, but it is also an excellent depiction of apathy toward others. Eichmann was not full of hatred or malice toward those he destroyed. Instead, he gave no thought to them or to their well-being at all. This disposition may seem like a simple intellectual vice, but it is not. He gave no thought to the deaths he aided and abetted because he did not care about those people. He was thoroughly apathetic toward them, their well-being, and their dignity as persons. Such apathy is far from harmless or morally neutral. It is a serious vice that causes tremendous harm. The apathetic person does not view other people's well-being or unity with them as a reason for action. Instead, he pursues his personal goals without considering their effects on other people. In principle, he is an egoist.

Apathy not only is harmful to others, but harms the self as well. One problem is that the apathetic person's indifference toward others harms his relationships. The apathetic person, like the hateful agent, cannot have the best kinds of relationships. Ingen describes this relational problem facing the agent who cares only for himself:

> Another significant human cost to consider in evaluating the appeal of the egoistic challenge to morality is the problem of the limitations of one's friendships and the absence of the best kind of friendship. Here we have an area of human

experience that, since Aristotle, has been considered an important part of human happiness; and yet the experience of genuine friendship is ruled out from the start by Edgar Egoist's normative approach to all other human agents.... All Edgar's so-called friends, whether they know it or not, will be friends incidentally because of the utility or pleasure that Edgar accrues from the relationship.[28]

Since the apathetic person lacks loving desires that are partially constitutive of friendships of virtue he cannot have the best kinds of relationships. Yet there are other harmful effects on the apathetic person's relationships.

Lester Hunt comments on how an exclusive focus on one's own well-being and apathy toward others devastates relationships. He explains,

> It also harms one's interest in a more immediate and possibly more devastating way. Anyone who, supposing it is possible, has this attitude toward others is obviously incapable of forming close personal attachments to other people, the sorts of attachments that are involved in love and friendship. Such attachments seem to be absolutely essential components of human well-being.[29]

The apathetic person loses the possibility of enjoyment from personal attachments such as those involved in love and friendship. His apathy toward others prevents him from bonding in relationships. He rules out the entire social world as a source of enjoyable ends in life. He will never take joy in celebrating a friend's success, in seeing his child flourish, or in the happiness of his lover. His world of potential ends is impoverished by his apathetic disposition. Anyone who completely loses the ability to form personal attachments is seriously disadvantaged in the pursuit of pleasure and fulfilled desires. The apathetic person can have exchange relationships, but not genuine mutual friendships. He can have a sexual relationship, but not a mutually loving relationship. Even the relationships he does have are less enjoyable, and contribute less to well-being, because the unity experienced within them does not fulfill a desire.

Jennifer Morse offers a description of the attachment-disordered person, who looks in many ways like our apathetic agent; he neither cares for nor bonds with others around him:

> The attachment-disordered person has a lot of trouble participating in long-term interactions. The argument that repeated interactions by themselves induce cooperative behavior goes out the window with these people. For the attachment-disordered child, other people are truly interchangeable with each other.
>
> From his own viewpoint, the attachment-disordered person is extremely limited in the kinds of transactions he can carry out. He can only engage in activities that do not require a particular person to interact with him for long periods of time. Unless he can truly restrain himself in the short run, using his rational calculating faculty, he will not be able to do anything very long-term.

This seems to be characteristic of these people as they age. They keep conning people. Since all persons are interchangeable to them, they continue to find a steady supply of new suckers.[30]

It is difficult to determine whether the apathetic person necessarily has all the traits of a person with attachment-disorder. Yet, one thing they share in common is their view of other people. Due to his indifference toward union with others, the apathetic person shares the attachment-disordered person's view concerning the complete interchangeability of all people. All people play the same fundamental role in his life as instrumentally useful tools for advancing desires. This attitude undermines all sorts of long-term relationships, not just friendships of virtue. Since everyone is potentially replaceable and no one is uniquely important to the apathetic person, she has fewer reasons to invest in longer-term relationships.

However, it is unclear to me that the apathetic person necessarily cons others and treats them as suckers. One difference between the apathetic person and the person with an attachment disorder might be that the apathetic person could seek to accomplish desires through long-term, mutually beneficial exchange relationships. Like the attachment-disordered person, he would not care at all for others' well-being or view them as unique. Furthermore, he would have difficulty maintaining such relationships long-term when they come into conflict with his own shorter-term desires. Nevertheless, we cannot entirely rule out the possibility of long-term relationships for the apathetic person.

However, even the relationships the apathetic person can have are less likely to occur and to last long-term. Consider Rebecca DeYoung's description of the traditional vice of sloth and its effects on relationships. Her insights concerning slothful indifference's negative effects on relationships are relevant to our discussion because this vice has effects that are remarkably similar to apathy's. She explains,

> For all its joys, any intense friendship or relationship like marriage has aspects that can seem burdensome. There is not only an investment of time, but an investment of self that is required for the relationship to exist and, further, to flourish. Even more difficult than the physical accommodations are the accommodations of identity: from the perspective of individual "freedom," to be in this relationship will change me and cost me; it will require me to restructure my priorities; it may compromise my plans; it will add obligations; it will demand sacrifice; it will alter the pattern of my thoughts and desires and transform my vision of the world. Stagnating and staying the same is easier and safer, even if ultimately it makes us more unhappy, than risking openness to love's transforming power and its claims on us.[31]

DeYoung's comments illustrate an important principle about relationships. The long-term viability of relationships is undermined by apathy toward them. Relationships require active efforts to pursue union, and to sacrifice for them that are incompatible with apathy. Apathy toward other persons allows rifts to form in relationships. Numerous small adjustments are needed to maintain unity in long-term relationships: investments of time and effort, temporary sacrifices to prioritize the other's needs or desires above our own, words or actions that affirm the relationship's value, and so forth. While the apathetic person could make similar gestures from a desire to maintain the relationship's instrumental value, at each step the apathetic person is less likely to take these actions because she does not really care for the other person. When she takes these actions she enjoys them less because she does not value the relationship as an end in itself. While apathy toward others may not have immediate and dramatic negative consequences, a long-term apathetic disposition typically undermines relationships and their benefits. Apathy may be easier in the short-term, but it is an imprudent long-term approach to life.

Another relational problem for the apathetic person is that her apathy toward others can undermine the well-being of others who are useful to her. If her apathy undermines the well-being of people she relies upon, then her own well-being is also harmed. Richard Kraut makes a similar point concerning the interdependent nature of well-being, "One other reflection shows how weak a theory egoism is. No human being acting in complete social isolation will go far with the project of promoting his own good."[32] Kraut's point is that there are so many ways that others contribute to our well-being, and so many resources they provide, that caring only for ourselves is unlikely to be an optimal strategy for acquiring well-being. If one is indifferent toward her children, spouse, parents, and friends it makes their failure more likely, yet their failure tends to harm the apathetic person as well.

A similar way that apathy toward others can harm the agent is through her dependence upon the surrounding community. If one's community descends into poverty or anarchy, such circumstances undermine the individual's opportunity to flourish. While an individual may survive a communal disaster with an every-man-for-himself mentality, the individual's well-being is connected to the community's well-being. Admittedly, failing to will the good toward large communities is unlikely to undermine the agent's well-being because it is unlikely to have much effect upon these larger groups. Yet in smaller communities one's care for others can make the difference between happiness and disaster for all.

A single free-rider who evades his taxes does little to undermine his country, while a single person who fails to pay his share of the rent puts the entire household in jeopardy. The selfish spouse, the free-loading friend, the irresponsible adult child, and the lazy co-worker all take risks in his apathy toward those around him. The extra strain their apathy puts on others may destroy the very communities they benefit from.

There is a final risk for the apathetic person. Others may respond negatively to his apathy. The social consequences of apathy, like the social consequences of hatred, vary based on how the agent carries out his apathy, his degree of cleverness, his society's norms, and how individuals choose to respond to him. Obviously, things did not ultimately go well for Eichmann or others who found themselves faced with criminal sanctions for pursuing their own interests regardless of the consequences for others. Yet criminal sanctions are hardly the only threat to the apathetic person.

There is also the risk that others will react in self-protective or aggressive ways. Since the apathetic person has no scruples against harming others to advance his own well-being, anyone who recognizes his disposition has good reason to act in self-protective or even aggressive ways against the potential threat he represents. While there are differences in how cultures and individuals react to apathetic people, many thinkers including Plato,[33] Aristotle,[34] Thomas Aquinas,[35] and Immanuel Kant[36] have identified a nearly universal interest individuals take in pursuing their own well-being. Therefore, regardless of cultural or individual differences there will be a strong tendency for anyone who recognizes the apathetic person's disposition to react self-protectively against the threat the apathetic person poses to his well-being. The apathetic person risks being avoided, fired, ostracized, divorced, or disowned. Each of these consequences would likely reduce the agent's pleasure and ability to fulfill desires.

In conclusion, the apathetic person harms himself in several ways. First, he harms himself through apathy concerning his own well-being and union with himself. Moreover, his disposition prevents him from having the best kinds of relationships. Even the relationships he can have are less enjoyable, less likely to last long-term, and less beneficial. He risks harming himself through his indifference toward others whom his well-being depends upon. He also risks social consequences stemming from his apathy.

6.6 INAPPROPRIATELY BONDED AGENTS: DESIRING THE WRONG KIND OF UNION

Another vicious disposition is the tendency to desire inappropriate types of union with persons. This agent may have any attitude toward people's flourishing, but desires relationally inappropriate bonds with them. However, this disposition does not include people who desire fewer bonds than appropriate or no bonds with people at all. Although such desires are certainly inappropriate, these dispositions are closer to our description of the apathetic, apathetic benevolent, and distant benevolent dispositions.

Some types of bonds or attachments to persons are not valuable, and are even destructive to those who form them. For example, Joseph Raz acknowledges the possibility of "irrational, and even pathological, and self-destructive attachments. Sometimes people form or maintain attachments against their better judgment, and keep them alive even when they cause them much suffering."[37] Furthermore, he warns that, "Not all attachments can confer value on their objects, only valuable attachments do so."[38] While Raz mentions the possibility of irrational, self-destructive, and worthless attachments, he does not offer clear criteria for recognizing them. However, we will focus on one type of self-destructive and therefore irrational attachment: a desire for a relationally inappropriate bond of union with people.

There is a considerable range of bonds within various relationships that are appropriate. For example, there are legitimate differences in the bonds formed within both individual friendships and the concept of friendship from culture to culture.[39] Such variety need not be inappropriate or harmful. However, other people seek bonds that go beyond this range of appropriate differences. Such bonds tend to be harmful to those in the relationship and to the relationship itself.

Just as other vicious dispositions entail vicious attitudes toward the self, the full disposition toward inappropriate bonding includes inappropriate desires toward the self.[40] One important aspect of union with the self concerns a person's desires toward his desires. For example, a person might be too strongly united with himself by being completely inflexible and unchanging.[41] Such a person would have a higher-order volition that none of his lower-order desires ever change. This disposition would undermine proper self-regulation, self-development, and self-improvement. For example, it would prevent him from benefiting from new information concerning the self-destructive nature of certain lower-order desires such as those for cigarette smoking or a fatty diet. It would also prevent him from adapting in appropriate ways to changing circumstances around him. Someone who could not adjust to new information or changing circumstances would be unlikely to fulfill as many desires or have as pleasurable a life as someone who could make such adjustments.

Another type of inappropriate bond with one's self concerns the relative strength of one's second-order desires. Such a person would have overly strong higher-order desires concerning desires that should be of secondary importance to the self. If someone had stronger higher-order desires toward first-order desires concerning his favorite sports teams, preferred colors, or diet, than toward first-order desires concerning his family, religion, or vocation, he would be inappropriately united with himself. Such a person would be more willing to abandon important relationships, his religion, or his vocation than these relatively trivial concerns. This disposition would harm the agent because he would sacrifice important desires that have a broader impact on his overall happiness in the pursuit of overvalued, but comparatively trivial, desires that have a lesser overall impact on his life.

There are also numerous ways for an agent to desire inappropriate union with others. A desire for union with others can be too strong, too weak, or have an inappropriate scope. Each disposition toward inappropriate love tends to be damaging to the agent. Like all nonloving agents, the inappropriate lover cannot have friendships of virtue, because they are partially constituted by loving desires.[42] However, his disposition causes additional relational problems as well. Relationally appropriate bonds are appropriate in part because they tend to be beneficial to both members of the relationships, tend to be attainable, and tend to be compatible with a full range of normal, helpful, and beneficial relationships within the structure of a particular society. By desiring inappropriate bonds, the agent seeks types of union that tend to be more difficult to attain and maintain, less socially acceptable, less compatible with other relationships, and harmful.

Due to her desire for inappropriate bonds with others, the agent often acts in ways that alienate others. For example, desires for union with others that include too great a scope harm the beloved by failing to give her enough autonomy, thereby alienating her. Similarly, while parenting children and mentoring apprentices are relationally appropriate expressions of love even though these relationships entail a degree of inequality, these desires are inappropriate and destructive in other relationships. Friendships and marital relationships are based on a considerable degree of relational equality. Relationships based on equality require respect for the beloved's autonomy that differs from the way one interacts with children. Appropriate forms of union within these relationships require respect for the other's autonomy regardless of one's own giftedness.

Someone with a broad disposition toward seeking inappropriate unequal bonds undermines his relationships. For example, such a person might desire to parent his spouse or mentor his supervisor and thereby risk alienating that person. Treating others in these relationships as inferiors damages these relationships and alienates the members of them.[43] Relationally inappropriate desires undermine relationships. They can lead others to distrust the agent. Even if the inappropriate agent does not lose these relationships entirely, he is harmed because these bonds change the nature of the relationship. He loses the opportunity to interact with others as equals, to learn from others, and to enjoy camaraderie with them.

As discussed in Chapter 4.4, a desire for union can also be relationally inappropriate and harmful by including too broad a scope. Parents who desire to control every aspect of their adult children's lives ignore the appropriate scope of the parent-child relationship. These desires are unloving regardless of how the parent views them. Some social psychologists refer to this pattern of inappropriate bonding with others as enmeshed. One psychologist describes patterns within enmeshed families:

> These families maintain emotionally close, but constraining, relationships, are overly committed to maintaining the status quo, and have great difficulty dealing with family conflict. Family tensions rarely rise to the surface because they are submerged beneath excessive expressions of love and demands for loyalty and unity among family members.[44]

Regardless of the benefits offered by these relationships, their overall effects are harmful. They squelch opportunities to improve relationships through resolving conflicts by refusing to acknowledge the existence of such conflicts. Their excessive demands for loyalty undermine outside relationships. Their constraining nature inhibits healthy autonomy and discourages fulfillment of an individual's goals. Unhealthy bonding is not limited to parents and children. Friends may become enmeshed with other friends and dominate each other's lives. Since we are examining the agent with the broad disposition toward desiring inappropriate union with others, the agents we are concerned with would seek inappropriate bonds in many of their relationships.[45]

Someone with these types of inappropriate bonds with others also tends to smother partners in relationships. They smother a small number of close relationships while leaving inadequate space in their own lives for other helpful relationships. Since humans have limited resources of time, attention, and energy, each inappropriate bond with others expends resources that cannot be invested into more productive, appropriate relationships. Even when this disposition does not alienate others, the agent is left with a less than optimal set of relationships and is unlikely to benefit from his relationships as much as he would have had he desired appropriate bonds in a larger number of relationships. Simply put, if the agent is deeply enmeshed in the lives of two or three friends, there will be little room left in life for other healthier relationships.

Accordingly, a desire for relationally inappropriate union with others harms the agent by wasting the agent's limited resources.[46] This problem manifests itself in various ways dependent upon the agent's pattern of inappropriately bonding. We have already examined this problem within the enmeshed pattern of relating to close friends and family. The obsessive fan who seeks inappropriate bonds with celebrities experiences a similar harm.

She harms herself by wasting limited resources on relationships that barely exist. While an appropriately bonded fan might enjoy fulfilling appropriate desires like getting her favorite stars' albums, reading about them in magazines, and seeing them perform, the inappropriately bonded fan wastes time and energy on desires that are unlikely to be fulfilled, such as desires for romantic relationships with celebrities. In extreme cases, such a person may even become a stalker. In all cases, wasting her mental energy and efforts on desires that are unlikely to be fulfilled undermines her well-being and hinders her from fulfilling more realistic relational desires with others.

The bonds of sexual union are another type of union that is inappropriate for many relationships. Eleonore Stump offers the example of a priest who desires to have sex with one of his young parishioners as someone desiring a type of union that is inappropriate for the relationship. She argues,

> To seek a kind of union with a person which is inappropriate for the office with him is thus to fail to desire his good and therefore also to fail to love him. So, for example, a priest who has sexual relations with a child entrusted to his care is not loving that child, however caring the priest may suppose himself to be, because in pursuing a kind of union with the child which is outside the bounds of the office he holds in the life of that child, what the priest desires is in fact not the good of the child.[47]

Since we are examining the agent with a broad disposition toward relationally inappropriate desires, the agent would not only desire sexual union in one inappropriate relationship, but would tend to sexualize all of his relationships. Someone with a tendency to sexualize all of his relationships risks serious social consequences by violating social norms in most societies, seeks a bond that alienates others within many relational contexts, and risks sexually transmitted diseases. This tendency also makes it difficult for him to have healthy nonsexual relationships, and to enjoy people for themselves and not just as sexual objects.

Let us expand Stump's example to a priest who tends to sexualize all relationships. Few people would knowingly trust themselves or their loved ones to the care of a priest with such views of sexuality. He undercuts his relationships, his vocational goals, and he may even be imprisoned. While sexual norms vary from society to society, most societies have prohibitions on sexuality within at least some relationships, so these consequences could not be avoided merely by changing cultural circumstances.

In conclusion, while there is a considerable range concerning what constitutes appropriate bonding within relationships, the agent who desires inappropriate union with others goes beyond these boundaries. Inappropriate bondedness to one's self harms the agent by encouraging attitudes toward one's own desires that undermine healthy self-regulation. By desiring bonds that tend to be harmful to others, he risks alienating others. These bonds are harder to attain and maintain than appropriate bonds, and when successfully established they tend to use the agent's limited resources inefficiently. Such bonds change the nature of the agent's relationships, causing him to lose enjoyable and useful benefits from relationships such as camaraderie with others and epistemic goods.

6.7 INCOMPLETE LOVE: MALEVOLENT LOVE

The following sections address four expressions of incomplete love. Someone with incomplete love is disposed toward having only one of love's desires. Incomplete love is expressed in both nonbenevolent love and disunified benevolence. In nonbenevolent love, the agent tends to desire relationally appropriate union with persons without desiring their good. The abusive spouse who wants a close relationship, but is indifferent toward his wife's well-being, displays nonbenevolent love. In disunified benevolence, the agent tends to desire the good for people without willing union with them. The distant parent who does not take a personal interest in her child, but cares for him by benefiting him monetarily, is an example of disunified benevolence. These two dispositions can each be subcategorized into two further expressions. The two types of nonbenevolent love are apathetic love and malevolent love. In apathetic love the agent is indifferent concerning the beloved's[48] well-being while the malevolent lover desires harm for the beloved. In both cases the nonbenevolent lover tends to harm herself.

Many of the harms from nonbenevolent love will be similar to harms caused by the hater's desire for harm for the hated and the apathetic person's indifference toward people's well-being. However, one important difference is that the nonbenevolent lover, unlike the hater and apathetic agent, necessarily desires relationships because union with others cannot be accomplished apart from them. Therefore, this agent needs relationships in a way other unloving agents do not. Yet without desiring the good of others relationships are difficult to maintain. All sorts of relationships are improved—and more likely to last long-term—when the agent cares for the well-being of others. Psychologists Catherine Rawn and Kathleen Vohs have observed,

> Intimate relationships are healthy when each partner can and will sacrifice his or her personal needs for the benefit of the partner and the relationships. What in the short term is a selfless act is often rewarded in the long term with stronger intimate ties. In this way, personal sacrifices lead to better relationships, which

in turn benefit the self. This relationship-supporting cycle, however, seems to be hindered by decreased self-regulatory abilities.[49]

As we shall see, both types of nonbenevolent lovers undermine the goal of union within relationships through their failure to desire the good of others as an end in itself.

The malevolent lover desires union with persons, but desires that they fail to flourish. This disposition may be formed because the malevolent person wants to be close to people with whom she can compare herself and judge herself superior, or because the agent desires to control those around her. It is also possible that she simply wishes to harm people around her because she enjoys it. Whatever the origin of the malevolent lover's desires, this disposition is inevitably harmful to herself. Most of the harm to the malevolent lover is similar to the harm caused by the hater's desire to harm the hated.

A good example of malevolent love can be seen in Joseph Goebbels's actions at the end of his life. As a leading Nazi at the end of World War II, with Hitler dead and the fall of Germany inevitable, he had his six children euthanized and committed suicide alongside his wife. While the Allied victory would have inevitably had terrible consequences for himself, there was no reason for him to believe that his wife and children would have failed to flourish. Yet he preferred unity with them in death over allowing them to survive. He desired a close kind of unity with his family, but he ultimately did not want the good for them.

A person with the full disposition of malevolent love will even desire harm for herself. Like the hater, she desires that the self be harmed and fail to have the goods constitutive of well-being. Since these harms are enumerated in Chapter 6.1, we will focus upon the harms an agent suffers as the result of malevolent love toward others even if he cares for his own well-being.

Like the hater, the malevolent lover undermines his relationships. However, this harm is even more significant for the malevolent lover. While both the hater and the malevolent lover lose resources from instrumentally valuable relationships, the malevolent lover suffers additional harm because alienating others hinders his goal of union with them.[50] Like all nonloving people, the malevolent lover cannot have friendships of virtue since such friendships are partially constituted by mutual love.[51] Even the relationships the malevolent lover can have are less beneficial than they could be because of his disposition. Many benefits of close relationships require the flourishing of both members of the relationship. An agent cannot receive physical and financial benefits from a relationship with someone who is not flourishing in these ways. When an agent desires harm for close friends and relatives, he desires a state of affairs that detracts from his own quality of life.

Like the hater, the malevolent lover risks harming himself by harming others on whom his well-being depends. Obviously, if one's close relatives are physically languishing then their practical hands-on contributions to the agent's day-to-day flourishing will be limited. The skills, energy, and income they bring to shared daily life become limited. In turn, this situation will typically require extra efforts from the agent to maintain the same standard of living.[52] Therefore, the malevolent lover will possess less time and energy to accomplish other personal desires and pursue pleasure. Moreover, since the malevolent lover desires union within relationships, his well-being is more closely tied to the well-being of others. Union[53] with others entails that their flourishing engender the agent's flourishing and harm to them also harms the agent.[54]

The agent's malevolence can also harm him by creating a barrier to fulfilling his desire for union with others. Unsurprisingly, many people react negatively toward those who desire to harm them. They may respond with similar malevolence or simply seek distance from him. In either case, this reaction makes it difficult for the agent to attain and maintain union with others.[55] He may yet succeed in finding people who are not repelled by his malevolence, but his malevolence creates an unnecessary barrier that frequently frustrates his relational goals.[56]

Like the hater, the malevolent lover does not merely undermine her well-being by undermining her close relationships, but also risks her place in society more generally.[57] Unlike the hater, she suffers an additional harm because she actually wants union with others in the community. While desiring harm for those close to the agent will likely undermine those relationships and make them less beneficial, she may also lose her place in society. Her lack of goodwill may be noticed and she may be punished, resulting in an additional loss of relationships. Some expressions of malevolence are criminal and have legal consequences. While societies differ considerably concerning their expectations of individuals and the consequences for rejecting those expectations, virtually all prohibit many forms of malevolence toward at least some members of society. Those who seek to harm others do so at their own risk.

The malevolent lover also undermines his own good by undermining the communities in which he participates. Consider the malevolent lover who works for a small company and enjoys his work there, but desires vocational failure for his co-workers.[58] He wills something incompatible with his own vocational success since his own goals require that many others in the company achieve at least modest success. He can hardly flourish vocationally if the company goes bankrupt. Furthermore, he sabotages his desire for union with his co-workers. If his company fails, then the unity with others in the company, *qua* fellow employees, will be impossible. Furthermore, if his malevolence toward others in the company is noticed he will experience social, vocational, and possibly legal repercussions. He may be socially ostracized, passed over for promotion, fired, or even sued.

One distinctly harmful aspect of malevolent love is that it provides the agent with a motive for self-destructive behavior. Just as love provides the lover with a motive for self-improvement,[59] the malevolent lover has a motive for self-destruction. Since she desires union with the beloved but does not desire his good, she should not desire her unity with the beloved to be a good for him. If someone possessed a fully integrated version of this disposition, she would want her relationship with the beloved to be burdensome, painful, and detrimental to the beloved. Perhaps some forms of teenage rebellion are rooted in this disposition. Destructive personal behaviors can be intended to hurt those who love them. Social scientist Andrew Greeley offers an example of such self-destructive behavior. He describes the self-destructive tendencies of people like the malevolent lover:

> They lose because they want to lose. Deep in the unconscious recesses of their personalities are powerful needs for failure and for hatred of those who tell them that failure is unnecessary.
>
> First of all, by defeating ourselves we punish those toward whom we feel aggressive. Does someone count on us? Is there anyone who wants us to succeed? Have we made a commitment to another person? Splendid! We can convert that person into a substitute parent and then punish him for having the gall to expect anything from us.[60]

Such a person's desire to harm close relatives motivates him to hurt himself in order to harm them. This self-destructive pattern harms both members of the relationship.

While self-destructive behavior is a logical option for the malevolent lover, many people are resistant to self-destructive tendencies. Of course, it is also possible to desire one's own well-being, union with others, and harm for others. While this combination of desires deters one from self-destructive actions, it also introduces considerable psychic disharmony. Union with others entails that whenever the self flourishes, others also benefit, and whenever the self is harmed, others are harmed as well.

For example, a malevolent daughter can try to succeed in her own life, but her success gives her parents a reason for happiness. The malevolent lover can flourish while frustrating her desire to harm those close to her, or she can fail to flourish in order to harm those close to her. While there are other ways that she may harm those close to her, the pursuit of her own flourishing runs counter to malevolent desires.

Malevolent love also introduces internal psychic disharmony in a second way. A desire for union with another person cannot be fulfilled if he does not flourish enough so that he continues to exist and is able to participate in the desired form of union. Obviously, if someone is on his deathbed or in excruciating pain the kinds of union that are possible with him are limited. Such a person can hardly engage in the typical activities of friendship. Therefore, if an agent desires union with another person and desires that he does not flourish at all, his desires are incompatible with one another.

A third way that malevolent love introduces psychic disunity results from the fact that union with others is often beneficial to them. A mutual friendship benefits both members of the relationship. To desire this relationship with another person is to desire something that benefits her. Most people find that union expressed in shared time, attention, and shared activities is pleasant and desirable. Therefore, whenever the malevolent lover desires shared time, attention, and activities with others, he desires something that benefits those he wants to harm. In each of the malevolent lover's relationships his desire for his own well-being, harm for others, and relationally appropriate union with others conflict with one another. This disposition results in unpleasant psychic discord and fewer overall fulfilled desires since his desires are largely incompatible with one another.

In conclusion, the disposition of malevolent love undermines relationships, makes relationships less likely and less beneficial, hurts the agent by harming those he is united to, undermines the community the malevolent lover's well-being relies upon, and introduces considerable disharmony into the agent's psyche. Such a person will have a less pleasurable life and fewer fulfilled desires as a result of this disposition.

6.8 INCOMPLETE LOVE: APATHETIC LOVE

The apathetic lover is indifferent concerning the flourishing of persons, but desires union with them. Like the apathetic person, the fully apathetic lover's indifference extends to her own well-being. The harmful effects of apathy toward one's own well-being are detailed in Chapter 6.4. We proceed by examining the harmful effects of caring for one's self while desiring relationally appropriate union with others, combined with indifference toward their well-being.

The most obvious harm from apathetic love is its role in undermining relationships. Like the apathetic person, the apathetic lover's indifference toward other's flourishing harms the agent's relationships. However, the apathetic lover's disposition also makes it more difficult to fulfill his desire for union with others. Like other nonloving agents, the apathetic lover cannot have friendships of virtue because they are partially constituted by mutual care.[61] Furthermore, apathy concerning the flourishing of those close to the agent often results in the loss of relationships or diminished relational benefits.

There are two distinct relational risks taken by the apathetic lover. First, he risks that others will react in negative ways to his indifference toward their well-being. Others may react to the apathetic lover in ways similar to negative reactions engendered by the apathetic person's disposition.[62] Others may distance themselves, cut off the relationship entirely, or take other self-protective measures if they realize that she does not care about their well-being. In principle, the apathetic lover is an egoist who does not view the well-being of others as a reason for action. Even a moderately reflective individual realizes that the egoist is willing to take advantage of him when it advances her well-being. Unsurprisingly, most people in most cultures respond negatively to such agents. Therefore, the apathetic lover risks alienating those with whom she desires union.

A second danger is that the agent's apathy toward others can affect them in ways that undermine her own well-being. Even if those around her do not react in self-protective or aggressive ways, her indifference toward them may undermine their well-being and leave them with fewer instrumentally useful resources that she can benefit from. When her apathy undermines the flourishing of those closely united to her, she simultaneously undermines her own flourishing.[63] She fails to desire a necessary condition for her own well-being, the well-being of those closely united to her. However, these negative consequences are less likely to occur for the apathetic lover than for the malevolent lover, since she does not actively desire harm for the beloved.

Like the apathetic person,[64] the apathetic lover risks her place within the community as well as within specific relationships. Her neighbors, co-workers, and others who interact with her may notice her apathy toward their well-being and react accordingly. They may also fail to flourish due to her indifference toward them, and she may lose benefits from those communities. In smaller communities, just as in intimate relationships, the apathetic lover's well-being is connected to the well-being of others. Indifference toward their well-being entails apathy toward a necessary condition for her own well-being.

In conclusion, apathetic love is not as harmful as many of the vicious dispositions we have examined. Apathetic love is probably less harmful than these dispositions because it is more similar to love than they are. Yet it is still necessarily harmful because it entails indifference to one's own well-being and makes it impossible to have friendships of virtue. Furthermore, the apathetic lover risks harm by undermining relationships, engendering social consequences, and undermining the well-being of others and communities that contribute to the agent's well-being.

6.9 INCOMPLETE LOVE: DISTANT BENEVOLENCE

The other category of incomplete love is disunified benevolence, which is to desire the good of people without desiring relationally appropriate union with them. This category of dispositions includes two expressions. One expression is distant benevolence, which is to desire the good of persons while actively desiring distance from them. Another expression is apathetic benevolence, which is to desire the good of persons while being apathetic concerning one's unity with them.

Failing to will union with distant people is incompatible with the full virtue of love. Even the most distant relationships call for some desire for union with others as fellow human beings.[65] Some close relationships call for a particularly strong desire for union. In closer relationships, there is a degree of overlap between love's two desires. For example, it is possible to will that one's children flourish in many ways without willing unity with them. Such a parent may be pleased to hear that his children are successful, but does not pursue a relationship with them. Yet it is not possible to will that one's children flourish completely without also willing unity with them since the flourishing of children requires parents who desire union with them.[66] Children need nurturance, guidance, and provisions from their parents in order to thrive.[67] Such a parent undermines his child's flourishing by failing to will the close parent-child relationship that contributes to the child's flourishing.

One may genuinely desire the good for others, but find unity with them undesirable. In distant relationships, this disposition could be an expression of racism or classism. Desiring a degree of the good for one's spouse, parents, or children without desiring union with them is also possible. Living in close proximity with others can be difficult. If one does not learn how to forgive then everyday frustrations and ordinary problems may undermine her relationships. Furthermore, pursuing union with others in close relationships expends limited resources. It takes time, effort, and attention. Pursuing union with others makes us vulnerable to them. It opens us up to personal rejection and criticism. Therefore, some people desire little or no union with close relatives.

The person with the full disposition of distant benevolence would even desire disunity with himself. The harms of this desire are enumerated in our discussion of self-hatred found in Chapter 6.2. Yet distant benevolence causes additional psychic disharmony. Since the distant benevolent person desires the good for the self, he undercuts that desire by willing disunity with himself. These conflicting desires introduce additional disharmony into a psyche that is already fractured by self-willed disunity with the self. Since the other harmful aspects of desiring disunity with one's self are addressed elsewhere, we will focus upon the person who wills unity with himself, but is disposed to reject union with others.

One harmful aspect of distant benevolence is that it undermines instrumentally useful relationships. Like other unloving persons, the distant benevolent person cannot have the best kinds of relationships since they are partially constituted by loving desires.[68] Even the relationships the distant benevolent person can have are undermined by his disposition. While distancing one's self from others may minimize the pain of frustrations and minor wrongs in close relationships, it also undermines those relationships. It introduces a self-willed emotional distance into relationships. Rejecting unity with others in close relationships entails rejecting a union of affections with others. Even when the agent is physically present to others, his attention will tend to be elsewhere. Forgiveness, reconciliation, and forbearing wrongs are better ways to minimize everyday pains in relationships without undermining them.[69]

Desiring an inappropriate distance from others tends to alienate them over time. Consider how others typically react toward those who reject relationally appropriate union with them. Imagine a young adult's reaction to her parents who are financially generous, but do not want to see her or be a meaningful part of her life. They have sent her off to a distant boarding school from an early age. While she may be thankful for their generosity, she will likely interpret their desire for distance as a form of rejection since their desire for distance from her is a rejection of union with her. After years of an unfulfilled desire for union with her parents, her desire may decrease or cease entirely. In time, distance in the relationship can become permanent. Even though the parents do not care about union with their daughter, they risk losing important practical benefits that children typically offer their parents such as personal care in old age. They also lose the joys of being involved in her day-to-day life such as sharing in her successes.

The distant benevolent agent weakens his relationship with others even when they are not alienated by his rejection of union with them. Relationships require ongoing commitment and attention if they are to last long-term. Withdrawing from relationships tends to undermine them regardless of the other person's reactions. Similarly, Aristotle commented on the importance of shared time and conversation together. He remarks that an absence of friendship-related activities does not immediately end a friendship. Nevertheless, he notes, "But if the absence is a long one, it seems to make people forget their friendship. Hence the proverb: 'Many friendships has lack of conversation dissolved.'"[70] The activities associated with pursuing union with others strengthen relationships and their absence weakens relationships. Of course, it is possible to will union with others in the absence of such activities, but when this is the case, the agent seeks other ways to strengthen the relationship. Instead, the distant benevolent person desires to avoid such activities.

Desiring disunity in relationships also makes them less enjoyable. Since the agent already wills that others flourish, a desire for relationally appropriate unity with them would increase the agent's pleasure by increasing his opportunities to enjoy and benefit from the beloved's flourishing. When distance is desired in a relationship, it decreases the relationship's contribution to well-being because unity in relationships thwarts this, desire thereby decreasing her well-being.

This disposition also introduces psychic disharmony in the agent. Union with others in close relationships contributes to their flourishing. As noted earlier, a parent's ongoing relationship, emotional closeness, physical closeness, and shared time with her children contribute much to their well-being. Parents who reject such union with their children undermine their well-being. Short of finding a surrogate or adoptive parent for them, the parent's desire for distance harms her children in ways that are difficult to recover from. By willing distance from one's children that undermines their well-being, the parents' desire that their children flourish is undercut.

A final detrimental aspect of distant benevolence is that it can lead to loneliness.[71] L. Vander Kerken argues that mere benevolence is insufficient to relieve loneliness:

> In this peaceful coexistence men regard each other with benevolence. Their relations are no longer exclusively determined by the profit to be derived from them, their motives have been widened and modified by a real inclination to help one another. Yet this inclination remains relative. First, it has not yet entirely emerged from the economic-exchange mentality. Next, and more important, the helpfulness is still to a great extent anonymous, it is aimed at the other person as somebody who is "a human being too," as all people are. This universal helpfulness does not yet advert to the unique subjectivity of "this" individual.[72]

Kerken claims that benevolence toward others does nothing to relieve loneliness, because it does not require closeness or even knowledge of one another's identity. Those who receive benevolence may be unknown to the giver. Instead, benevolence in the context of a mutual relationship is needed to relieve loneliness that cannot be alleviated by benevolence alone.

Kerken's critique can be expanded further; since even benevolence in close types of relationships can fail to relieve loneliness if emotional distance and lack of union allows others to become intimate strangers. This problem can occur if one shares time, space, and resources with another person, but there is no closeness in the relationship. Since the distant benevolent person wills a lack of union in the relationship he will be more susceptible to loneliness. However, this harm is contingent upon the agent actually having some sort of unmet relational desire.

In conclusion, the distant benevolent agent is harmed in a number of ways. She wills disunity with herself. She cannot have virtue-based friendships. She introduces psychic disharmony into herself by willing the good of others, but undermining others' good in close relationships by distancing herself from them. She makes her relationships less enjoyable and makes them contribute less to her well-being. She risks losing instrumentally useful resources by alienating those around her. Finally, she increases her risk of loneliness by distancing herself from others.

6.10 INCOMPLETE LOVE: APATHETIC BENEVOLENCE

The disposition of apathetic benevolence is closer to the full virtue of love than distant benevolence is since it includes no desires that are actively opposed to love. Therefore, we should expect it to have fewer and less severe consequences than distant benevolence. Yet it shares some of distant benevolence's harmful aspects. Like the distant benevolent person, this agent genuinely cares for the well-being of others. Unlike the distant benevolent person, she is indifferent toward union with others.

This disposition may be formed for motives similar to those that often lead to the distant benevolent disposition. Like the fully apathetic person, a thoroughly apathetic benevolent person would even be indifferent toward his unity with himself. These harms have already been investigated in section 4.4's examination of the apathetic disposition. Therefore, our examination focuses on the agent who has at least some desire for union with himself, but does not desire relationally appropriate union with others.

Apathy toward unity with others undermines instrumentally valuable relationships that promote well-being. Like agents with other nonloving dispositions, the apathetic benevolent person cannot have friendships of virtue.[73] Furthermore, union within relationships promotes and reinforces the relationship's bond, thereby increasing the relationship's long-term viability. Apathy toward union with others entails indifference toward the bonds that hold relationships together. Therefore, the apathetic benevolent person allows relationships to wither. Of course, a relationship is affected by the actions and attitudes of both of its participants. The apathetic benevolent person may be lucky and benefit from others who desire union with her. Since the agent is apathetic toward union with others, she will allow union to occur if others desire it and it does not hinder her other goals.

To illustrate the potentially harmful nature of desiring to benefit others without desiring an appropriate kind of unity with them, consider this example of flawed benevolence offered by Robert Adams:

> Suppose that a friend of mine, seized (as he at least supposes) by benevolent impulse, takes it into his head one day to confer a benefit on a number of people. The means he chooses for this purpose is to give each of them twenty dollars. Making his rounds, he comes to me. He pulls a twenty-dollar bill from his pocket and holds it out to me, saying, "Here, Bob; I'd like to give you this." Perplexed, I respond, "Well ... thank you. But why?" He replies, "I just wanted to do something nice for you."
>
> I do not know exactly what I would do at this point, but one thing is clear: my friend has not succeeded in doing something nice for me. He has only created an awkward situation. I will feel embarrassed about it—and underneath that, perhaps a little insulted. If he wanted to do something nice for me, why didn't he pay me a compliment? Or why didn't he invite me to lunch? That might have cost him no more, but would have been a gracious rather than an awkward thing to do.[74]

Perhaps not everyone would agree that Adams's friend has failed to do something nice for him. Nor would everyone share Adams's standoffish reaction to his friend's awkward display of benevolence. Yet, his comments illustrate that many people prefer that a friend benefit them through an insightful compliment that shows he knows and thinks well of them or by sharing time together over a meal. Both of these benefits would demonstrate the friend's desire for unity and closeness, while economic benevolence alone expresses something inadequate for close relationships. This example also illustrates that benevolence without a desire for unity can actually harm a relationship. A person who consistently made such relational errors would risk alienating many of his friends. Perhaps, Adams's friend could compensate for such errors by initiating other relationship building activities intended to promote unity in the relationship. Yet the apathetic benevolent person has no desire for such activities, because they are precisely the sort of activities he is indifferent toward. Therefore, he is unlikely to initiate them and strengthen the relationship.

Like other nonloving dispositions, apathetic benevolence also harms the agent by making relationships less enjoyable. The agent does not care whether there is closeness and union within relationships. Since union within relationships does not fulfill a desire, the union that takes place within relationships contributes less to the agent's well-being and is less enjoyable than if he possessed fully loving desires.

Finally, the apathetic benevolent agent fails to will something that makes his desires more likely to be fulfilled. Willing union with friends and close relatives typically contributes to their well-being. Since the agent is indifferent toward union with his parents, spouse, children, and friends, he makes their flourishing less likely (thereby lowering the chances that his desire for their flourishing will be fulfilled).

Overall, the apathetic benevolent disposition is less damaging to the agent and relationships than many other nonloving dispositions, because it is more similar to a loving disposition. However, the agent still suffers from his failure to will unity within his own psyche and his failure to will an ongoing unity of his future self with current desires. He also cannot have friendships of virtue. Furthermore, he risks undermining relationships through his failure to will union with others, he makes his relationships less enjoyable, and he makes it less likely that his desire that others flourish will be fulfilled.

6.11 A STRATEGY TO AVOID HARM FROM UNLOVING DISPOSITIONS: INSTRUMENTAL CARE FOR OTHERS

One strategy for avoiding some drawbacks of unloving dispositions is to will the good of and union with others instrumentally to promote the agent's own good, but not as final ends. This strategy is potentially useful for agents who lack one or both loving desires toward others. Yet this strategy cannot be used by those who are apathetic toward themselves, since it requires instrumental desires toward others that aid in fulfilling an already existent desire for one's own good held as a final end.

This strategy is also less promising for agents who possess desires that oppose the desires of love, because it would entail psychic disharmony. For example, if the hateful person who desires to harm others as a final end also wills that others flourish to promote his own good, he introduces disharmony into his psyche. The hater cannot cause the hated to be both harmed and benefited overall. At best, the hater might desire harm for others in some ways, while desiring that they flourish in other ways that benefit him. Since this strategy is more complicated and less promising for the hater and other agents with desires actively opposed to love, we will focus on the apathetic person who seeks to promote his well-being by instrumentally motivated desires for the good of and union with others.

This strategy might protect the agent from some harm resulting from non-loving dispositions. For example, this strategy would prevent harm to an agent who would otherwise allow her apathy to undermine the good of those her well-being depends upon. She also decreases her risk of social consequences since she acts as if she cares for others. In a discussion of egoism, Kraut offers this depiction, which helps explain the instrumental lover's motives:

> Egoism holds that there is only one person whose good should be the direct object of one's actions: oneself. It allows one to take an indirect interest in others, and to promote their well-being, but only to the extent that doing so is a means toward the maximization of what is good for oneself.[75]

Kraut correctly identifies a challenge for the instrumental lover. He wants to promote his own well-being while avoiding unnecessary efforts that accompany altruistic care for others. This tension leads to a question concerning the instrumental lover: does he care for others wholeheartedly or only as it seems necessary to promote his own well-being? There are problems with either option. Since he only cares for others in order to promote his own well-being, it would be sensible to care for others in only limited ways. This approach allows the agent to save resources for pursuing his own interests. Yet, there are dangers with this approach.

First, he may be mistaken concerning which people's well-being he can benefit from. One's closest family and friends are plausible candidates for people it would be prudent to care for. After all, relationships with friends, parents, siblings, children, and spouses tend to be long-term and tend to include many shared areas of life. Yet, there are risks if he limits his care to these people. After all, there are many others around him for whom he could care and from whom he could potentially benefit. A cousin may someday become a successful businessman and remember the agent's encouragement and care. Caring for co-workers may improve the agent's work environment or even save his job by improving the company's financial stability.

It is also unclear which aspects of others' well-being will contribute to his own well-being. Obviously, the health and financial well-being of close family members is desirable. A sick relative is unlikely to be of much instrumental use. Similarly, a poor family member is less likely to be useful than a rich one. Yet, it is unclear how much he should care for their feelings, emotions, and day-to-day preferences in order to advance his own well-being. If he ignores these aspects of their well-being, then he can save additional resources for pursuing his own interests, yet his indifference entails additional risks.

First, genuine care for other close friends and relatives is typically associated with concern for the whole person rather than care for just their health and finances. If he is consistently callous and unhelpful in other areas then he risks revealing that he does not truly care for them. He may also alienate them—even if they do not discover his underlying apathy. The instrumental lover may also fail to recognize all aspects of others' well-being that affect his own. For example, someone may recognize that his wife's financial success helps his own flourishing and be supportive of it, but fail to realize that her enjoyment of close friendships aids in his flourishing by giving him more networking opportunities and by re-energizing her so that she has more energy to invest in their relationship. If others flourish in these ways then it may benefit the agent considerably. He spends time in the company of his family for much of his day. That time will likely be more pleasant if they are happy and emotionally fulfilled. Even if he ultimately cares only for himself, there are benefits to caring about all aspects of others' well-being. If he limits his desire for their good to areas where he identifies clear and immediate benefits to himself then he still risks undermining important benefits to himself.

In contrast, if he decides to act as if he cares wholeheartedly he faces other problems. First, he must use enormous amounts of limited resources. This choice is inefficient and wastes resources. Furthermore, if he is going to act as if he cares wholeheartedly for others, he would be better off if his concern were genuine. Genuine concern for others would cause him to enjoy these efforts more and cause them to contribute to his well-being by fulfilling desires he cares about as ends.

Regardless of whether the instrumental agent cares wholeheartedly for others or limits his care he must use an amount of deception. Lester Hunt considers the risks if the agent does not deceive those close to him.

> If people were to realize that I act as if I value their well-being simply in order to get something out of them, all sorts of results that are bad for me will tend follow: to one extent or another, other people will object to being 'used' in this way and will refuse to cooperate with me. They will also dislike me, and they will think I am a bad person. However, it is good for me that others cooperate with me, like me, and think I am a good person; thus, to the extent that these results can be expected to follow from it, egoistic behavior undermines the aim of egoism.[76]

In many of his relationships, the agent cannot allow others to realize that he cares for them only because he benefits from them. In the most vulgar of exchange relationships, this attitude is acceptable, but in anything approximating an intimate relationship, a friendship, a close working relationship, or a familial relationship, such realizations engender at least some relational and social consequences. Yet deception in relationships brings its own problems, which will be considered in the next section.

Furthermore, someone who lacks genuine love for others may be quite bad at acting as if he cares for others. His underlying indifference toward them may still be discovered. The alienated person may react by ending the relationship entirely or eliminating the benefits the agent seeks to gain. Most people do not like being used. The agent using the instrumental strategy is still an egoist in principle who only cares for others because it ultimately seems beneficial to him. If the relative benefits of rejecting others ever appeared to outweigh the benefits of caring for others, he would be perfectly willing to abandon or harm them.

In conclusion, the potential of the strategy of instrumental care is limited. First, it cannot be used to avoid the harms of apathy toward the self. Second, it can only be employed by those who lack love's desires rather than those who have desires that are incompatible with love. It requires a careful calculus that seeks to maximize one's own benefits in relationships without investing too heavily in return. It risks alienating those we seek to benefit from. Finally, it requires deceit. The next section examines the risks of the deceptive strategy.

6.12 ANOTHER STRATEGY TO AVOID HARM FROM UNLOVING DISPOSITIONS: DECEPTION

One major source of harm for the nonloving person is the reaction of others to his character. At least some of this harm can potentially be avoided through deception. This strategy for obtaining the benefits of virtue, without possessing virtue, was examined long ago by Plato in the *Republic*. He considered the possibility that the benefits of justice do not come from being just, but merely from looking just. He considered that the unjust man who appears just might gain the advantages of both justice and injustice. Plato described the gain for the unjust man who successfully deceives those around him:

> He rules his city because of his reputation for justice; he marries into any family he wishes; he gives his children in marriage to anyone he wishes; he has contracts and partnerships with anyone he wants; and besides benefiting himself in all these ways, he profits because he has no scruples about doing injustice. In any contest, public or private, he's the winner and outdoes his enemies. And by outdoing them, he becomes wealthy, benefiting his friends and harming his enemies.[77]

The argument in favor of vice and injustice is that an unjust person can attain the same social benefits as the just person through deception while also enjoying the benefits of injustice.

Ingen similarly observes that the sensible egoist, like most of our unloving agents, should recognize that achieving his goals largely depends on hiding his disposition from others. He claims,

> The most distinctive characteristic of the egoist's calculations, which radically differentiates it from all other deliberation procedures, is the *maintenance of secrecy* about her egoism and about her total absence of genuine good will. It is very inefficient to *appear* to be completely biased in her own favor. Especially in everyday affairs, which are highly repetitive and consistently cluttered with the same group of human resources and obstacles, one of the most efficacious tactics possible is to avoid being categorized as having a selfish character, much less being a card-carrying egoist. The clever egoist realizes that inefficient strategies or tactical moves at inopportune moments may be self-defeating and needlessly tip her hand.[78]

Prudent unloving agents realize that the optimal strategy for accomplishing their goals requires hiding their disposition from others. There are at least some relational and social benefits that might be gained through deception. When the unloving person's deception is successful, he will be treated as well as the loving person. Others may treat him as if he actually cares for them and will become more trusting, generous, and useful for fulfilling desires and gaining pleasure.

However, there are problems with the deceptive strategy. First, it can only protect from harm stemming from the reactions of others. Yet, fully vicious dispositions also entail harmful attitudes toward one's own well-being or union with one's self. Neither these harms, nor the harms caused by psychic disharmony introduced by some unloving dispositions, can be avoided through deception. Finally, deception does nothing to prevent harm to the agent caused by her destruction of or indifference to individuals and communities her well-being relies upon.

Not only does deception fail to prevent many kinds of harm, but it entails its own set of problems for the deceiver. Ingen points out that the deceiver cannot have certain important relational experiences. He explains,

> Given Edgar's strategic need for secrecy about the nature of his agency, he cannot share *who he really is* with any other human being. Yes, Edgar can share some, or even many, of his wants with some other persons when it is tactically safe and efficient to do so *vis-à-vis* the steady application of his normative program. But whatever is shared about who he is must always fall short of disclosing that essential element of an accurate description, that he is an amoral personal egoist and what that means.... This human need, to share with some other person who one is, I take to be a very strong need, and to give up the

opportunity to satisfy this need is to pay a high price. A corollary of this sacrifice is that Edgar can never have a genuine confidant in his life.[79]

Ingen may be incorrect in claiming that the deceiver would have no opportunities at all for self-revelation. For example, assuming the deceiver has not committed any major crimes, she could reveal herself to a nonjudgmental counselor or to a priest at confession. Yet the deceptive strategy eliminates widely desired relational experiences from her options. Revealing her true self to friends and family would make her vulnerable to serious social and relational consequences. Avoiding these consequences is at the heart of the deceptive strategy. Therefore, any pleasures or fulfilled desires that require revealing one's self to friends and family are lost by the deceptive strategy.

While I do not know whether Ingen is correct in claiming that self-revelation is a universally experienced human need, the claim seems plausible. Moreover, while there are many studies that identify friendship as beneficial, at least one study suggests that having a confidant is among friendship's most valuable benefits. Lucas and Dyrenforth report "Pennebaker (1990) has shown that opening up to individuals about one's problems has beneficial health consequences. It may be that having a friend in whom one can confide provides the strongest benefits [from relationships]."[80] Whether or not these broader claims concerning the benefits of self-revelation are correct, there is a distinct pleasure that most people experience when confiding in friends and relatives who love them. Yet the deceiver cuts herself off from such experiences.

Rosalind Hursthouse also offers an analysis of why deception is bad for the deceiver. She says that honesty is preferable for many reasons including:

> It's so much easier than being dishonest; you do not have to keep a constant guard on your tongue and worry about the details of what you should say—mostly you just tell the truth. Lying is usually so pointless and silly. People know and you just look a fool, trying to pretend that you never make mistakes or are admirable when you're not. It's such an essential part of good relationships that there should be trust between you.... And who would want to be loved and respected for a façade one presents rather than what one is?[81]

Let us examine each of Hursthouse's claims individually. Is honesty easier than dishonesty? Honesty is easier in that the agent does not need to expend extra efforts of imagination to fabricate a believable story that is compatible with the facts the deceived have available to them. The honest person also does not need to remember and distinguish between what actually happened and what he wants others to believe happened. Furthermore, the honest person rarely worries about whether others will believe him. Therefore, deception requires an unnecessary expenditure of time, energy, and resources that could be invested into other pleasure-producing or desire-fulfilling activities.

While Hursthouse's claim concerns dishonesty in general, consider the specific challenges faced by one who wants to succeed in the systematic deception of others concerning his attitude toward their well-being. An optimal chance of deception would require the nonbenevolent agent to *act* consistently as if he cares for their well-being even though he does not. He must examine any public action, word, or nonverbal communication that might reveal his character and mask his internal life. To succeed he must show concern for other's well-being consistently enough that his motives rarely come into doubt. Even if he succeeds, it would require so much effort in closer relationships that genuine care for others would be a more strategic use of his energy because he could use the additional time and energy needed for deception to achieve other goals.

Another problem Hursthouse identifies is that deception undermines the trust needed for close relationships. We have already established that unloving dispositions undermine relationships and make the best types of relationships impossible. The issue of trust is important for many of the deceiver's goals. If the deceiver is going to benefit from his relationships then a certain amount of trust is necessary to achieve his goals. Yet deceit is more destructive to relationships than some other vicious activities are to their goals. One may occasionally overeat without seriously undermining one's goal of physical health or indulge in a pridefully high view of one's self without forever raising doubts about one's character. In contrast, deception is extremely destructive to relationships since even one or two clearly recognized cases of deception may destroy a relationship or cause significant distrust in future interactions. Someone with a recognized willingness to deceive can have a very hard time regaining trust.

Hursthouse also claims that successful deception necessarily undermines some relational goods. One enjoyable aspect of relationships is being close to people who know, love, and appreciate you. Yet, if an agent is systematically deceptive in relationships then others do not know, love, or appreciate the real person, but only the artificial façade she has projected. The deceiver can take no joy in praise or affection within the relationship except as evidence of successful deception. Hursthouse is correct that the deceiver loses these pleasurable experiences, though if it allows the deceiver to advance his goals, he may view this loss as trivial. A more serious problem for the deceiver is that deception undermines the quality of other goods gained through relationships. For example, one important instrumental benefit of relationships is the insight and advice given by others. But if others are deceived about the deceiver's character and goals, then their insight and advice will be less useful and accurate.

Hursthouse also claims that lying is silly and pointless in the sense that it is unlikely to be successful. This claim is important because any benefit from deception requires its success. If lying is silly and pointless, then the liar has wasted all sorts of resources, lost access to enjoyable relational experiences, and lost epistemic goods without gaining anything in return. Yet, the accuracy of her claim is less than obvious. The clever deceiver would not make unrealistic claims, such as pretending to never make mistakes. Instead, the clever deceiver would make considerable efforts to ensure the plausibility of his claims. Furthermore, the systematic deceiver might become experienced at deception and more adept at it than Hursthouse assumes. The deceiver would not be guaranteed success, but neither would he be guaranteed failure.

While Hursthouse raises a number of interesting issues, she raises two particularly important questions. Is the deceiver likely to succeed? What are the costs for that chance of success? Obviously, harm from the reactions of others will not always be prevented by deception. Furthermore, if the agent's deception is discovered he will be even more likely to lose relationships and their benefits than someone who is merely unloving. When the deceiver is recognized, she is not viewed only as apathetic or hostile toward those she pretends to love, but also as manipulative and untrustworthy. The additional vices increase the probability that others will reject her, distance themselves from her, or act against her interests if deception is unsuccessful. Moreover, there is reason to think that egoists would be inept at imitating loving behavior. Hugh LaFollette suggests,

> Friendly people have skills conducive to intimacy: listening attentively, expressing concern, or showing affection. They did learn these skills, but not in a skills seminar run by their company. If they have these skills, they acquired them by experience and careful instruction, not rote (Aristotle 1985). These skills are not isolated behaviors, easily mimicked by others. Rather, they are habits embodying an individual's deeper-disposing traits. They are part of who she is, her self.
>
> People listen to their intimates not because they acquired some specified set of behaviors to parrot, but because they care for each other. The range and tone of care is framed by the kind of person we are. If we are basically selfish people, preoccupied with our own interests and problems, then we will not be able to really care; concern for ourselves will always get in the way. That is why we care for others to the extent that we are good (virtuous) people. And virtue is acquired (if at all) over a lifetime, not during an intensive weekend conference on social skills. Thus, unless we are at least somewhat morally good, we cannot establish close personal relationships.[82]

LaFollette claims the acts of friendship that build close relationships require virtuous character, something akin to the virtue of love. The egoist's problem is that preoccupation with his own interests necessarily shapes his interactions with others. He may learn some deceptive tricks. He may learn how to feign many aspects of sincerity. Yet nothing is an adequate substitute for sincerity long-term. It may be possible to fool most others on a short-term basis, but increased interactions inevitably increase the probability of being discovered.

Even if his deceit is not discovered, a relationship based on deception is less enjoyable and more costly than a relationship based on love. While the relationship may be instrumentally beneficial, it is not enjoyable in itself since it does not satisfy one of the agent's ends. Furthermore, if deception is to have the optimal chance of success, the agent must expend the energy of a genuinely loving person along with the energy required by deception.

Consider the difference between how a genuine loving friend and a deceptive egoistic friend might act if they both helped an acquaintance move across town, which is a typical act of friendship. Despite the deceiver's best efforts, he has difficulty behaving like the true friend. The true friend will be happy to help, will tend to exert himself wholeheartedly, and will ultimately be more helpful. The false friend may show up to help, but will feel distracted and inconvenienced. His efforts may be halfhearted. He may spend the afternoon thinking "What is in this unpleasant exertion for me?" Even if he reminds himself that these actions will help build a useful relationship, ingratiate his friend, and that he can ask for a reciprocal favor, he will not enjoy the afternoon more than an instrumentally useful trip to the dentist. Furthermore, his actions may reveal his egoism. Therefore, he risks discovery since his acts of friendship are unlikely to come across as fully sincere. Of course, the egoist may try to cut corners and avoid the most costly acts of love, but each time he indulges in this strategy it increases the chances of discovery. Overall, the egoist's fear of discovery, his failure to enjoy the relationship and activities associated with the relationship for themselves, and the constant need to feign insincere priorities and emotions are all inherently negative even if he succeeds.[83]

All of these considerations together demonstrate that deception is not a promising strategy for unloving agents. It offers no protection from many of the harms that typically come from vicious dispositions. It requires a considerable effort for the mere chance of protecting the deceiver from the reactions of others. It is an inefficient strategy because it expends considerable resources in activities the agent does not enjoy. It also requires that the agent not pursue his goals in direct, identifiable ways. Furthermore, it prevents widely enjoyed relational experiences, such as revealing yourself to friends and having them know, appreciate, and love you. It also decreases the usefulness of others' advice. Therefore, deception is unlikely to make unloving dispositions beneficial to the agent.

6.13 HOW THE VICIOUS MIGHT FLOURISH

What is the upshot of this chapter? After examining these harmful aspects of unloving vices and the unpromising nature of the two best strategies for avoiding these harms, it might seem that the unloving cannot flourish under any circumstances. Yet this conclusion goes beyond my claims. This chapter has demonstrated that unloving vices necessarily entail certain harms. Furthermore, these dispositions are typically harmful to the agent overall and are not a prudent approach to life. However, these claims are compatible with the possibility that vicious people may occasionally flourish. An unloving person with considerable financial resources, cleverness, charisma, or luck may be able to avoid many harmful consequences of vice. He may even flourish, in part, as a result of his vice. Just as love in unusual circumstances can result in an overall loss to well-being, unloving dispositions can sometimes result in an overall increase in well-being.

In this way, my claims are not as ambitious as the claims of some virtue theorists. For example, Taylor categorically states of the seven vices she examines, "They [the vices] are similar also in that in each case they are destructive of that self and prevent its flourishing."[84] My account is closer to the view of the vices implied by MacIntyre's definition of virtue in *After Virtue*. He explains, "A virtue is an acquired human quality the possession and exercise of which tends to enable us to achieve those goods which are internal to practices and the lack of which effectively prevents us from achieving any such goods."[85] Implicitly, he views a vice as something which does not prevent a life of pleasure or fulfilled desires, but only prevents the enjoyment of a particular type of good. The goods relevant to love would include a certain type of relational good. Therefore, what is necessarily lost through unloving vice is primarily this relational good, but it does not ensure that a life of overall pleasure or fulfilled desire would be impossible.

However, this claim must also be qualified. The most serious problem for vicious individuals is that fully unloving dispositions entail destructive desires toward the self. If someone desires harm for himself or is apathetic toward his own well-being, this disposition would be extremely unlikely to result in an increase in the individual's well-being. Similarly, a disposition toward desiring psychic disunity or apathy toward psychic unity entails serious internal barriers to well-being. Unloving attitudes toward the self are extraordinarily destructive because the agent is in a unique position to harm the self. Therefore, people with fully developed vicious dispositions including unloving attitudes toward the self will not benefit from these dispositions and are extremely unlikely to flourish overall.

Of course, it is unsurprising that unloving attitudes toward the self are destructive to the agent. The more controversial question is whether the agent who loves himself, but has vicious attitudes toward others might benefit from this disposition.[86] The barriers to these vices resulting in a long-term overall increase in well-being are considerable. First, the vicious person must overcome the loss of friendships of virtue. Second, he must overcome the substantial relational challenges entailed by unloving vices. Vices often alienate others and necessarily make relationships less enjoyable. Third, he must avoid additional harms from some unloving vices such as psychic disunity.[87] Finally, these agents lose the benefits of love including final ends, psychic unity, motive to develop additional supporting virtues, improved relationships and epistemic benefits.

How might an unloving person overcome the harms of a vicious disposition? Since the most common harms of these vices come from their effects on relationships with others, the unloving person is best off if he cares little for relationships in themselves while simultaneously finding ways to obtain desirable resources typically provided by other people. First, there are certain kinds of relational desires that he ought to avoid. He needs to avoid desiring friendships of virtue. If he does not desire relationships based on virtue, then his inability to have these relationships will have a smaller effect upon his well-being. He would also be better off if he did not desire that others know him well since many unloving dispositions tend to alienate others who gain knowledge of his disposition. These attitudes toward relationships would minimize many of the harms entailed by unloving dispositions. If close relationships and relationships based on virtue are not desired, then failing to have them does not undermine well-being according to the desire-fulfillment model. Similarly, if an agent does not particularly care about such relationships, she experiences less pain if her disposition undermines them.

Second, in order to flourish the vicious person needs to find other ways to attain the resources and help typically offered by close relationships. Even if the unloving person does not want relationships, it is a rare person who can be completely self-sufficient. Everyone starts life as a completely helpless individual, and almost all of us continue to need the help of others in times of physical, financial, or emotional hardship. Even apart from times of hardship, others have numerous resources that can contribute to our well-being in less strained times. The unloving person cannot gain the help of others through genuine friendships of virtue, but he may still obtain social support through flattery, false promises, veiled bribes, emotional manipulation, seduction, threats, or honest exchange relationships. Each of these strategies contains risks or limitations, but a clever and lucky agent will be able to gain many resources without virtue.

Furthermore, the unloving person would have a better chance at flourishing if she found an alternative way to attain the benefits of love. At least some of love's benefits can be obtained elsewhere. Final ends can be obtained apart from love. The epistemic benefits of love may be obtained elsewhere. This claim is more controversial, but at least according to many accounts psychic unity and other virtues can be obtained without love.[88] So, the lucky or clever unloving person may still obtain some of love's benefits as well.

At this point, it is necessary to distinguish between the person who flourishes despite his vice and the agent who benefits from his vice. An unloving person born to an utterly privileged family may be able to live a life of pleasure and fulfill most of his desires because of the vast resources available for purchasing things and hiring help. Yet this case might not truly be an example of someone benefiting from vice. Such a person still might have enjoyed life more and had more desires fulfilled if he had been a loving person. The fact that his vast resources allowed him to maintain a pleasant life despite his vices does not necessarily imply that he benefited from them. In such a case, unusual resources merely mitigate some harmful effects of vice.

The more interesting case would be a genuine example of someone who is better off as a result of a thoroughly unloving disposition: an unloving person who is able to gain substantial resources because of his willingness to harm others and ignore his choices' effects on them. In turn, these resources might be used to live a life with more pleasure and fulfilled desire than otherwise possible.

Consider the example of the happy immoralist offered by Steven M. Cahn:

> Consider Fred, a fictitious person, but an amalgamation of several people I have known. Fred's life has been devoted to achieving three aims: fame, wealth, and a reputation for probity. He has no interest whatever in friends or truth. Indeed, he is treacherous and thoroughly dishonest. Nevertheless, he has attained his three goals and is, in fact, a rich celebrity renowned for his supposed integrity. His acquiring a good name while acting unscrupulously is a tribute to his audacity, cunning, and luck. Now he rests self-satisfied, basking in renown, delighting in luxuries, and relishing praise for his reputed commitment to the highest moral standards.[89]

Cahn's example demonstrates the pattern an unloving person would need to follow in order to gain well-being from vice. He must have no interest in genuine friendships. Yet, he must find a way to gain the resources usually gained through close genuine relationships. And he must have a combination of luck and skill in order to be successful at his vicious ploys. Such a person would be an indubitable example of an unloving flourishing individual.

Of course, it is possible to question whether such a person is a real possibility. Even Cahn implicitly admits that he knows of no real instance of such a person. One might object to Cahn's example that no one could successfully carry on such deception long-term or that such a person is necessarily wracked by guilt or loneliness. Perhaps a historical example will bolster Cahn's case that a vicious unloving person could successfully live a life of pleasure and fulfilled desire. Such an example is found in the life of Joseph Stalin. As a leader of the Soviet Union from the time of the 1917 revolution and the *de facto* dictator of the country from the middle of the 1930s until his death in 1953, Stalin gained incredible privileges as the result of his ruthless behavior. While the precise numbers are unknown, during his rule millions of Soviet citizens were killed as a result of his policies of forced resettlement, imprisonment in the harsh conditions of the gulag, and execution.[90] His harsh treatment of others seems to have extended to his family. His cruel treatment of his son Yakov led him to attempt suicide. Historian Robert Conquest records,

> Stalin also disapproved of Yakov's first marriage, and then of his second marriage (to a Jewish woman), Yakov's "gentleness and composure," we are told, infuriated Stalin. When Yakov attempted suicide after a few years of this, his failure led to Stalin's comment, "Ha! He couldn't even shoot straight."[91]

Nor was Stalin uniquely harsh to his son. His harshness similarly extended to his second wife, who is reported to have committed suicide in 1932.[92]

Stalin is a good example of an unloving person who found final ends in the pursuit of power and did not put a high priority on personal relationships, but whose ruthlessness enabled him to gain every resource imaginable for pursuing his desires. And while it is possible that he was secretly lonely or wracked by guilt, there is no compelling reason to believe this was the case. While idealists might be tempted to believe that vicious agents like Stalin could not truly be happy, it is likely that an individual with as much power, influence, and resources as Stalin had a life with much pleasure and fulfilled desire.[93]

Yet the fact that a rare unloving person might benefit from her vice does not undercut my central argument. It is somewhat telling that both examples I have provided here are far from typical people. Cahn's example of the happy immoralist may be purely theoretical and not a real possibility at all. While Stalin may have had an enjoyable life as a successful dictator, most who pursue such ambitions are unsuccessful; even those who achieve such power do not always keep it and often die violently at the hands of their rivals. Such an approach to life could theoretically result in considerable well-being for the extraordinarily lucky and clever person with an unusual set of desires, but it can hardly be recommended as a generally prudent strategy for life.

As I claimed in the previous chapter, virtue is a prudent approach to life in the same way that typical temperate dietary and lifestyle advice is prudent.[94] Even though an occasional cigarette smoker may live a hundred years without tobacco-related health problems and gain considerable tobacco-related pleasure from this lifestyle, the current medical advice against smoking is still the only prudent advice on the matter. Similarly, an occasional lucky unloving person may avoid many of the harms of her vice and attain an overall increase in well-being. Yet, this fact does nothing to undercut the claim that it is imprudent for a person to live a life of unloving vice.

6.14 CONCLUSION

We examined the connections between the virtue of love and well-being. Historically there have been three general views.[95] The first view is represented by Immanuel Kant, sentimentalists, and others who reject any inherent connection between love and well-being. A second common view can be traced back to the speech of Aristophanes in Plato's *Symposium*. According to this view, love primarily benefits the lover through relationships. The third view is found in Thomas Aquinas, who claims that love benefits the agent because it is needed to fulfill humanity's final end. This view maintains a strong necessary connection between love and well-being, but depends upon controversial philosophical conceptions such as an objective final end for humanity.

My argument departs from each of these views. I have argued that love necessarily benefits the lover in a number of distinct ways, typically results in a net increase in the lover's well-being, and is the only prudentially advisable disposition toward people. This view is incompatible with the Kantian position. It also departs from Aristophanes's account of love and well-being because I identify many of love's benefits that are independent of relationships. Furthermore, I avoided the vagueness of this account and demonstrate how love improves relationships. Finally, I depart from the Thomistic view by demonstrating that a connection between love and well-being need not depend upon controversial ideas such as an objective end for humanity. The connection I establish between love and well-being exists on all four mainstream contemporary accounts of well-being: the hedonistic account, the desire-fulfillment account, the objective list account, and the *eudaimonistic* account.

I develop my account of love from Aquinas's account of *caritas*. My Neo-Thomistic account construes love as *a disposition towards relationally appropriate acts of the will, consisting of a disinterested desire for the good of the beloved and a disinterested desire for unity with the beloved, held as final ends*. I argue that this account of love is preferable to the current philosophical

accounts of love offered by Harry Frankfurt, J. David Velleman, Hugh LaFollette, and Niko Kolodny. In this argument, I used the following criteria. First,
an adequate account of love needs to be flexible and apply to a broad range
of relationships. Second, an account of love should explain the normative
experiences associated with love including the unique nonreplaceability of
the beloved, the tenacity of loving relationships, emotional vulnerability in
loving relationships, and the joy found in community with the beloved. Third,
an account of love should offer guidance for reconciling ethical concerns
arising from the perceived conflict between partial love and impartial morality. Finally, an account of love should allow love to be construed as a virtue,
should explain what is excellent and admirable within love, and should distinguish between ideal love and inferior expressions of love.

We identified five benefits of possessing a loving disposition. Direct benefits gained by the loving person include final ends that motivate enjoyable
activity and the integration of the psyche. Love also acts as a motive for
self-improvement and self-perfection, and also promotes self-knowledge.
Indirect benefits to the loving person include fulfilling a necessary condition
for entering into relationships of mutual giving and receiving and making
relationships more harmonious and enjoyable. As a result of these benefits,
the virtue of love necessarily benefits the lover in a number of distinct ways,
typically results in an increase in well-being on the whole, and on relevant
matters is the only advisable disposition to develop.

Finally, we concluded that unloving dispositions are harmful to the agent.
Vicious dispositions are inferior to love at producing fulfilled desires and
pleasure, they undermine relationships, they make some benefits of relationships completely impossible, and they make life and relationships less
enjoyable. Even when benefits are gained by a vicious agent these benefits
typically require an unnecessarily high expenditure of time and energy that
could have been avoided. While there are rare circumstances in which an
unloving disposition could actually help an agent attain well-being, such
a disposition is typically destructive to the individual and is not a prudent
approach to life. To fail to love is to live imprudently.

ENDNOTES

1. Gabriele Taylor, *Deadly Vices* (New York: Oxford University Press, 2006), 9.
2. While it is also possible to have one hateful desire and to be apathetic concerning love's other desire, I will not address these dispositions separately from hate and
apathy since the harm from these dispositions can be deduced from an examination
of hate and apathy.

3. *Cf.* Thomas Aquinas, *Summa theologiae* I-II.34.

4. In this context I am using the term "distance" metaphorically as an antonym for "relationally appropriate unity." It does not necessarily refer to physical distance.

5. The hater may or may not desire that the hated possess vice. It depends on whether she views vice as a bad for the hated.

6. Frances Berenson, "What Is This Thing Called 'Love'?" *Philosophy* 66 (1991): 71.

7. *Cf. The Prudence of Love*, Chapter 4.3.

8. Aurel Kolnai, "The Standard Modes of Aversion: Fear, Disgust and Hatred," *Mind* 107 (1998): 590.

9. It is theoretically possible that such a person might consistently be incorrect about the effects of her choices and attempt to choose harmful things that are actually helpful, good, and pleasurable for her instead. However, even in this implausible case, such a person would suffer from the consistent pain of unfulfilled desires as she is frustrated in her pursuit of the bad for herself.

10. For more details concerning the harm of a disharmonious psyche, see *The Prudence of Love*, Chapter 5.3.

11. Eleonore Stump, "Willed Loneliness," *Wandering in Darkness* (Oxford University Press, forthcoming).

12. Richard E. Lucas and Portia S. Dyrenforth, "Does the Existence of Social Relationships Matter for Subjective Well-Being?" in *Self and Relationships*, eds. Kathleen D. Vohs and Eli J. Finkel (New York: The Guilford Press, 2006), 254.

13. Aristotle, *Nicomachean Ethics*, trans. Roger Crisp (Cambridge: Cambridge University Press, 2000), 1155a.

14. Lucas and Dyrenforth 2006, 257.

15. Aristotle, *Nicomachean Ethics*, 1156a.

16. Of course, it is possible that the hater will attempt to hide his hatred. We will examine such cases in Chapter 6.12.

17. Charles Hartshorne, *The Zero Fallacy and Other Essays in Neoclassical Philosophy*, ed. Mohammad Valady (Chicago: Carus Publishing Company, 1997), 189.

18. Alasdair MacIntyre, *Dependent Rational Animals: Why Human Beings Need the Virtues* (Chicago: Open Court Publishing Company, 2002), 99.

19. John Van Ingen, *Why Be Moral? The Egoistic Challenge* (New York: Peter Lang Publishing, Inc., 1994), 168.

20. While this example focuses upon Nazi Germany, I claim that other 'hateful' societies and subcultures fit the pattern of this model. Whether it is the racist society of the Ku Klux Klan, the violent subculture of the Mafia, or the terrorist culture of Al-Qaeda in each case there are groups that are acceptable to hate and others that are unacceptable to hate. While the increased acceptability of hatred makes these social environments more hospitable to the hater, none of these groups accepts hatred expressed toward their own members.

21. *Cf.* Faith McNulty, *The Burning Bed* (New York: Harcourt Brace Jovanovich, 1980).

22. Richard Kraut, *What Is Good and Why: The Ethics of Well-Being* (Cambridge, MA: Harvard University Press, 2007), 51.

23. Grainne Fitzsimons, "Pursuing Goals and Perceiving Others: A Self-Regulatory Perspective on Interpersonal Relationships," in *Self and Relationships*, eds. Kathleen D. Vohs and Eli J. Finkel (New York: The Guilford Press, 2006), 32.

24. *Cf. The Prudence of Love*, Chapter 5.3.

25. Christine Swanton, *Virtue Ethics: A Pluralistic View* (New York: Oxford University Press, 2003), 42–43.

26. Laura Waddell Ekstrom "Autonomy and Personal Integration," in *Personal Autonomy*, ed. James Stacey Taylor (New York: Cambridge University Press, 2005), 147–148.

27. Christine McKinnon, *Character, Virtue Theories and the Vices* (Toronto, CA: Broadview Press, 1999), 146.

28. Van Ingen 1994, 172.

29. Lester Hunt, "Flourishing Egoism," in *Human Flourishing*, eds. Ellen Frankel Paul, Fred. D. Miller, Jr., and Jeffrey Paul (New York: Cambridge University Press, 1999), 87–88.

30. Jennifer Roback Morse, "No Families, No Freedom: Human Flourishing in a Free Society," in *Human Flourishing*, eds. Ellen Frankel Paul, Fred. D. Miller, Jr., and Jeffrey Paul (New York: Cambridge University Press, 1999), 300.

31. Rebecca DeYoung, "Resistance to the Demands of Love: Aquinas on the Vice of *Acedia*," *The Thomist* 68 (2004): 198–199.

32. Kraut 2007, 40.

33. *Cf.* Plato, *Meno*, in *Plato: Five Dialogues*, 2d ed., trans. G. M. A. Grube (Indianapolis, IN: Hackett Publishing Company, Inc., 2002), 77c–78c.

34. *Cf.* Aristotle, *Nicomachean Ethics*, 1097a–b and 1155b.

35. *Cf.* ST I-II.5.8.

36. *Cf.* Immanuel Kant, *Critique of Practical Reason*, trans. and ed. Mary Gregor (New York: Cambridge University Press, 1997), 5:25.

37. Joseph Raz, *Value, Respect, and Attachment* (New York: Cambridge University Press, 2001), 17 n 6.

38. Raz 2001, 16.

39. *Cf. The Prudence of Love*, Chapter 4.6.

40. In Chapter 4.6, I discuss one's relationship with the self. As in other relationships, one who loves himself desires an appropriate type of union with the self.

41. Note that such a disposition would not be harmful to a God or other perfect being since such a being would have no need to change. Inflexible bondedness with the self is only harmful to imperfect beings.

42. *Cf. The Prudence of Love*, Chapters 5.5 and 6.3.

43. These claims do not imply that friends and spouses are absolutely equal in their knowledge, skills, or virtues. One person may genuinely know more about or be more adept at cooking, automotive repair, public speaking, practicing religion, or be more virtuous. Nevertheless, desiring bonds that control others in these areas expresses arrogance. Such bonds are not appropriate in these sorts of relationships. Furthermore,

inequalities are rarely absolute. Without humility, the inappropriate lover misses opportunities to learn from and appreciate others around him.

44. Oscar A. Barbarin and Mildred Tirado, "Enmeshment, Family Processes, and Successful Treatment of Obesity," *Family Relations* 34 (1985): 115.

45. Obviously, it is possible that someone would only seek inappropriate bonds in a single or small range of relationships, but that is not the fully vicious agent we are examining in this section.

46. Of course, this pattern would not hold for someone desiring fewer connections with others than appropriate. However, we address this disposition in our discussions of apathy, apathetic benevolence, and distant benevolence.

47. Eleonore Stump "Love, by All Accounts," *Proceedings and Addresses of the American Philosophical Association* 80 (2006): 32.

48. For simplicity's sake, I refer to the object of incomplete love as the "beloved" even though this label is not completely appropriate.

49. Catherine D. Rawn and Kathleen D. Vohs, "The Importance of Self-Regulation for Interpersonal Functioning," in *Self and Relationships: Connecting Intrapersonal and Interpersonal Processes*, eds. Kathleen D. Vohs and Eli J. Finkel (New York: Guilford Press, 2006), 21.

50. Of course, this pattern does not hold in every situation. Those who enjoy harming others do sometimes build relationships with people who possess masochistic tendencies. Yet malevolent love tends to alienate others, and if the malevolent lover can only have long-term relationships with others who possess masochistic tendencies, this limitation will severely limit his relational options.

51. Cf. *The Prudence of Love*, Chapters 5.5 and 6.3.

52. The exception to this pattern would be the rare situation of those who are so independently wealthy that they do not need the unpaid practical help of close friends and relatives.

53. Note that the malevolent lover truly desires a relationally appropriate union with others, so she will not avoid this harm by avoiding union with the beloved.

54. I will later examine some possible ways that the vicious person might try to avoid such harm, but I will conclude that these efforts are typically unsuccessful. *Cf. The Prudence of Love*, Chapter 6.11–12.

55. I do not deny that in some cultural situations, the agent's victims will not be able to escape him easily. Yet, even in these cultures, others will be able to harm or escape the malevolent lover. At the very least, his malevolence gives others a broadly rational motive, regardless of culture, to avoid union with him.

56. For a more detailed discussion of the social risks of desiring to harm others, *Cf. The Prudence of Love*, Chapter 6.3.

57. *Cf. The Prudence of Love*, Chapter 6.3.

58. If the agent only desires failure for one of his co-workers his risks are reduced, but they are not eliminated. Furthermore, such an agent would not really have a fully developed disposition of malevolent love.

59. *Cf. The Prudence of Love*, Chapter 5.4.

60. Andrew M. Greeley, *The Friendship Game* (Garden City, NY: Doubleday and Company, Inc., 1970), 69.

61. *Cf. The Prudence of Love*, Chapters 5.5 and 6.3.

62. *Cf. The Prudence of Love*, Chapter 6.5.

63. *Cf. The Prudence of Love*, Chapter 6.5.

64. *Cf. The Prudence of Love*, Chapter 6.5.

65. *Cf. The Prudence of Love*, Chapter 4.4.

66. Even if an adoptive parent can contribute to a child's well-being as well as a natural parent, someone must fulfill such a role in the child's life if she is to flourish fully. Anyone in the role of "parent" who fails to will relationally appropriate union with the child undermines her flourishing.

67. While some of these responsibilities might be fulfilled by a proxy, other responsibilities, such as emotional support, cannot be completely fulfilled by a proxy without harm to the child and to the parent-child relationship.

68. *Cf. The Prudence of Love*, Chapters 5.5 and 6.3.

69. This depiction of distant benevolence should not be confused with prudent expressions of love where unusual circumstances require the lover to distance himself from the beloved for the good of both the lover and the beloved. For example, in Chapter 4.4 we demonstrated that distancing oneself from a physically abusive spouse is compatible with love.

70. Aristotle, *Nicomachean Ethics*, 1157b.

71. We will consider the possibility of an agent who has no desire for relationships with others in a later section. *Cf. The Prudence of Love*, Chapter 6.13.

72. L. Vander Kerken, SJ, *Loneliness and Love*, trans. J. Donceel, SJ (New York: Sheed and Ward, 1967), 34.

73. *Cf. The Prudence of Love*, Chapters 5.5 and 6.3.

74. Robert Adams, *Finite and Infinite Goods: A Framework for Ethics* (New York: Oxford University Press, 1999), 142.

75. Kraut 2007, 39.

76. Hunt 1999, 75.

77. Plato, *Republic*, trans. G. M. A. Grube (Indianapolis, IN: Hackett Publishing Company, 1992), 362 b–c.

78. Van Ingen 1994, 50.

79. Van Ingen 1994, 171.

80. Lucas and Dyrenforth 2006, 263.

81. Rosalind Hursthouse, *On Virtue Ethics* (New York: Oxford University Press, 1999), 168.

82. Hugh LaFollette, *Personal Relationships* (Cambridge, MA: Blackwell Publishers, 1996), 157.

83. Of course, the egoist might try to avoid these difficulties by pursuing relationships with those who have low expectations of others. Yet, this strategy seems undesirable since it severely limits the people with whom the egoist can pursue relationships. Furthermore, one reason they may have low expectations of others is due to their own unwillingness to invest much into relationships themselves.

84. Taylor 2006, 1.

85. Alasdair MacIntyre, *After Virtue*, 2d ed. (Notre Dame, IN: University of Notre Dame Press, 1984), 191.

86. For example, this question is at the heart of Plato's *Republic* and discussed in Aristotle's *Nicomachean Ethics*.

87. In the interest of brevity, I will avoid discussing all of the other possible harms of unloving dispositions in this section. It is sufficient to note that all harms that are external to the agent can be avoided at least occasionally through skill or chance. It is only internal harms, such as psychic disharmony, that can absolutely never be avoided.

88. For Aquinas's arguments against these possibilities see *The Prudence of Love*, Chapters 3.1 and 5.3.

89. Steven M. Cahn and Jeffrie G. Murphy, "Happiness and Immorality," in *Happiness: Classic and Contemporary Readings in Philosophy*, eds. Steven M. Cahn and Christine Vitrano (New York: Oxford University Press, 2008), 262.

90. Robert Conquest, *Stalin: Breaker of Nations* (New York: Penguin Books USA, 1991), 171–235.

91. Conquest 1991, 128.

92. Conquest 1991, 169.

93. Of course, if one judges that such a person could not truly be happy, one might use the counterintuitive nature of Stalin's flourishing as a reason for rejecting hedonistic and desire fulfillment accounts of well-being.

94. *Cf. The Prudence of Love*, Chapter 5.8.

95. These views can be found in *The Prudence of Love*, Chapter 1.1.

Works Cited

Adams, Robert. *Finite and Infinite Goods: A Framework for Ethics.* New York: Oxford University Press, 1999.

Aquinas, Thomas. *De caritate.* Trans. Lottie H. Kendzierski. Milwaukee, WI: Marquette University Press, 1960.

———. *Summa theologiae.* Trans. Alfred Freddoso. Accessed at http://www.nd.edu/~afreddos/summa-translation/TOC-part1.htm.

———. *Summa theologiae.* Trans. Eric J. Silverman.

———. *Summa theologiae.* Trans. Fathers of the English Dominican Province. London: Burns, Oates, and Washburne, Ltd. 1920–1942.

Aristotle. *Magna Moralia.* In *The Metaphysics,* 2 vols. Trans. Hugh Tredennick and G. Cyril Armstrong. Cambridge, MA: Harvard University Press, 1977–1980.

———. *Nichomachean Ethics.* Trans. J. A. K. Thompson. New York: Penguin Books, 1955.

———. *Nicomachean Ethics.* Trans. Joe Sachs. Newburyport, MA: Focus Publishing, 2002.

———. *Nicomachean Ethics.* Trans. Roger Crisp. Cambridge: Cambridge University Press, 2000.

Augustine. *The Confessions of St. Augustine.* Trans. Edward Bouverie Pusey. New York: Modern Library, 1949.

———. *The Confessions of St. Augustine.* Trans. Eric Silverman.

———. *The Confessions of St. Augustine.* Trans. Jack K. Ryan. New York: Doubleday, 1960.

Badhwar, Neera K. "Love." In *The Oxford Handbook of Practical Ethics.* Ed. Hugh LaFollette, 42–69. New York: Oxford University Press, 2003.

Barbarin, Oscar A. and Mildred Tirado. "Enmeshment, Family Processes, and Successful Treatment of Obesity." *Family Relations* 34 (1985): 115–121.

Berenson, F. M. *Understanding Persons: Personal and Impersonal Relationships.* New York: St. Martin's Press, 1981.

Berenson, Frances. "What Is This Thing Called 'Love'?" *Philosophy* 66 (1991): 65–79.

Cahn, Steven M. and Jeffrie G. Murphy. "Happiness and Immorality." In *Happiness: Classic and Contemporary Readings in Philosophy*. Eds. Steven M. Cahn and Christine Vitrano. New York: Penguin Books USA, 2008.

Calcutt, Daniel. "Tough Love," *Florida Philosophical Review* 5 (2005): 35–42.

Conquest, Robert. *Stalin: Breaker of Nations*. New York: Viking Penguin Books, Inc., 1991.

DeYoung, Rebecca. "Resistance to the Demands of Love: Aquinas on the Vice of *Acedia*," *The Thomist* 68 (2004): 173–204.

Driver, Julia. *Uneasy Virtue*. New York: Cambridge University Press, 2001.

Ekstrom, Laura. "Autonomy and Personal Integration." In *Personal Autonomy*. Ed. James Stacey Taylor, 143–161. New York: Cambridge University Press, 2005.

Emmons, Robert. *Psychology of Ultimate Concern*. New York: Guilford Press, 1999.

Fitzsimons, Grainne. "Pursuing Goals and Perceiving Others: A Self-Regulatory Perspective on Interpersonal Relationships." In *Self and Relationships*. Eds. Kathleen D. Vohs and Eli J. Finkel, 32–56. New York: Guilford Press, 2006.

Frankena, William. *Ethics*. 2d ed. Englewood, NJ: Prentice Hall, 1973.

Frankfurt, Harry. *Necessity, Volition, and Love*. Cambridge: Cambridge University Press, 1999.

———. *The Reasons of Love*. Princeton, NJ: Princeton University Press, 2004.

———. *Some Mysteries of Love*. Lawrence, KS: University of Kansas Press, 2001.

———. "Freedom of the Will and the Concept of a Person." *Journal of Philosophy*, LXVII (1971): 5–20.

Gilson, Etienne. *Thomism: The Philosophy of Thomas Aquinas*. Trans. Laurence K. Shook and Armand Maurer. Toronto: Pontifical Institute of Mediaeval Studies, 2002.

Greeley, Andrew M. *The Friendship Game*. Garden City, NY: Doubleday and Company, Inc., 1970.

Hartshorne, Charles. *The Zero Fallacy and Other Essays in Neoclassical Philosophy*. Ed. Mohammad Valady. Chicago: Carus Publishing Company, 1997.

Hooker, Brad. "Is Moral Virtue a Benefit to the Agent?" In *How Should One Live?* Ed. Roger Crisp, 141–156. New York: Oxford University Press, 1996.

Hunt, Lester. "Flourishing Egoism." In *Human Flourishing*. Eds. Ellen Frankel Paul, Fred. D. Miller, Jr., and Jeffrey Paul, 72–95. New York: Cambridge University Press, 1999.

Hursthouse, Rosalind. *On Virtue Ethics*. New York: Oxford University Press, 1999.

Ingen, John Van. *Why Be Moral? The Egoistic Challenge*. New York: Peter Lang Publishing, Inc., 1994.

Jollimore, Troy. "Impartiality." In the *Stanford Encyclopedia of Philosophy*, April 18, 2006. http://plato.stanford.edu/entries/impartiality/ accessed on September 19, 2007.

Kant, Immanuel. *Critique of Practical Reason*. Trans. and ed. Mary Gregor. New York: Cambridge University Press, 1997.

———. *Groundwork of the Metaphysics of* Morals. Trans. H.J. Paton. New York: Harper and Row Publishers, Inc., 1964.

———. *Metaphysics of Morals.* Trans. Mary Gregor. New York: Cambridge University Press, 1996.

Keenan, James. *Goodness and Rightness in Thomas Aquinas's Summa Theologiae.* Washington, DC: Georgetown University Press, 1992.

Kerken, L. Vander. *Loneliness and Love.* Trans. J. Donceel, SJ. New York: Sheed and Ward, 1967.

Kolnai, Aurel. "The Standard Modes of Aversion: Fear, Disgust and Hatred." *Mind* 107 (1998): 581–595.

Kolodny, Niko. "Book Review: The Reasons of Love." *The Journal of Philosophy* 103 (2006): 43–50.

———. "Love As Valuing a Relationship." *Philosophical Review* 112 (2003): 135–189.

Kraut, Richard. *What Is Good and Why: The Ethics of Well-Being.* Cambridge, MA: Harvard University Press, 2007.

Kraut, Robert. "Love *De Re.*" *Midwest Studies in Philosophy* 10 (1986): 413–430.

LaFollette, Hugh. *Personal Relationships.* Cambridge, MA: Blackwell Publishers, 1996.

Lucas, Richard E. and Portia S. Dyrenforth. "Does the Existence of Social Relationships Matter for Subjective Well-Being?" In *Self and Relationships.* Eds. Kathleen D. Vohs and Eli J. Finkel, 254–273. New York: The Guilford Press, 2006.

MacIntyre, Alasdair. *After Virtue.* 2d ed. Notre Dame, IN: University of Notre Dame Press, 1984.

———. *Dependent Rational Animals: Why Human Beings Need the Virtues.* Chicago: Open Court Publishing Company, 2002.

McDougall, Rosalind. "Parental Virtue: A New Way of Thinking about the Morality of Reproductive Actions." *Bioethics* 21 (2007): 181–190.

McKinnon, Christine. *Character, Virtue Theories and the Vices.* Toronto: Broadview Press, 1999.

McNulty, Faith. *The Burning Bed.* New York: Harcourt Brace Jovanovich, 1980.

Morse, Jennifer Roback. "No Families, No Freedom: Human Flourishing in a Free Society." In *Human Flourishing.* Eds. Ellen Frankel Paul, Fred. D. Miller, Jr., and Jeffrey Paul, 290–314. New York: Cambridge University Press, 1999.

Murray, Sandra L. "A Leap of Faith? Positive Illusions in Romantic Relationships." *Personality and Social Psychology Bulletin* 23 (1997): 586–604.

Nussbaum, Martha. *Upheavals of Thought: The Intelligence of Emotions.* New York: Cambridge University Press, 2001.

———. "Compassion: The Basic Social Emotion." *Social Philosophy and Policy* 13 (1996): 27–58.

Plato. *Apology.* In *Plato: Five Dialogues.* 2d ed. Trans. G. M. A. Grube. Indianapolis, IN: Hackett Publishing Company, Inc., 2002.

———. *Meno.* In *Plato: Five Dialogues.* 2d ed. Trans. G. M. A. Grube. Indianapolis, IN: Hackett Publishing Company, Inc., 2002.

———. *Republic.* Trans. G. M. A. Grube. Indianapolis, IN: Hackett Publishing Company, 1992.

———. *The Symposium.* Trans. Benjamin Jowett. Mineola, NY: Dover Publications, 1993.

Rand, Ayn. *The Virtue of Selfishness.* New York: The New American Library, 1964.

Raz, Joseph. *Value, Respect, and Attachment.* New York: Cambridge University Press, 2001.

Schneider, Helga. *Let Me Go.* Trans. Shaun Whiteside. New York: Walker Publishing Company, Inc., 2001.

Schockenhoff, Eberhard. "The Theological Virtue of Charity (IIa IIae, qq. 23–46)." In *The Ethics of Aquinas.* Ed. Stephen Pope. Washington, DC: Georgetown University Press, 2002.

Shakespeare, William. *Othello.* Naperville, IL: Sourcebooks, 2005.

Sherwin, Michael S. *By Knowledge and By Love: Charity and Knowledge in the Moral Theology of St. Thomas Aquinas.* Washington, DC: The Catholic University of America Press, 2005.

Slote, Michael. *Morals From Motives.* New York: Oxford University Press, 2001.

Soble, Alan. "Love and Value, Yet *Again.*" *Essays in Philosophy* 6 (2005): online journal, accessed at http://fs.uno.edu/asoble/pages/soble2rev.html.

Solomon, Robert. *The Joy of Philosophy.* New York: Oxford University Press, 1999.

Stump, Eleonore. *Wandering in Darkness.* New York: Oxford University Press, forthcoming.

———. "Love, By All Accounts." *Proceedings and Addresses of the American Philosophical Association* 80 (2006): 25–43.

Swanton, Christine. *Virtue Ethics: A Pluralistic View.* New York: Oxford University Press, 2003.

Taylor, Gabriele. *Deadly Vices.* New York: Oxford University Press, 2006.

Velleman, J. David. "Beyond Price." *Ethics* 118 (2008): 191–212.

———. "Love as a Moral Emotion." *Ethics* 109 (1999): 338–374.

Veltman, Andrea. "Aristotle and Kant on Self-Disclosure in Friendship." *Journal of Value Inquiry* 38 (2004): 225–239.

Williams, Bernard. *Moral Luck: Philosophical Papers.* New York: Cambridge University Press, 1981.

Wolterstorff, Nicholas. *Lament for a Son.* Grand Rapids, MI: William B. Eerdmans Publishing Company, 1987.

Zupko, Jack. "John Buridan." In *The Stanford Encyclopedia of Philosophy.* July 10, 2006. http://plato.stanford.edu/entries/buridan/, accessed on Dec. 5, 2007.

Index

Vita Auctoris

Eric J. Silverman is assistant professor of philosophy and religious studies at Christopher Newport University. He earned a bachelor of arts from Rutgers University and a master of arts from Baylor University before receiving his doctoral degree from Saint Louis University. His research interests include medieval philosophy, ethics, and philosophy of religion. *The Prudence of Love* is his first monograph.

Breinigsville, PA USA
12 March 2010
234097BV00002B/5/P